BUSINESS GROWTH STRATEGIES FOR ASIA PACIFIC

BUSINESS GROWTH STRATEGIES FOR ASIA PACIFIC

Willie Chien
Stan Shih
Po-Young Chu

John Wiley & Sons (Asia) Pte Ltd

This publication is designed to provide accurate and authoritative information in regard
to the subject matter covered. It is sold with the understanding that the publisher is not
engaged in rendering professional services. If professional advice or other expert assistance
is required, the services of a competent professional person should be sought.

Other Wiley Editorial Offices

John Wiley & Sons, 111 River Street, Hoboken, NJ 07030, USA
John Wiley & Sons, The Atrium Southern Gate, Chichester PO19 8SQ, England
John Wiley & Sons (Canada) Ltd, 22 Worcester Road, Rexdale, Ontario M9W 1L1, Canada
John Wiley & Sons Australia Ltd, 33 Park Road (PO Box 1226), Milton,
    Queensland 4064, Australia
Wiley-VCH, Pappelallee 3, 69469 Weinheim, Germany

Library of Congress Cataloging-in-Publication Data

0-470-82172-8

Typeset in 10/12 points, Photina by C&M Digitals (P) Ltd.
Printed in Singapore by Saik Wah Press Ltd
10   9   8   7   6   5   4   3   2

CONTENTS

ACKNOWLEDGEMENTS

Stan Shih:

My gratitude goes to Dr. Willie Chien and Dr. Po-Young Chu, with whom I have had the honor of co-authoring this book. Between us, we have had many years' global business experience of passing our accumulated knowledge onto others through this book and others as well as Aspire Academy. It therefore gives me great pleasure to be able to share some of the invaluable materials and insights we have acquired in doing business in Asia. I am confident that my 30-year experience in founding and developing Acer, BenQ, and Wistron, which between them had revenues exceeding US$20 billion in 2004, will be of benefit to anyone looking to establish or expand a business in the Asia Pacific region.

Willie Chien:

My appreciation first of all goes to my wife, Catherine, and my daughters, Mercedes and Tiffany, for their unconditional support. My special tribute goes to my Mom, who encouraged me to pursue my dreams but never forget where I come from. For me, a Chinese American born in Taiwan, it has been an amazing experience to have lived and worked in such places as Australia, Canada, China, Hong Kong, Taiwan and the US for the past 20 years. These overseas assignments have enabled me to appreciate the subtleties of different cultures and to share their passions. If I ever grow wiser, it will only be because of this special journey, the great books I have read, and the remarkable people I have been lucky to be associated with. I feel privileged to work closely with Stan, who is truly one of the most brilliant businessmen of our time. I also want to thank Po-Young for his support throughout this project. It is my sincere wish to generate discussion with the readers of this book at williechien88@hotmail.com.

Po-Young Chu:

Most of the insights in this book are based on the experience and vision of my co-authors, Willie and Stan. Their hands-on experience was invaluable in developing the materials and case studies, which we feel sure will help readers master the principles of doing business in Asia. Through these joint efforts, I hope we have developed a useful management textbook for those business executives who are involved in developing business strategy in Asia and those graduate students who are in MBA and EMBA programs. I would like to thank Morris Chang, Lu-Pao Hsu, Ding-Hua Hu, and my many students for their encouragement and feedback over the years to help me develop better courses in the EMBA program at National Chiao Tung University (NCTU). The data collection, figure drawing and table preparation related to the case studies by Peter Lin, May Tseng, Yvonne Yu, Chuan-Yi Yang, Min-Hsien Liu and Ya-Ting Yang are also greatly appreciated. Finally, my appreciation goes to my wife, Hsueh-Fen, and my children, Philip, Jennie and Loa, for their support and love.

FOREWORD

As one of the most successful entrepreneurs in the information technology (IT) industry today, Stan Shih has been an inspiration to many young executives and entrepreneurs.

When Stan founded Acer in the burgeoning personal computer industry 28 years ago, his goals were considered ambitious and probably too optimistic. At that time, the industry was dominated by Western multinationals and some Japanese companies and many core industry competencies, such as semiconductors and computer software, were not within the reach of Acer or any other Asian company. But rapidly evolving technology and the shifting of manufacturing competence to Asia eventually changed the industry's landscape. Under the legendary leadership of Stan Shih, Acer has proven to be a formidable player in this highly competitive industry, matching the rapid changes in the IT market environment to the point where it is now No. 5 in global PC rankings and No. 1 in Europe for notebooks. Such a strong track record gives Stan the undisputed credentials to speak on global or Asian business strategies.

I am pleased to see Stan join forces with Dr. Willie Chien and Dr. Po-Young Chu to lend their combined experience and insights gleaned from various industries and different Asian countries to develop the next generation of CEOs. I am convinced that this book will benefit a new generation of managers across Asia.

Readers will find this book useful as a guide to understanding Asian business from both the macroscopic and microscopic standpoints. The macro factors such as national economic characteristics, cultural differences and varying market environments are always fundamentally important for any company trying to formulate a business strategy. The micro factors such as competitiveness, technology and cost positioning are equally critical in forming the foundation of a business plan. Once these basic factors are properly understood and mastered, an effective business strategy for Asia Pacific can then be defined using the systematic approach proposed in this book.

As this book makes clear, more and more Asia-based companies are rising up to the global standards of sales, profitability, technology and productivity. There is growing evidence that Asia-based companies will, increasingly, set the benchmark for global competition. It is clear that the future success of a company will be increasingly dependent on having a prudent business strategy and meticulous execution. Such a fundamental change is going to have a profound impact on the competitive conditions of all industries. Any company that wishes to win in Asia must properly develop and train its managers to think strategically and to execute effectively. This book is one of the best available to help serve this purpose.

Koh Boon Hwee
Chairman
Singapore Airlines

PREFACE

It is a great honor for me to recommend this book. Many foreign investors participating in Asian markets have frequently had hard lessons to learn because they had not developed a comprehensive business strategy and implementation plan to address Asian culture, the realities of the market and the expectations of customers in a very different competitive environment. With international companies becoming increasingly reliant on the Asian market for their continued growth, such lessons can be both painful and costly.

But there are also many success stories of foreign companies who clearly understand the subtle differences between Asia and their home markets. These companies — although not necessarily No. 1 in their industry segment globally — tend to focus on building on their unique competencies and mobilizing local resources effectively to achieve medium- and long-term success.

In this book, the authors have used numerous practical examples and case studies from a broad range of industries to highlight the critical importance of defining a strategy for Asia with local market characteristics. Where they have excelled is in their systematic use of analytical models to describe the complex business environment. For example, Stan Shih's "Smiling Curve" model, originally proposed in 1992, is here expanded into a number of innovation-based industry segments. The income distribution models proposed are also intriguingly enlightening for market planning. The authors further elaborate on quantitative measures to define business strength matrix and strategic directional matrix, which are crucial in formulating an Asia Pacific business strategy, and they fine-tune tried and trusted methodologies such as Michael Porter's five-force model to take into account the numerous factors related to Asian market conditions. I believe that readers will unlock the value of this book when they start following the models proposed to plan for their Asia Pacific business strategy.

Jim Morgan
Chairman and CEO
Applied Materials

LIST OF ABBREVIATIONS

ASEAN	Association of Southeast Asian Nations
BOT	Build, Operate and Transfer (a major infrastructure from a private investor to a government)
BRIC	Brazil, Russia, India, and China
BSM	Business Strength Matrix
CCV	Critical Customer Value
CMMS	Component Modules Manufacturing Services
EBITDA	Earnings before interest, tax, depreciation and amortization
EMS	Electronic Manufacturing Services
GDP	Gross Domestic Product
HDI	Human Development Index
IPR	Intellectual Property Rights
IMF	International Monetary Fund
MES	Market Economy Status; a set of measurements imposed by the EU and the US to track if China has fulfilled her commitments as a member of the WTO
METI	Ministry of Economy, Trade and Industry in Japan
NEA	Northeast Asia, comprising China, Japan, Korea and Taiwan
NIC	Newly Industrialized Countries; commonly used in reference to Hong Kong, Korea, Singapore and Taiwan, also called "Tiger Economies"
NPV	Net Present Value
OEM	Original equipment manufacturer, such as IBM and Cisco, but later also referring to the contractor that provides manufacturing services to an OEM

ODM   Original design manufacturing; includes design or
        co-design capabilities by the supplier
PPP   Parity Purchasing Power; a measurement of the actual
        purchasing power based on a basket of goods and services
        that are directly related to the cost of living in a country
ROI   Return on investment
RMT   Regional management team
SDM   Strategic Directional Matrix
SBU   Strategic Business Unit
TQM   Total Quality Management
WMN   A Western multinational; a company whose business
        activities, corporate functions, and headquarters are based
        largely in the Western world
WTO   The World Trade Organization

INTRODUCTION

Judging from the sheer size in land area and population, the Asia Pacific region is gigantic and seems to provide unlimited opportunities for future business growth. In addition, the impressive economic growth in the region including Japan (prior to 1990), the newly industrialized countries (NICs — Korea, Taiwan, Hong Kong and Singapore), and ASEAN countries (prior to 1997) and the rise of China and India have caught the eye of global investors in recent years. Many overseas investors rushed into Asia in a manner similar to the US gold rush of the 1800s. In 2002, China dethroned the US as the leading recipient of foreign direct investment (FDI), with a staggering US$50 billion. In 2003, despite the SARS epidemic in the first half of the year and the constant friction with major trading partners, China received a total inflow of US$53 billion in FDI. The first 10 months of 2004 saw that figure exceeded. Western multinational companies (WMNs), under tremendous pressure to improve or to sustain their profitability, continue to look at Asia — and, in particular, at China — as a safe bet in their global strategic planning.

There are many marketing, competitive and organizational factors that may determine the success or peril of a business in the Asia Pacific. Contrary to conventional wisdom, an international company that is highly successful in its traditional markets may be substantially less so in Asia, even though its technical supremacy and flawless quality remain unchallenged. For readers with a Western cultural background, this book provides a pragmatic approach based on hands-on experience in various industries, as well as numerous case studies from diversified executive

MBA programs. For those readers with an Asian cultural background, this book can serve as a guide in improving their understanding of the strengths and the weaknesses of WMNs in general. It is hoped that this book can help stimulate intellectual debate on globalization strategy, be it for the Asia Pacific region or for the rest of the world.

Although the fundamental principles for running a successful business remain the same, some of the strategies taken for granted by Western executives must be tailor-made or adapted to suit the unique cultural background and different market conditions of Asia. As we have learned from years of experience, the subtle difference between the success and failure of an investment in Asia sometimes lies in the marketing concept, the sales approach, the formulation of a business plan, the empowerment of people or other very basic business principles.

This book is divided into three parts. Part I focuses on macroscopic factors, including national wealth, individual income, government policy, financial stability, Asian cultural background and business practices, and rising market opportunities, that are fundamentally important in defining a business growth strategy for the Asia Pacific. Part II deals with microscopic competitive factors, including conducting competitor analysis, assessing the technology and innovation factor, and using best practice for cost competitiveness, that are important in defining the competitive advantages under the framework of a business growth strategy. Part III incorporates a step-by-step approach to formulating a business growth strategy. It also proposes different investment options and ways of developing an effective organization through maximizing human resource potential, and implementing and tracking the business growth strategy. To make this book as practical as possible for the reader, we have included numerous examples throughout the text to illustrate the particular point under discussion. At the end of each chapter, there is a case study comparing a well-known WMN and a successful Asian company from the same or a similar industry segment using the principles and planning methods outlined in this book. There are lessons to be learned from these case studies by both WMNs and Asian companies.

As history has taught us repeatedly, those countries that are capable of learning from their rivals and turning past failures into competitive advantages always have a chance to recover from defeat, even though it might take several decades or even centuries. Companies unfortunately do not have the luxury of time to go through too many painful lessons, since the average lifespan of a medium-size or large company is only 20 to 30 years. This applies to global giants, too: of the companies listed in the Fortune 500 in 1980, some 60% are no longer on the current list, and only one company, General Electric, that was on the original list of the Dow Jones 30-Industry Index remains so. Essentially only those companies that are capable of instituting a learning culture, building an effective team, and constantly evolving in an ever-changing market environment through systematic strategic planning and constant business review can survive as long-term winners.

PART I

A MACROSCOPIC VIEW OF THE ASIA PACIFIC REGION

CHAPTER 1

STRATEGIC VIEWPOINTS ON ASIA PACIFIC

The vast diversity of marine life reveals the amazing adaptation of the natural world over years of evolution.

ECONOMIC IMPORTANCE

Pre-industrial period (prior to 1769)

Up until the Industrial Revolution in 18th-century Europe, population size and stability were the main drivers of economic activity. People in all parts of the world struggled with rampant disease, natural disaster and social inequality in feudal societies. Commercial trading activities mainly took place in a few ancient civilizations and limited clusters of human gathering. The Middle Kingdom, established along the banks of the Yellow River and the Yangtze River, was numbered among the active trading nations which, at different times, included the Persians in the Gulf region, the Indians in South Asia, the Egyptians in the Mediterranean and the Romans in Europe.

The Middle Kingdom, thanks to its relatively large population, advanced scientific knowledge, and goods such as silk and porcelain, emerged as the largest economy in the world, reaching its peak during the Ming Dynasty in the early 15th century. A number of important Chinese inventions such as gunpowder, the compass, paper, cartography, and dyestuff are thought to predate their Western counterparts by some

500 years. Under the command of General Tseng He, four Chinese fleets of more than 800 vessels circumnavigated the world between March 1421 and October 1423.[1] Chinese sailors and concubines from those great fleets settled in Malaysia, India, Africa, North and South America, Australia, New Zealand and other islands across the Pacific Ocean. The great discovery of the New World by the Chinese was at least 60 years before Columbus, who was reputed to have relied on a Chinese map. At this stage, the main purpose of the great voyages was the search for precious merchandise or unique animals that were to be brought back as tribute to the Emperor. Some economists have estimated that at its peak the Middle Kingdom made up around 35% of global GDP, based on a total global population of around 400 million. This compares with the 27% of global GDP of the current superpower, the United States.

Colonial period (1769 to 1945)

With the onset of industrialization in Europe, great military powers such as the United Kingdom, Holland, Spain and Portugal were able to dominate through their "gunboat diplomacy" and the world entered a new era of economic confrontation and cooperation. As at every other stage of mankind's history, there were winners and losers. Through the ready supply of raw materials, cheap labor, and rudimentary value-added goods from their various colonies, the wealth of Western countries grew rapidly and out of all proportion to the efforts of the overall population of these countries. Those countries with a sound government structure, such as the UK, tended to be the most successful in sustaining prosperity during this colonial period. The success of the British Empire from a mere business viewpoint suggests that a sound management system and government support are always essential in guiding economic development. As a result, the UK — with colonies that covered nearly all continents and all major islands — came to dominate in both West and East. UK-based trading houses such as Jardine and Hutchison were considered the model of how to run an international business in the Oriental world. Even though the carrot-and-stick style of trading was commonly supported by unfair treaties imposed on the colonized nations by the Western powers, it is important to recognize that many crucial modern technologies came to the East during this period. Likewise, many international trading companies benefited greatly from their first full-scale encounter with the East.

In the East, Japan was the first Asian country that woke up to the threats and opportunities presented by Western modernization and undertook comprehensive reform of its industry, its education system and its armed forces. Because of the unique ability of its culture to appreciate, embrace and adapt technology from the outside world to its own ends, Japan was the first Asian nation to succeed in adapting to the new realities. As a result, Japan transformed itself from a country of fragmented warlords into a centralized empire with great economic power and eventually followed the same path as its Western counterparts to colonize its neighboring countries. Through international trade, Japan emerged as the largest economy in the Asia Pacific and set the standard for technology and international trading within the region. The other Asian countries were either being held back as a result of being colonized or were simply being pulled apart by endless civil wars.

Post-World War II period (1945 to 1978)

After World War II, the world was clearly divided into two different economic systems: Communist countries, led by the USSR, concentrated on the planned economy while the rest of the world adopted the free-economy system of the United States. These two economic blocs were entirely independent of each other, regardless of geographical proximity. With the whole of Europe devastated by war, the US became the undisputed economic power in the world, with roughly 47% of world GDP. While the US dominated the free world, Japan re-emerged as the economic powerhouse in Asia. This came about partly as a result of the post-war re-building efforts of the US, and partly because of its own solid industrial base. Most important in this process, however, was the work of a committed government backed by the efforts of an extremely diligent people. During the post-war era, Japan grasped the golden opportunity to supply all kinds of non-military goods to the US; first, during the Korean War and, later, the Vietnam War, at the same time improving its knowledge of consumer behavior in the world's largest economy. The poor-quality image associated with Japanese products such as umbrellas, appliances and clothes in the early days of trading with the US quickly improved as export-oriented Japanese companies learned from their deficiencies and embarked on a course of continuous quality improvement. Many famous management gurus, including Edward Deming and Joseph Juran, were invited by Japanese conglomerates and the government to teach Japanese workers and management one of the most important factors in providing customer satisfaction — quality. The focus on quality-management systems, which was grossly neglected by many Western multinationals, turned out to be one of the most effective differentiation tools used by Japanese companies. As Japanese companies exported more and more to the US and other countries, many world-class companies started mushrooming in Japan and became extremely competitive in the global market.

The first Oil Crisis in 1973, basically a political showdown between oil-rich Arabian countries and the oil-hungry Western world, presented another golden opportunity for Japan to enter a very important industrial segment: the automotive sector. Suddenly, the fuel-thrifty Honda cars that had arrived in the US without drawing too much attention in late 1960s were in hot demand to replace the "gas-guzzling" monsters supplied by Detroit. The consistency in quality and the reliability of Japanese cars impressed American consumers and earned Japanese manufacturers a prestigious image that was later to prove highly valuable in almost all manufacturing segments.

At the same time, the sustained high growth of Japan's economy over the previous 30 years had seen the yen appreciate from 360 to the US dollar in the 1950s to around 120 to the dollar in the late 1970s, and many Japanese companies were enticed to set up their fully owned transplants or joint-venture factories in other low-cost Asian countries. This shifting of the production base was considered one of the main thrusts to drive part of the Asian economy out of the doldrums when both capital investment and technology were not readily available to compete in the global market. Another main driver was the import-substitution and export-oriented government policy adopted by many newly emerging economies such as South Korea, Taiwan, Hong Kong and Singapore. In the case of Korea and Taiwan, the government not only set up bonded export-processing zones but also provided financial loans to certain industrialists such as the Hyundai Group, in South Korea, or the Formosa Plastics Group, in Taiwan, to spearhead the aggressive economic expansion plan. The direct involvement of Asian governments in micro-managing the economy was considered highly successful at this stage because most of those countries also had an abundant supply of competent engineers and well-disciplined workers to cope with relatively low requirements for product design and manufacturing technology. Somewhat ironically, it was the generally stable but authoritarian regimes in these countries that facilitated economic development in its infancy. Labor-intensive industries, including electronics, textiles and toys, turned out to be the pillars supporting the development of several emerging Tiger economies in Asia. Southeast Asian countries, long considered a safe haven and a favorite destination by Japanese investors, also grew in leaps and bounds, though at a lesser pace and on a smaller scale than their Northeast Asian neighbors.

"Emerging Asia" period (1979 to 1990)

After experiencing robust economic growth for more than three decades in most countries, Asia now became more than a low-cost production base for Western multinationals. Across Asia, the sentiment was one of optimism bordering on euphoria. Japan continued its relentless thrust to become the global leader in nearly all industrial segments — automotive, capital goods, computer hardware, construction, consumer goods, metals, telecommunications and banking. As business boomed, the upbeat corporate and consumer sentiment reached an all-time high. The multiplier effect from the accumulated wealth through trade surplus and domestic investment led to an outrageous rise in real-estate and stock values which, in turn, benefited the banking segment, at least on the books. By the late 1980s, Japan was regarded by many Western scholars (most notably by Professor Vogel of MIT[2]) as the "Rising Sun" that would soon replace the US as the most powerful economy. At its peak in the late 1980s, the Japanese banking segment had nine out of the top 10 banks in the world. Under the threatening shadow of Japan Inc., nearly every WMN launched catch-up programs such as providing Total Quality Management (TQM) training for all its managers and employees.

The four emerging economies — South Korea, Taiwan, Singapore and Hong Kong — were held up by many economists as examples of how to outgrow poverty through development based on export-oriented industry, strong government support, hard-working people and entrepreneurship. South Korea's gigantic *chaebols* started entering the global arena in steel, electronics, shipbuilding and chemicals, threatening to replicate or exceed the successes of their Japanese counterparts. Taiwan and Singapore, on the other hand, devoted substantial resources into information technology-related segments in addition to their prior investments in petrochemicals (Taiwan) and oil refining (Singapore).

Some parts of Southeast Asia, particularly in Thailand and Malaysia, also grew tremendously during this period, thanks to strong inbound investment, the generally stable political environment, and reasonable infrastructure (particularly in Malaysia). The high growth in certain Southeast Asian countries or cities unfortunately did not generate greater benefits to the general public as many of the ASEAN members continued to struggle with their own domestic political issues. Nevertheless, the rosy growth prospect seemed to be taken for granted by most Southeastern countries as the momentum of economic growth picked up all over the Asia Pacific region.

Since 1979, China, after 30 years of economic isolation, has announced the establishment of four special economic zones along its coastal provinces of Guangdong and Fujian with a view to attracting the foreign investment necessary for the transformation of its planned economy into a market-oriented economy. Most foreign companies did not respond to the open-door policy immediately, but many overseas Chinese — particularly those who had suffered from rising costs in Hong Kong and Taiwan — quickly joined the first wave of investors and rapidly built up foreign-funded enterprises near the border with Hong Kong or across the Taiwan Strait. The initial success stories for investing in China came mostly from export-oriented enterprises. For the first-wave of investors who entered the domestic-oriented market, the success rate was much lower because there was a fundamental lack of purchasing power for the general public and regulations governing domestic trading were stifling. Even up to 1990, the average GDP in China was less than US$400 per capita which, by the definition of the United Nations, could cover only food, clothing and basic appliances. However, once the seeds of a free economy are planted, and wherever risk-taking can be properly rewarded, entrepreneurship soon blossoms. As the gateway for investment in China, Hong Kong enjoyed the benefits as the most important investment channel in what was potentially the largest market in the world.

The growth engine for the world's economy? (1990 and beyond)

Just as a formidable emerging Asian market was gradually taking shape in the late 1980s, Japan's bubble economy started to decline, as bad debt and business failures surfaced in 1990. Behind the decline lay excessively overvalued stock and real-estate markets that would never be able to fulfill their obligations to the financial institutions. The cheap capital that once helped Japan power ahead to become the global economic giant during a period of ambitious expansion now turned its long overdue adjustment into a financial nightmare.

Regardless of the daunting task faced by Japan to fix its chronically ill companies and financially distressed institutions, other Asian countries managed to escape what could have become the first regional financial crisis and maintained the growth pattern into the early 1990s. Having gone through the sharp economic downturn and embargo imposed by Western countries shortly after the Tiananmen Square crackdown in 1989, China's paramount leader, Deng Xiaoping, made a high-profile visit to Southern China in 1990 and 1991 to reconfirm the government's commitment to the market reform policy. Robust economic development soon returned to China, followed by a heavy inflow of foreign investment that pushed China to the number-two spot in the world for foreign direct investment by 1997. Deng also handpicked Zhu Rongji, one of the most visionary and determined economic architects, to take charge of economic development. Zhu's major accomplishments included laying down a modern fiscal and finance framework, upgrading the basic infrastructure for future economic development, and negotiating accession to the WTO to enable China to become fully integrated into the global economy. As the investment gained momentum, China surpassed the United States as the leading recipient of foreign direct investment in 2002. The following year, this went up again to reach US$53 billion, despite the SARS epidemic sweeping through the country in the first half of the year. As of mid 2004, foreign countries had invested more than US$500 billion in China since the mid 1990s, mostly in the manufacturing sector. The strong inflow of investment as well as the mammoth foreign trade surplus will no doubt continue to make a significant contribution to China's economy. Today, foreign-invested enterprises are the main contributors behind the impressive trading growth figure that, as of the end of 2003, stood at US$851 billion, and surpassed US$1 trillion in 2004 as the top three in the world.

After years of experimenting with socialism, another potentially big economy, India, under Atal Bihari Vajpayee, decided to adopt market-oriented policies and initiated a string of deregulations which were aimed at allowing more foreign investment and stimulating the economy into a sustainable growth mode. Even though it is too early to quantify the real benefits of this to the Indian people, the new economic policy has helped create one of the most robust economic growth periods in the modern history of India. The declining interest rate made middle-class consumers more willing to purchase and to borrow, which led to a multiplying effect on overall economic growth. For the first time, Indians began to enjoy a high rate of growth without being penalized by high interest rates as the country's economy became more market-driven and connected to the global economy. The reform policy came at an ideal time because globalization of information technology gave Indian software engineers, scientists and the English-literate population virtually unlimited access to the global market from an extremely advantageous cost position. India, therefore, has become another hot spot for economic growth — although at a lesser pace than China, mostly as a result of having inferior infrastructure. Even though India's oldest political party, the Congress Party, and its communist ally replaced the incumbent Bharatiya Janata Party (BJP) in May 2004 in an election upset that sent a wave of jitters in the global business community, it is unlikely that the Indian government will stop its massive economic reforms completely. The new prime minister, Manmohan Singh, a former finance minister and a champion of financial reform, has committed to continuing the reform path spearheaded by the BJP while seeking to relieve the massive poverty — estimated to affect at least 25% of the total population — in the rural areas, and the 40% illiteracy across the country.

In 1993, the International Monetary Fund (IMF) described the remarkable economic achievements of the Four Tigers (also called NICs, or newly industrialized countries), the ASEAN countries, China and India as "the Asian Miracle". The upbeat economic sentiment found in all these countries took the form of an insatiable appetite for new capital and additional manufacturing capacity as if Asia would soon catch up with the rest of the developed world. Unfortunately, the boom-and-bust economic cycle hit Asia in 1997 after prolonged abuse of capital in numerous non-productive investments. The event that triggered the financial meltdown was the failure by the Thai government to maintain its currency-pegging policy to the US dollar after coordinated attacks by international speculators on the Thai baht. In mid 1997, international banks announced default on 26 Thai financial institutions which, in effect, proclaimed the onset of the first catastrophic regional financial crisis. Adding to these woes, similar and worse non-performing loan (NPL) problems were discovered almost simultaneously in South Korea, Malaysia and Indonesia. Those Asian countries that did not have suffi-cient foreign-exchange reserves to fulfill their foreign-debt payment obligations were forced to undergo massive financial restructuring by the IMF. The domino effect this created represented the worst setback in the entire history of economic development in Asia. Restructuring of foreign debt meant the immediate shutdown of the non-performing enterprises, which automatically triggered massive lay-offs. Domestic consumption for many non-essential segments came to a virtual stand-still. Bankruptcy rates hit an all-time high in all affected countries. It took up to five years for these countries to get back on track after implementing the necessary financial and banking reforms required by the IMF and paying back the IMF's rescue loans. South Korea, the first to pay off the debt within two years, learned from the humiliating lesson and became very careful to keep its US-dollar reserves at a sufficiently high level — US$100–150 billion. Thailand, thanks to its diversified economic base and its use as a production hub for the ASEAN market by the multi-nationals, managed to return to a growth pattern under the leadership of Prime Minister Thaksin Shinawatra. Indonesia, Malaysia and the Philippines, too, have quietly implemented financial disciplines that are gradually restoring the confidence of their own people and foreign investors alike.

Meanwhile, China and India have continued their remarkable economic expansion and are the envy of the world during a rather stagnant post-dot.com period. China recently climbed to sixth place in global GDP rankings, while India is also approaching the top 10. According to the projections of numerous economists, the 21st century may become another turning point for the global economy. In late 2003, Goldman Sachs[3] projected that the total GDP of BRICs (Brazil, Russia, India and China) would surpass the US and the EU combined as the dominant economic centers within 30 to 50 years. It is worthwhile noting that such a robust projection was based on many hypotheses that are yet to be proven. For example, the study by Goldman Sachs assumed the availability of abundant natural resources and the ability of all of these BRIC countries to improve their infrastructure and to eliminate the growing income disparity in order to sustain the anticipated growth. Simplistic as the logic sounds, however, the study clearly highlights that the economic balance of the West and the East is shifting rapidly. It is vital for business executives to be mindful of the rise of Asia and to develop adequate business strategies to capture the full benefit of the growth opportunities that become available.

DEFINING THE ASIA PACIFIC REGION

A definition

In most management textbooks, a definition of Asia usually includes Northeast Asia (NEA) and Southeast Asia (SEA) but normally does not include India, Australia and New Zealand, citing differences cultural background and/or business practice. However, for the purposes of strategic business planning, it is important to include India, Australia and New Zealand in the Asia Pacific region. Most Western multinationals consider Australia and New Zealand, quite apart from their geographical proximity to Asia, as a major source of Western management talent at a reasonable cost compared to other expatriate options from the EU or the US. Indeed, the adventurous and down-to-earth nature of most Aussies can normally contribute a lot to the regional management team. As the costs associated with expatriates become a general concern to the multinationals, the option to mobilize seasoned managers from Down Under is normally considered a plus.

India is gradually removing its entry barriers and seeking closer economic ties with its Asian neighbors while setting ambitious goals on the global stage. As India and China both embark on their own journey of economic development, it is natural that these two most populous countries and old rivals are going to have more competition as well as more cooperation. For business planning purposes within the WMN, including India within the definition of the Asia Pacific actually provides a broadened view on market similarities, intensity of competition, and the talent pool — in particular, R&D capabilities — within the region. As average Indian purchasing power is more similar to that of other Asian countries, in particular China, than to most Western countries, there are substantial synergies to be gained between India and the rest of the Asia Pacific region in conducting market analysis, selecting raw-material suppliers, identifying suitable local products, benchmarking the best R&D center, and sharing management experience.

Defining the sub-region

In principle, the Asia Pacific region can be divided into Northeast Asia, Southeast Asia, India, and Australia and New Zealand (ANZ). Sometimes, Japan and China are classified under a separate sub-region because of the volume of business and the complexity associated with having a holding company that includes many subsidiaries and joint ventures.

In any event, the definition of sub-region is becoming less important as borders are rendered less distinct by the process of globalization and the availability of Internet technologies. A hierarchy of sub-regional management is no longer the priority in organizing business activities. Instead, a market-facing and business-oriented management structure, with a primary focus on business and a secondary focus on administrative and legal support, is preferred nowadays. An ideal regional team ought to consist of key members spread across different countries in the region. With the advancement of IT, this is becoming a way of life for many multinationals. All sub-regions should fall under the umbrella of a global business team that is the main driver of business and operational activities, while the regional and sub-regional teams should be focusing on coordinating and supporting the global objectives with a tailored regional implementation scheme. The sub-region definition is mostly for the purposes of defining different business plans to meet specific market requirements and tracking business results in a systematic way.

In addition to these four sub-regions, within the multinationals Arabian or Muslim countries are frequently managed directly by the EU or classified as a Middle East (or Near East) sub-region under the EU region. There is no obvious benefit to be had by WMNs in including the Middle East in the Asia Pacific region or, indeed, in excluding it because, with the exception of certain industries such as petro-chemicals, defense, and construction, there are generally limited new-business opportunities in the Middle East. Many Indian trading firms and some Asian companies have long captured the routine business requirements. With a relatively stagnant economy, which is heavily dependent on the export revenue from the sales of oil and its primary derivatives, the Middle East has not yet developed a strong manufacturing base and lacks a sizeable middle-class, which are essential for long-term economic prosperity.

POPULATION, GDP, PPP AND HDI

Accounting, as it does, for more than half the world's population, there is no doubt that Asia carries substantial weight when a measurement is related to population and demography. Out of the top 10 countries in population terms worldwide, Asia has six spots: China (1.24 billion); India (1.05 billion); Indonesia (212 million); Bangladesh (135 million); Japan (127 million); and Vietnam (80 million). However, it is very important to keep in mind that the majority of the population in the Asia Pacific region still live in poverty and have no substantial purchasing power. Take China, for example. Regardless of the ultra-modern coastal cities that are as impressive as the metropolitan cities in the West, there are at least 700 million people living in underdeveloped rural areas or on completely undeveloped farm land. About 30% of these people have a meager GDP, typically less than US$200 per capita. Likewise, India also has a large portion of its population constantly struggling to feed themselves and their families. It is therefore critical that any business plan designed for Asia must clearly define its target customers. A bridge factor commonly used in the Western countries to draw a rough comparison between a known market and a new market must be strictly avoided in any study of an Asia Pacific market. A market study without a proven customer base is equivalent to no market study. Worse still, it is destined for a disastrous outcome in the lifespan of the investment project.

Gross Domestic Product

Asia as a whole makes up roughly 20% of world GDP (see Figure 1.1 for individual regional rankings). Korea is the second Asian country (along with Japan) to meet the standards defined for adequate individual wealth and total national economic power to qualify as a member of the Organization for Economic Cooperation and Development (OECD). Being on the OECD list also implies that Korea is a strong industrial power (12th in the GDP rankings) and a consumer-oriented country similar to developed countries in the West.

Currently, China and India enjoy the highest GDP growth in the region and, indeed, in the world. However, to become a true economic powerhouse, each will need to sustain growth for at least three decades. Only recently has the burgeoning middle class of these two countries become a critical factor to spur the domestic consumption of capital items such as housing, vehicles, consumer electronics, personal computers, jewelry and family vacations.

Parity Purchasing Power

As Figure 1.2 clearly shows, the respective economic rankings of Asian countries are very different when looked at in terms of Parity Purchasing Power (PPP). PPP is the composite index of the actual purchasing power, measured in US dollars, based on the conversion of local purchase of a basket of goods and services related to general living standards. These goods and services include housing, transportation, education, medical treatment, food, clothing, appliances, computers, and so on. After a long period of self-sufficiency during the era of the planned economy, China has the capabilities to produce nearly all industrial goods and consumer products on its own. But it was as a result of several major devaluations of the Chinese currency, the RMB, vis-à-vis the US dollar between 1983 and 1994 that the Chinese currency started

Countries	GDP ($ billion)	Rank	GDP per capita ($ dollar)	Rank	GDP Growth Rate (%)	Rank
Japan	3,978.8	1	31,293	1	2.72	10
China	1,237.1	2	966	9	8.01	2
India	515.0	3	491	12	8.10	1
Korea, Rep.	476.7	4	10,006	6	2.70	12
Australia	410.6	5	20,969	2	2.70	11
Taiwan	281.5	6	12,500	5	3.30	9
Indonesia	172.9	7	817	11	4.10	8
Thailand	126.4	8	2,052	8	5.22	4
Malaysia	95.2	9	3,915	7	5.20	5
Singapore	87.0	10	20,886	3	2.25	13
Philippines	77.1	11	964	10	4.56	7
New Zealand	58.2	12	15,035	4	4.65	6
Bangladesh	47.3	13	349	14	–	–
Vietnam	35.1	14	436	13	7.04	3
Cambodia	3.7	15	294	16	–	–
Lao PDR	1.7	16	304	15	–	–
Brunei	–	–	–	–	–	–
Myanmar	–	–	–	–	–	–

Figure 1.1 Regional GDP rankings of key Asia Pacific countries and economic entities

Source: EIU, 2004[4]

carrying stronger purchasing power than its nominal value. As a result, China has a much lower nominal living cost for housing, compulsory education, medical treatment, public transportation, rice, cooking oil, and charcoal for winter heating than almost any other country in the world, and the PPP for China is about five times that of its actual GDP when the US economy is used as the baseline for comparison. This is the primary reason that China, as of mid 2004, already accounted for nearly 40% of the total global consumption of cement, 29% of steel, 25% of aluminum, 33% of rice, and 20% of mobile phones, while her

Year: 2003

Countries	GDP ($ billion)	Rank	PPP ($ billion)	Rank	PPP ($ per capita)	Rank	Population (million)	Rank
Japan	3,978.8	1	3,558.8	2	28,000	2	127.1	5
China	1,237.1	2	6,007.9	1	4,690	9	1,281.0	1
India	515.0	3	2,966.7	3	2,830	12	1,048.3	2
Korea, Rep.	476.7	4	836.8	4	17,580	6	47.6	10
Australia	410.6	5	559.0	6	28,520	1	19.6	13
Taiwan	281.5	6	551.3	7	24,500	4	22.5	12
Indonesia	172.9	7	738.8	5	3,490	11	211.7	3
Thailand	126.4	8	426.3	8	6,920	7	61.6	8
Malaysia	95.2	9	161.4	11	6,640	8	24.3	11
Singapore	87.0	10	113.5	12	27,030	3	4.2	16
Philippines	77.1	11	317.2	9	3,970	10	79.9	7
New Zealand	58.2	12	86.5	13	22,170	5	3.9	17
Bangladesh	47.3	13	–	–	–	–	135.7	4
Vietnam	35.1	14	191.6	10	2,380	13	80.5	6
Cambodia	3.7	15	–	–	–	–	12.5	14
Lao PDR	1.7	16	–	–	–	–	5.5	15
Brunei	–	–	–	–	–	–	0.4	18
Myanmar	–	–	–	–	–	–	48.9	9

Figure 1.2 Showing GDP, PPP, PPP per capita and population of key Asia Pacific countries and economic entities

Source: EIU, 2004[5]

GDP is only around 3.3% of the global figure. In reality, if the latter figure is multiplied by a factor of five and then normalized by the total PPP figure, China has a 14% share of global PPP. The significance of this becomes clear when compared with the United States, the global leader, which has 26% of global PPP.

Likewise, India and other Southeast Asian countries all benefit from a better purchasing power than the face value (GDP) would indicate, and receive extra bonus points on the total size of the economy when it is measured in PPP. Under the definition of PPP, India's economy is roughly US$3.0 trillion, or a 7% global share. This is the main reason why India's economy is so vital for business development on a global scale.

Japan, on the other hand, has fallen to number two in the Asian PPP rankings because of its higher cost of living than that in the US, which is used as the benchmark for indexing. The relatively low PPP in Japan can also imply that in reality average Japanese consumers cannot afford as many luxury items as may be otherwise suggested by the face value of its income level.

The importance of PPP must be kept in mind in the study of the Asian economy, particularly in China, Japan and India where there is a substantial gap between GDP and PPP. It is important to remember that PPP is the true measure of how much people can afford to spend in day-to-day purchasing activities under a local market environment. GDP, on the other hand, is what the multinationals can convert back to US dollars and put under their globally consolidated P&L statements. A more detailed explanation of the planning of business strategy will be given in Chapter 3.

Human Development Index

When measured under the Human Development Index (HDI), the Asia Pacific region is actually not as successful as it is on the GDP and PPP scales because the aggressive pursuit of economic development by Asian countries has usually been carried out strictly on GDP growth rates (see Figure 1.3). In the past, most Asian countries tended to measure their own success by comparing the growth of per-capita GDP under their reign against that of their rivals. It is quite common to observe that GDP-centric planning by Asian governments was usually done at the expense of concerns about the environment, political reform, a pluralist culture or social security systems. The generally low HDI score for most Asian countries, except Australia, Japan, Singapore and New Zealand, reflects the compromises made in the quality of life for most Asians. However, through the influence of the mass media and modern information technology, there is a growing awareness amongst most Asian countries of the need to give greater consideration to these more "spiritual" aspects of life. This growing shift in focus away from GDP towards HDI provides another golden market opportunity that will be discussed later in Chapter 3.

Countries	HDI Value	HDI	Rank in Asia Pacific	HDI rank in the world
Australia	0.946	High	1	3
Japan	0.938	High	2	9
New Zealand	0.926	High	3	18
Singapore	0.902	High	4	25
Korea, Rep.	0.888	High	5	28
Brunei	0.867	High	6	33
Malaysia	0.793	Medium	7	59
Thailand	0.768	Medium	8	76
Philippines	0.753	Medium	9	83
China	0.745	Medium	10	94
Indonesia	0.692	Medium	11	111
Vietnam	0.691	Medium	12	112
India	0.595	Medium	13	127
Cambodia	0.568	Medium	14	130
Myanmar	0.551	Medium	15	132
Lao PDR	0.534	Medium	16	135
Bangladesh	0.509	Medium	17	138
Taiwan	–	–	–	–

Figure 1.3 HDI scoring and ranking for Asian countries, 2002

Source: United Nations[6]

Key geographic areas for business growth

Geographically, China and India undoubtedly possess the greatest potential for business growth. Each has a large population; each is in the early stages of economic development and enjoys other favorable conditions such as widespread entrepreneurship, a rapidly growing middle-class, competent engineers, solid scientific capability, diligent labor and pragmatic government policy. Japan can always be an important area for business growth provided that a market potential can be realized by offering differentiation instead of commonality. Likewise, substantial business opportunities exist in Korea in selected segments such as finance and advanced technology. As to the rest of the region, similar growth opportunities are possible provided that a thorough analysis is done in a systematic way. However, the intensity of competition in Asia in most cases is greater than that in the US or in the EU because it is manifest across the board, from low-end to high-end products. There will be further discussion of business growth opportunities in Chapter 3.

GEOPOLITICAL ISSUES

Any strategic planning in business inevitably must start by investigating the political risks of doing business in the selected countries. In making decisions on fixed-asset investments, it is vital that any strategic planning must cover major external risks for at least 10 to 15 years. Although we have no intention of dwelling on political ideology in a highly diversified region, it is very important to recognize the potential risks in certain countries; among which some can be very risky in the eyes of investors. It is important to recognize that there is no direct correlation between a specific political system and the success of its economy within the current Asia Pacific context. Democracy is no guarantee of successful economic development; just as having a successful economy is not always dependent on democracy. However, it is generally agreed that a highly developed economy must rely on liberating the brainpower of its people; that is, the ability to innovate without constant interference from a bureaucratic system. Such a highly innovative society can only exist under an advanced democracy based on accumulated experience.

The historical divide

Asia is among the world's most volatile geopolitical areas, having endured a long history of confrontation between neighboring countries, not least during the Cold War era, which came to a symbolic end with the pulling down of the Berlin Wall and the collapse of the Soviet Union. The historical divide was, and is, clearly marked along the border between North and South Korea and in the Taiwan Strait between the People's Republic of China (PRC) and the Republic of China (Taiwan). As the world's only superpower, the United States is constantly seeking to impose its values and standards on the PRC and North Korea which, for their part, have no desire to commit to any political reform faster than their own agendas dictate. As a result, the Korean Peninsula and the Taiwan Strait have the potential to precipitate massive military confrontation. While the general consensus reached by Koreans is for a reunification of the two regimes over an unspecified timetable, Taiwanese public opinion is divided on the issue of reunification, let alone a timetable for its implementation. As the opinion polls show that neither pro- nor anti-independence parties can command a majority vote, the status quo seems to be the natural choice and is probably the best way to preserve the first democratic system in a Chinese-dominated society. Therefore, the biggest challenge for the political leaders across the Taiwan Strait is to handle this highly explosive topic responsibly in steering clear of the brink of catastrophe. Taiwan's political leaders must bear in mind their historical mission to make Taiwan the shining example of both economic success and democratic triumph. The flip side of not being able to deal with such a monumental issue is to marginalize Taiwan's economic position or to turn Taiwan into one of the high-risk destinations for fixed-asset investment in Asia. Under such a scenario, Taiwan would risk blunting the appetite of investors and, despite its favorable location and abundant expertise, losing out in the race to capture the massive growth opportunities in China.

Other geopolitical conflicts in the region carry less risk. Even though the row between two other nuclear powers, India and Pakistan, over Kashmir at times may sound serious enough for investors to step away, the possibility that the brinkmanship will turn into large-scale military action has lessened substantially as both countries are now focusing on building their respective economies. The chances of a destructive military confrontation taking place will more likely depend on the political stability of the regime in Pakistan than that in India. As a well-established democratic country, the chances of India declaring war unilaterally against another country are very slim.

It is worthwhile noting that even if there is a military confrontation between the PRC and Taiwan or between India and Pakistan, it is highly unlikely that this will have a long-term impact on the economic ambitions of the PRC and India. The potential damage to the smaller economies involved in such conflicts can be more devastating and may be much more difficult to recover from than for the two Asian giants. The two old foes, China and India, have also reconciled substantially since the past focus on ideology has been gradually replaced by a focus on economy. The recent exchange visits by high-level government officers and a joint military exercise on combating maritime piracy underscore the priority for both nations.

For the rest of the Asia Pacific region, the only obvious political risk is related to the existence of terrorism and terrorist groups in Indonesia, the southern Philippines and small parts of Malaysia. The negative image associated with terrorism not only hurts the country in receiving foreign investment but also directly affects the overall economic activities in these countries. However, the deeply rooted hatred embedded in much of the recent terrorist activity goes far beyond what can be resolved by the people of this generation, particularly under the iron-fisted unilateralism of current US foreign policy. The impact on the economy of terrorism and the so-called war on terrorism will be far-reaching and will present a major challenge to the governments concerned in the years to come.

Ongoing rivalry versus regional cooperation

In addition to contributing to the high-profile Asia Pacific Economic Cooperation (APEC) Annual Meeting covering all major economies within the Pacific Basin, Asian countries that aspire to develop their economy are all aggressively pursuing sub-regional cooperation treaties in the form of free-trade zones or preferential taxation treatment. Following Singapore's success in signing a bilateral free-trade treaty with the United States in 2003, many Asian countries are actively expanding their cooperation within the Asia Pacific region. For example, China and Japan have recently reached an agreement with ASEAN countries on reducing tariffs, which will lead to free trade in the medium term. India, in fear of losing its competitive edge to the Northeast Asian countries, stepped up its economic cooperation with ASEAN, particularly Thailand, through a mutual reduction in tariffs in order to boost its presence in these countries.

It is therefore important for all Asian countries not to be left without a chair when the music stops. Those Asian countries that have not positioned themselves in a regional or sub-regional cooperative treaty are bound to be the losers in the long term. Among these countries that have not established substantial intra-regional connections, Taiwan stands out as the most controversial. With a GDP of US$281.5 billion and an annualized foreign trade of more than US$324 billion, it is unthinkable that Taiwan, which is ranked at number 22 in the world's economies, is being kept out of any important regional cooperative treaty. There is a great urgency for Taiwan to find relief from the economic isolation that will otherwise hurt its future competitiveness on the global arena.

The impact of political system on economic development

Unlike the United States or EU countries that prefer using macro-economic measures such as government fiscal policy and monetary policy to promote economic development, many Asian governments actually define their national economic development plans based on a four- to six-year cycle, in addition to the two government policies commonly used by the Western governments. Therefore, the invisible hand described by Adam Smith as managing a free economy and its market-oriented activities always has another dimension in most Asian countries. The most significant effect of such government manipulation of the economy is the distortion of the supply-and-demand principle that forms the basic theory of Western management. As the supply can be funded by a public pool of money based on the judgment of a selected group of government planners, leading scientists, industrialists and economic scholars, the fundamental principle of adjusting supply in accordance with market demand can possibly take place at the wrong time or on the wrong scale or may be totally inappropriate, to the detriment of the general public. In addition, the impressive successes of the government-led investment plan by Japan's METI in advanced electronics materials, by the Taiwanese government in semiconductors, and by Korea in the steel and auto industries have frequently disguised the fact that most government-supported capital projects are usually wasted in non-productive areas. In countries where the competency level of the small elite groups is limited or the stakeholders have a vested interest in making investment decisions, the outcome can, not surprisingly, be viewed as corrupt by the general public.

It is quite evident that beneath the surface of many Asian enterprises there is a large portion of government equity. Although it is difficult to quantify the exact ownership of private industry by the governments in Asia, Western business executives must keep in mind that the supply in Asia is not necessarily determined by market demand within a specific country or a target marketplace. The role of most Asian governments is therefore inseparable from daily economic activities and major business negotiations.

The "all-mighty government" concept was attributed to the economic success of Japan, the NICs and China and is evident in daily business activities in most Asian countries. Hence, a seasoned business executive must constantly examine the background of the customers, suppliers and competitors. When there is heavy government involvement in a particular industrial segment, the usual rules of supply and demand may not be valid. It is important to keep in mind that the major reasons for the 1997 Asian financial crisis, as Professor Paul Krugman of Stanford University has rightly pointed out, were the stagnant return on investment and deteriorating productivity despite the heavy flow of capital into the region.[7] Most of these non-performing loans were originally based on short-term working capital requirements but were channeled into numerous speculative investments — some were even borrowed or guaranteed by the governments of the countries affected.

THE TRANSPARENCY INDEX AND ITS IMPLICATIONS

Since most Asian governments have a tendency to manage their economy under the tight control of a privileged group, it is vital that the style of each government is properly scrutinized before making a major investment decision. A group of German social scientists and political scholars have come up with a systematic appraisal of governments across the world based on a set of standards that include visibility, efficiency, integrity, clarity of government regulations, and openness of public bidding to foreign investors. This system is known as the Transparency Index, which is usually updated annually. A recent ranking of Asian governments is listed in Figure 1.4.

While there is inevitably some subjectivity involved in the process of such an appraisal, the general trend as shown on Figure 1.4 matches the common view of business executives who have worked in the Asia Pacific region for extended periods. It is not the authors' intention to point the finger at any particular Asian country. As a matter of fact, the humiliating collapse in the United States of Enron and WorldCom, to name but two, as the consequence of poor corporate governance confirms again that greed and corruption can exist anywhere. Cultural factors are never the main reason for corruption; rather, it is a universal greed that goes beyond checks and balances. Our purpose is to share published data that have won both praise and criticism from several Asian governments, some of whom see this type of appraisal as simply another human rights report published by Western countries. Some take a more serious view and reflect on their own weaknesses. China, for example, has been sending many of its party cadres to Singapore, the most corruption-free Asian country, and Western management schools

Country	2003 Score	Rank in Asia Pacific	Rank in the World	Surveys Used	Standard Deviation	High-low Range
New Zealand	9.5	1	3	8	0.2	9.2–9.6
Singapore	9.4	2	5	12	0.1	9.2–9.5
Australia	8.8	3	8	12	0.9	6.7–9.5
Japan	7	4	21	13	1.1	5.5–8.8
Taiwan	5.7	5	30	13	1	3.6–7.8
Malaysia	5.2	6	37	13	1.1	3.6–8.0
South Korea	4.3	7	50	12	1	2.0–5.6
Cambodia	3.7	8	59	11	0.5	2.7–4.4
China	3.4	9	66	13	1	2.0–5.5
Thailand	3.3	10	70	13	0.9	1.4–4.4
India	2.8	11	83	14	0.4	2.1–3.6
Philippines	2.5	12	92	12	0.5	1.6–3.6
Vietnam	2.4	13	100	8	0.8	1.4–3.6
Indonesia	1.9	14	122	13	0.5	0.7–2.9
Myanmar	1.6	15	129	3	0.3	1.4–2.0
Bangladesh	1.3	16	133	8	0.7	0.3–2.2

Figure 1.4   Transparency Index rankings, 2003
Source: Transparency International[8]

such as the Harvard Business School, to learn and to develop proper ways to overcome numerous problems associated with its political system.

FINANCIAL STABILITY AND RISK ANALYSIS

Common Asian financial characteristics

As a result of accumulated trade surpluses over the years, by April 2004 many Asian countries commanded leading positions in the global rankings of foreign reserves: Japan led, with US$700 billion; China was in second place, with US$440 billion; Taiwan was third, with US$228 billion; South Korea was fifth, with US$164 billion; and Hong Kong (US$124 billion), India (US$113 billion) and Singapore (US$103 billion) occupied the next three positions. The sound financial position of these countries lays a solid foundation for stable economic conditions such as low inflation rates, low interest rates and sustainable domestic investment.

Unfortunately, the conservative fiscal policies adopted by most Asian countries prior to 1990 have been gradually replaced by a public-funded deficit policy, either to stimulate the economy following the Asian financial crisis or — as more democratic ideas took hold in Asia — to win votes. In China, however, the issue of financial stability is very different from the rest of Asia. On one hand, having the highest foreign direct investment and the second-highest foreign reserves in the world seems to put China in a very healthy financial position. Nevertheless, China has a massive non-performing loan problem in the order of US$500 billion or 20–25% of total outstanding loans. There is also a huge under-funding of social security pension liabilities in the order of US$300 billion owed to retirees and future pensioners. With limited investment channels available in China for average citizens, the Chinese government has for years used the high domestic savings, trade surpluses, and foreign investment to fund the dismal finance sector and social programs. As the reduction of non-performing loans through asset write-offs or discount sales of underperforming assets is constantly hampered by risky real-estate loans and white-elephant infrastructure projects, financial stability in China very much depends on how quickly the government can put in place a modern finance and fiscal system. Under the leadership of President Hu Jin Tao and Premier Wen Jia Bao, China will have to work aggressively towards fulfilling her obligations to open up various market sectors — retailing, finance and banking, for example — to international competitors before the end of 2006. The government also has the daunting social responsibility to look after the unemployed and the underprivileged, who make up some 20% of the population, mostly in the rural areas. This is why China must strike a balance between economic growth and social fairness in order to avoid the mistakes committed by the former Soviet Union. The current Chinese leadership clearly understands the hardship of the impoverished and, therefore, insists on using macroeconomic controls to cool the occasionally overheated economy. For the first time, legislation is now being drafted by the National People's Congress to safeguard the interests of farmers and migrant workers. Until China can lift the income of the poorest (currently averaging US$200 per capita) to the still-modest level of US$500 per capita, economic development in China will be constantly subject to scrutiny and control.

Current-account status and government fiscal policy

Having developed their economies through export-oriented industry, most Asia Pacific countries in general have a healthy trade balance, especially after the painful lessons of the 1997 financial crisis. However, as politicians in general tend to protect their own political interests, the fundamental financial weakness in the region normally comes from a lack of the fiscal discipline necessary to achieve a balanced government budget. Such a weakness can be observed in most democratic countries, where incumbent and opposition parties fight hard to win the public vote while ignoring their responsibilities to future generations. Figure 1.5 shows the current-account balance status for countries in the Asia Pacific.

The current-account balance is closely linked to the ability of these Asian countries to pay their outstanding foreign debt obligations and to borrow for future major infrastructure projects. Normally when a country does not have an adequate current-account balance to cover its financial obligations, the chances of incurring a major financial risk are clear. The only exception to this rule is the United States, which is dependent on a massive inflow of foreign capital (estimated at US$2 billion per day as of mid 2004, notably from Asian countries) to finance its mammoth current-account deficit. As the largest owners of US debt, Asian countries are forging a special political tie that will be very difficult to break. China, for example, is one of the major subscribers to US Treasury Bills and its low-cost imports have helped to relieve inflationary pressures in the US in recent years. This complex economic interdependency helps to stabilize the political relationship between the two countries.

Government monetary policy

As the export-oriented economic policies of Asian countries are more dependent on the US economy than on that of the EU, their monetary policies in general tend to follow the lead of the US Federal Reserve Board. The routine announcements of the Board's chairman, Alan Greenspan, effectively set the pace of interest-rate adjustments in the rest of the world, including Asia.

Countries	Current Account Balance ($ billion)	GDP ($ billion)	Current Account Balance/GDP (%)	Rank
Singapore	20.3	87.0	23.3	1
Malaysia	11.9	95.2	12.5	2
Taiwan	24.8	281.5	8.8	3
Thailand	7.6	126.4	6.0	4
Philippines	4.2	77.1	5.5	5
Indonesia	6.6	172.9	3.8	6
Japan	125.7	3,978.8	3.2	7
China	35.4	1,237.1	2.9	8
Korea, Rep.	11.4	476.7	2.4	9
India	2.6	515.0	0.5	10
Vietnam	−0.2	35.1	−0.6	11
New Zealand	−2.0	58.2	−3.5	12
Australia	−25.9	410.6	−6.3	13
Brunei	−	−	−	−
Cambodia	−	3.7	−	−
Myanmar	−	−	−	−
Lao PDR	−	1.7	−	−
Bangladesh	−	47.3	−	−

Figure 1.5 Current-account balance for Asia Pacific countries, 2003
Data Source: EIU[9]

Again as a result of export-oriented government policies, foreign-exchange rates, too, are essentially pegged to the US dollar, which gives most Asian countries a predictable basis for pricing their export products. But, after prolonged delay in adjusting to market supply and demand, the pegging policy also has a tendency to create a bubble economy, where the accumulated foreign reserves far exceed normal foreign capital requirements for investment or trading. Most consumers in Japan, Hong Kong, Singapore, Taiwan and China have, at various stages of economic development, been victims of their governments' rigid monetary policies which have had the effect of driving up the real-estate and stock markets, and the consumer price index to unreasonable levels. Most of these countries did not fully enjoy the benefits of the massive foreign trade reserves and failed to convert these into a higher quality of living for the general public.

Competitiveness by country

Before making a major fixed-asset investment in another country, a company has to consider the political and financial risks involved. However, as free trade and information technology continue to blur international borders, it is equally important to take into account the relative competitiveness of each country or, more appropriately, each economic entity. In the 2004 World Competitiveness Yearbook,[10] nine regional economies, including Bavaria (Germany), Maharashtra (India) and Zhejiang (China), are highlighted because of their unique characteristics in global competition. In order to establish a comprehensive comparison, four competitiveness categories are defined and graded numerically. These are as follows:

- economic performance (domestic economy, international trade, international investment, employment, prices);
- government efficiency (public finance, fiscal policy, institutional framework, business legislation, societal framework);
- business efficiency (productivity, labor market, finance, management practices, attitudes and value) and;
- infrastructure (basic, technological, scientific, health, environment and education).

The Yearbook, which covers 60 national and regional economies, reveals encouraging progress made by Asia Pacific countries as shown in Figure 1.6. Not surprisingly, the strategically focused Singapore is ranked second globally and is top regionally. Australia is ranked number four in the world because of its high score in infrastructure, economic performance and government efficiency. Taiwan, a world-class venue for venture capital and technological innovation, is ranked number 12 in global competitiveness, despite the potentially explosive political situation and massive challenges in infrastructure and government fiscal policy. Malaysia makes an impressive entry into the global number 16 position, mainly because of excellent infrastructure and improved political transparency. Japan, with a global ranking of 23rd, is only one spot ahead of China,

Country/Territory	The World Competitiveness Scoreboard 2004	Ranking	Investment Creditworthiness 2003	Ranking
Australia	86.046	4	91.72	14
China	70.725	24	61.52	42
India	62.971	34	54.92	48
Indonesia	38.095	58	40.05	58
Japan	71.915	23	90.02	21
Korea, Rep.	62.201	35	67.67	36
Malaysia	75.919	16	62.13	41
New Zealand	74.394	18	87.09	26
Philippines	49.666	52	51.33	50
Singapore	89.008	2	89.11	22
Taiwan	79.543	12	79.76	32
Thailand	68.235	29	59.51	46

Figure 1.6 The World Competitiveness Scoreboard (2004) and Investment Creditworthiness (2003) for Asia Pacific Region

Note: The lower the creditworthiness, the higher the investment risk.

Source: IMD World Competitiveness Yearbook 2004

because of the slow pace of political reform and the ongoing struggle towards achieving a sustainable economic recovery. China continues its marvelous economic growth but still lags behind in the sphere of government efficiency. India, with a global ranking of 34, trails China by 10 places mainly because of the poor basic infrastructure and social framework. South Korea takes only 35th position because of numerous domestic issues such as labor unrest, stagnant local investment and a confrontational legislative council. Indonesia, potentially the next big frontier for business growth in Asia, is ranked at number 58 globally because it has not demonstrated sufficient progress in all four competitiveness categories. Unfortunately, no specific data on Vietnam and Bangladesh are available yet from this IMD report.

It is worth mentioning that IMD also tabulates the global rankings on investment creditworthiness for these 60 economic entities. Even though some Asia Pacific countries such as Australia, Japan, Singapore and New Zealand score very high marks, not a single Asian country is in the top 10, which clearly highlights that Asia Pacific countries still need to devote substantial resources to improving their credit-reporting systems and integrating these with the global credit-report data bank. The tremendous progress made by China in investment creditworthiness since the initiative spearheaded by former premier Zhu Rongji provides a good example of how building a reliable software infrastructure is crucial for a sustainable economic growth.

Case Study:

GE vs. HAIER

With top-line sales figures for 2003 of US$9.8 billion, Haier of China would seem to have little scope for a comparative case study alongside GE, whose sales for the same period reached US$134 billion. Yet, with Haier's growth pattern revealing a doubling every two to three years, it is possible that the company could reach annual sales of US$50 billion within 10 years. GE, with frequent portfolio pruning and acquisition, will most likely stay between US$150–US$200 billion.

Bold or blunt as it may sound, it is very important to recognize how far entrepreneurs in China have progressed in the past 20 years. Take Zhang Rei Ming, chairman and CEO of Haier, as an example. As a typical collective enterprise during the Communist days, Haier's predecessor was an ordinary state-owned factory that produced under the direction of a centrally planned economy. There was no need to pay attention to market demand or customer preference because the government decided what the people needed and what they could afford through allocation. However, Zhang Rei Ming, as the plant manager of the collective enterprise, grasped the first wave of market reform in the coastal city of Qingdao and began an amazing metamorphosis from stifling control into vibrant entrepreneurship. After smashing a number of sub-standard refrigerators in front of the plant management committee and uncommitted workers, Zhang championed the boldest campaign to improve the shabby-quality image of the Communist regime and did so with technology from the West acquired via a joint venture with a German company. The learning process imposed by such a unique leader mirrored what Jack Welch had done when he took over at GE in the late 1980s.[11] Welch saw that the competition from Japan clearly cast a long shadow on the viability of the old industrial conglomerate and was determined to move GE onto a totally different path from what it had done successfully over the previous 150 years.

Both men started with a clear vision and a determination to shape the company or to face the inevitable shakeout. The tremendously successful transformation

	GE			Haier		
Financial Results	2003	2002	2001	2003	2002	2001
1. Revenue (US$ million)	134,187	131,698	125,913	9,750	NA	NA
2. Net income (US$ million)	15,002	14,118	13,684	193	NA	NA
3. Total assets (US$ million)	647,483	575,244	495,023	NA	NA	NA
4. Return on equity, or ROE (%)	18.9	22.2	25.0	NA	NA	NA
5. Return on assets, or ROA (%)	2.3	2.5	2.8	NA	NA	NA
6. EBITDA (US$ million)	26,860	24,889	26,790	NA	NA	NA
7. EBITDA/Sales (%)	20.0	18.9	21.3	NA	NA	NA
8. Net income/sales (%)	11.2	10.7	10.9	NA	NA	NA
9. Sales growth (%)	1.9	4.6	−3.0	NA	NA	NA

Figure 1.7 GE and Haier: A comparison of financial performance

Source: Mergent Online database[12]

of GE from a mostly manufacturing conglomerate to a value-based, diversified giant has been well documented elsewhere and is not our focus here.

What we wish to pinpoint here is the ambition, the aggressive business plan, and the pursuit of best practice carried out by Haier. In the white-goods industry that GE also covers, Haier has not only become the undisputed leader in China but is rapidly closing the gap with the global leader, Whirlpool. By 2003, Haier had captured a 50% market share for small refrigerators and a 60% market share for wine coolers in the US, climbing to fifth spot in the world rankings. By mid 2004, Haier had surpassed GE to become the fourth-largest producer of white goods in the world. Haier's impressive progress is only partly due to having the lowest cost base of all the global players. Where it really excels by comparison with Western companies who are trying to develop their business in Asia is in providing quality service to customers in a cost-effective way. It is standard practice for Haier's service teams to provide punctual, free installation of appliances and genuine after-sales service. Any complaint or issue raised by the customer is met with an immediate, free follow-up service. Only when the customer is completely satisfied with the installation is the matter closed. Most Western companies doing business in China or elsewhere in Asia find it difficult to match such service. As a result, Haier is building an image as a service leader in the white-goods industry. However, through harnessing synergies with other electronics and electrical industries, Haier is expanding rapidly beyond being a pure appliance player. While customer-service teams in the field report encouraging feedback on substantial quality improvements, additional innovative products, such as washing machines specifically designed for families living in agricultural areas, have been introduced. These take care of washing vegetables as well as drying farm products effectively.

Besides leading the appliance market in China, Haier has now positioned itself in overseas markets by setting up 22 offshore manufacturing facilities, including one in South Carolina in the US. The company's marketing approach in the US closely resembles that used by Honda in the early 1970s to attract entry-level users who have limited funds. Today, in the US Haier is perceived as the leading entry-level appliance supplier, mostly through college dormitories and rental apartments. However, as these young graduates start families, Haier goods stand a very good chance of being their first choice because of reliable quality, good service and low cost.

The potential for Haier to gain market share is promising because each of its manufacturing sites has a design team to focus on differentiated products within the selected market. Today, Haier boasts an R&D spending of 4% of total sales revenue — a very respectable figure, even by international standards.

In another example of its customer-oriented business growth strategy, Haier designs air conditioners specifically for Middle East countries to give maximum cooling and improved durability under harsh conditions. In the US, Haier engineers design refrigerators not only to fit into the confined dormitory space but also to provide extra functions such as acting as a foldable computer desk for college students. For Japanese customers, Haier is focusing on quieter and smaller models that fit comfortably into the confined living space of the average Japanese apartment. Haier is also among the few Asian companies that have established an R&D center and factory in India in pursuit of further marketing opportunities.

As a result of its unprecedented success in transforming a typical socialist enterprise into a modern international conglomerate and reshaping its entire business organization in order to meet the customer's requirements, Haier has now become the focus of many Western management school studies. The business model adopted by Haier basically defines the financial responsibility of each employee within its organization. For example, R&D employees keep a continuous track on the revenue generated by their product against the total cost, until the R&D cost is completely paid off and shows economic return. Likewise, production managers are asked to track sales revenues against total cost so that prudent business decisions can be made in response to customers' demands.

GE, which no longer considers itself a manufacturing company, naturally will focus more on the high-end home appliances, particularly through the integration of multiple electronics appliances via remote control and artificial intelligence. GE will also try to capitalize its strength by providing financial services or capital loans to its distributors. It will no doubt continue to be one of the most admired companies in the world because it has a brilliant management team and an excellent business portfolio that allows it to benefit from different stages of the global economic cycle and broad geographic coverage. However, GE's share of the electronic appliances market will decrease as various commodity segments continue to migrate to specialty segments. What GE and other multinationals need to bear in mind is that Haier is expanding rapidly into highly diversified areas such as financial services, pharmaceuticals, hotels, restaurants and other industry segments. History shows that massive diversification can turn a highly successful company into either an unstoppable giant or a dinosaur destined for extinction.

CHAPTER 2

UNDERSTANDING ASIAN CULTURE AND BUSINESS PRACTICE

In the mad pursuit of excessive profits, it was the greed of the chiefs and their confidants that caused irreparable damage. It was never about a race or a culture.

UNDERSTANDING ASIAN CULTURE

Key cultural elements

Deeply influenced by Confucianism, Buddhism, Hinduism, Taoism and feudalism, traditional Asians normally behave quite differently from Western people. These differences are, to a large degree, attributable to an Asian identification with the group, as opposed to the more individualistic behavior of Western culture. Confucianism, for example, preaches that respect for the elderly, the educated and those in authority forms the basis of society. Students of traditional Asian society must commit themselves to understanding complex etiquette and to studying classical literature reflecting on the wisdom acquired over thousands of years. During the Song Dynasty in China (960–1279 AD), the emperor usually appointed a top officer to supervise examination boards and create a highly complicated examination system for the screening of talent. It was not unusual for participants to study in isolation for decades before they could excel in the examinations. The government recruited only those with the highest marks from the millions who participated in the examination system. Having survived this tough screening system, the elite few were rewarded with treasure and official positions in accordance with their ranking. Naturally, most of those chosen became vigilant guardians of the rules, rituals and formalities of the old society. The same etiquette and literature were likewise passed on without compromise to the next generation. Thus, Confucianism itself is a powerful tool to guide a large population on a predictable path. It teaches people to focus on studying in chaotic times so as to avoid getting into political trouble. This pragmatic approach is woven into the social fabric of most of the Oriental world. Confucianism places great emphasis on social harmony and imposes moral standards on the general public. It teaches people to respect knowledge and the well-educated. All of these virtues have proved to be very valuable in the pursuit of economic development.

Buddhism and Hinduism have their origins in India. Central to each is a belief in reincarnation based on the karma of a previous life and each teaches people to practice and accumulate good deeds in order to earn a better next life. The inherent value of these two religions lies in assisting people to endure the hardships and uncertainties of life. As neither required Christian-style baptism and practices, there was little formal structure. Throughout the harsh and frequently brutal history of feudal society, the role of Buddhism and Hinduism was mostly to cleanse the mind and to elevate the soul of believers to a higher spiritual world. Even today, there is no doubt that both philosophies help keep most Asian people content and peaceful in their dealings with life, nature and society.

The third major religion within Asia is Taoism. It is not really about worshipping a god or gods. It is more of a philosophy shaping a life of purity and simplicity. A person who achieves liberation from the trappings of superficial materialism may become a saint. The supreme state of Taoism allows for the possibility of turning people into gods, a state that may be hastened through serving society. Although Taoism also provides another means of guiding, and thus controlling, a huge population, it can form a quasi-society in itself. The group activities within Taoism actually form another channel for serving the public and provide another safe haven for average people in a turbulent society.

The last, but not the least, major factor that dominated Asian culture for thousands of years is feudalism. Like their counterparts in the West, the privileged few in the East enjoyed the majority of wealth in a generally impoverished society, the only difference being that the dark age of feudalism had a much longer history in the East and its effects have been longer lasting. The heavy-handed and frequently ferocious approach taken by most tyrants, warlords and government officers no doubt instilled constant fear in the people whose dreams were often limited to bare survival. Chinese history, for example, has recorded many instances of the brutal suppression of those who opposed government policy, sowing the seeds of fear and distrust towards government officers. Silence is not only golden but was the safest way to guarantee the continued existence for many Oriental people. Even today, a marked reluctance to speak in public, especially in the presence of the boss or other figures of authority, is a distinguishing characteristic in many Asian countries. It is less than 100 years since the first, ill-fated, Asian democracy, the Republic of China, was set up by Dr Sun Yat Sen. However, this regime, beset by civil war and rampant corruption, was eventually replaced by the Communist People's Republic in 1949 and retreated to Taiwan. Even though freedom of speech was granted to many Asian people after World War II, liberation from feudalism in Asia wasn't really achieved until the past two decades, when successful economic development in several Asian countries brought about a general transformation of democratic ideology into a political system.

Balancing Asian and Western values

By putting so much emphasis on collective interests, including the importance of family and relationships with others, Asian values, from time to time, tend to stifle individualism. Asians also tend to give higher priority to hierarchical structures than to egalitarian ideas, emphasizing authoritarian decision-making over the more open discussion and dispute that marks Western decision-making processes.

Of course, there are differences between various Asian countries in the degree to which such cultural values are evident. Yet only a few Asian countries, namely those dominated by Westerners, including Australia and New Zealand, do not properly fall within the traditional value system described above.

The downside of Asian values usually comes from the formidable mindset to protect the interests of family and close friends at the expense of the public interest. The interpretation of family can be expanded to include the inner circle or the loyal subordinates or even government officers. Within the intertwining group there is a great deal of trust that can often transcend the requirements of the law. Major transactions can be executed without resorting to complicated legal due diligence and commercial procedures. This type of gentlemen's agreement was quite commonly respected in traditional Oriental society, where business relationships usually lasted for a long time. While such arrangements can be powerful and effective when key decisions must be made within a pressing timetable, they also prove to be a common source of corruption when respect for law and public interest are compromised. Therefore, before anyone enters negotiations with an Asian partner or begins business operations in Asia, they must have a clear understanding of the subtleties of Oriental social and business culture.

Turning Asian values into management strengths

During the boom years of the Asian economy, Lee Kuan Yew, the well-respected architect of Singapore's political, social and economic success, attributed the great economic achievements of Japan and the Four Tigers to their inherited cultural values. The frequently used term "Asian values" connoted a passion for knowledge, the excellence of teamwork, the unselfish sacrifice of self for the betterment of the family, the willingness to save money to invest in tomorrow, and so on. By a broad definition, Asian values appeared to highlight collective benefits, as opposed to the drawbacks of individualism commonly found in Western culture. Many Western scholars actually echoed or acclaimed Asian values because Japan was about to overtake the US as the biggest economy in the late 1980s and the Four Tigers appeared to be about to replicate that success on the global stage.

Indeed those virtues associated with Asian values can be tremendously beneficial for building the solid groundwork for a country's prosperity when diligent people are guided by a group of competent economists and technocrats. A high savings rate for an economy in its infancy is one of the immediate benefits to be derived from Asian values because it is critical to accumulate enough capital for sustainable economic growth. In China today, the average savings rate as a percentage of income is around 50% — one of the highest in the world. The passion for higher education, if properly planned by government, can lead to an abundant supply of educated labor and high-quality engineers. For example, Chinese universities turn out about 400,000 scientists and engineers each year. Likewise, Asians tend to be more disciplined than Westerners because of the strict doctrines imposed by society and the schools. As a result of all these behavioral differences in performing well-defined routines, Asian countries are frequently considered to be preferred manufacturing destinations. Disciplined workers tend to produce higher product quality at higher throughput. It is interesting to note, too, that Singapore, Taiwan and South Korea all have two or three years of compulsory military service for young men aged between 18 and 24. The cadet training helps many young people to fit into a group activity. They also learn to manage a platoon of soldiers, which is very similar to managing a small factory. Standard military training normally includes mastering the chain of command, maintaining supplies, practicing teamwork and developing interpersonal communication skills. Such activities can also be found in China, where most students go

Cultural Element	Positive Influences	Negative Influences
Confucianism	(1) Imposes ethical standards and work discipline (2) Respects the elderly and the educated (3) Cultivates learning habit	(1) Difficult to innovate outside the box (2) Old guard only allows incremental progress (3) Lack of balance between theory and practice
Buddhism	(1) Reinforces people-centric management culture (2) Helps people endure uncertainty during times of change	(1) Loosely organized (2) Tends to be too passive in dealing with corruption and misconduct
Hinduism	(1) Pacifies the soul and spirit in turbulent times (2) Harmonizes group relationships	(1) May mislead people to accept class society (2) May tolerate unfairness
Taoism	(1) Accepts higher moral ground for the common benefit of society (2) Less dependent on materialistic incentives	(1) Acting as a group may be a trade-off for individualism
Feudalism	(1) Accepts management power	(1) Difficult to develop two-way communication (2) Hard to stand up against management's abusive use of power and unethical conduct

Figure 2.1 Major Asian cultural elements and their influence on management practices

through paramilitary training sessions at some stage of their schooling. It seems natural, therefore, for Asians to be adept in the areas of manufacturing in the early stage of economic development. For Western business executives working in Asia, it is important to recognize the strengths of the East that may not be available in their home countries. If Asian values are properly managed, they can become tremendous assets for Western multinationals.

ASIAN AND WESTERN THINKING AND BEHAVIOR COMPARED

Because of differences in culture and values between East and West, there are considerable differences in the way Asians conduct business. A summary of the key differences in thinking processes and business behavior is set out below:[13]

	Asians	Westerners
Way of thinking		
Subject	holistic	individualistic
Social status	hierarchical	egalitarian
Relationship	beyond business	business networking
Logic	interrelated	sequential
Approach	authoritarian	open to discussion
Means	enforcement of order	fact-oriented
Channels	relationship	information
Duration	long-term	short- or medium-term
Business behavior		
Etiquette	formal	mostly informal
Meeting format	multiple objectives	clear objectives
Delegation	limited	authorized
Responsible party	normally unchanged	frequently changed
Information exchange	need-to-know basis	open exchange
Business proposal	arrived at indirectly	direct and open
Negotiation style	passive but persistent	direct and less patient
Priority setting	favorable total deal	principles and objectives
Expected partnership	long-term	business-driven

ASIAN BUSINESS CHARACTERISTICS BY CULTURAL GROUP

Chinese ethnics

Since the Chinese are the largest single ethnic group in the world and China is the largest growing market, its business characteristics deserve special attention. Of all the common Asian characteristics, face — that is, social recognition — stands out as the most important element in any dealings with Chinese. If Chinese are made to suffer a loss of composure or, worse still, total embarrassment in front of others, superiors or subordinates, this most likely will lead to a business disaster or even the pursuit of revenge of some sort because face is the most important measure of social success for a Chinese, regardless of whether he is born in mainland China, Thailand or Taiwan. What Westerners may consider a minor social blunder, when it causes loss of face it is much more serious in the eyes of Chinese. After all, face is about the social status that the individual has been building over his entire life.

Another critical business characteristic is the way that Chinese, in particular mainland Chinese, are highly skilled at using persistence as a weapon to succeed in whatever they consider to be the most important goal. Many Westerners, confident that they have succeeded in persuading their Chinese business partners on a particular point after long sessions of negotiation, eventually discover, just as they are about to wrap up the deal and go home, that there is still something left unresolved. A Westerner's approach to negotiation is generally based on logical, sequential steps. For most Chinese, however, negotiation consists of a series of isolated subjects that are eventually all connected together based on the value of the total deal. Such an approach requires persistence and endurance, and can be a powerful tool for Chinese business negotiators, who generally are able to outlast their Western counterparts to secure the point they are seeking or, at least, to achieve compromise at the final moment.

Indian

Indians have a reputation for being extremely intelligent and sophisticated in their business dealings. Any formal business negotiation with Indian partners must be well thought through by the Western company's representatives before any official meeting takes place. Indians seem to have the ability to remember every single detail that has been discussed and debated. This, together with the ability to prepare legally smart documentation, can often give the Indian partner an edge in any subsequent business dispute unless the Western partner ensures that it maintains detailed and accurate legal records of its own.

The long history of British rule in India and the various political and social institutions the British left behind have given Indians considerable experience of what works and what doesn't work under Western management systems. The fact that English is the official language of this vast and diverse country has also given educated Indians a greater understanding of how Westerners think, and has removed some of the barriers to open communication. Indians have a deserved reputation for their mathematical, scientific and English-language skills — all of which make them attractive to a WMN. On the other hand, Indian society is still riven by deep-rooted social and religious divisions that often lead to infighting or prolonged internal debate that is detrimental to productive teamwork and economic development.

There is a certain cynicism amongst many educated Indians regarding politics and social injustice in their country and an awareness of this is important for doing business in India. Westerners should understand, too, that the inevitable dealings with government can be very complicated and time-consuming. For many years, the Indian government has been recognized by the global business community as being very inward looking because of its slow adoption of international trade rules. The onerous tax regulations and frequent government intervention in business activities are two further obstacles for foreigners wishing to do business in India. Even though the Indian government, principally under the leadership of the BJP, has made great efforts to integrate its economy into the global community, it is clear that further improvements are needed in the areas of introducing greater transparency of government regulations, upgrading infrastructure to bring it closer to international standards, and in reducing the frequency of anti-dumping charges being brought against its trading partners.

Japanese

Japanese people have an official name for themselves as the People of Great Harmony, and the search for harmonious relationships with society, with the elderly and with authority underpins traditional Japanese life. Not surprisingly, perhaps, consensus-building is one of the most important traits of Japanese culture. But the same spirit that has created a much-admired passion for detail and contributed to the building of superior-quality products also imposes the most challenging obstacle for Westerners wishing to deal with the Japanese business community. With isolated exceptions such as Sony and Toyota that do not have complicated cross-ownership with gigantic conglomerates, most Japanese companies take a long time to reach important strategic decisions on such issues as re-engineering the business, streamlining certain non-performing business units, deciding on major investment projects or forming joint ventures overseas. Ironically, the worst enemy faced by the mighty Japanese conglomerates today as they struggle with the rapid change of the global business environment is one inherited from its own cultural traits.

A seasoned Western executive normally finds out who the decision-makers are for a particular project after engaging in prolonged contacts with different people or third-party intermediaries in a Japanese company. Nevertheless, having identifying the key decision-makers does not mean that it is no longer necessary to maintain close contact with other people in purchasing, manufacturing, planning, site management, and so on. No part of the whole business process should be skipped, because this could lead to a possible gap in consensus. Naturally, doing business with a Japanese company will require a lot of patience, local knowledge and inside contacts. It is, therefore, very important to build a long-term relationship with the targeted Japanese customers through a visible, preferably high-profile or well-respected, local presence within the company rather than through a distributor.

Korean

Korean people are known to be extremely hard-working, patriotic and very proud of what they have accomplished in rebuilding their home-land after the devastation of the Korean War. Any suggestion or impli-cation that is seen to question national achievements is, quite naturally, regarded as an insult to the Korean people. Throughout the years of shaping the "Miracle of the Han River", Koreans have gained a lot of confidence in building world-class steel, automotive, marine transport, semiconductors and telecommunications industries. The primary interest of Koreans working with a foreign business is to gain access to critical technological know-how. Any WMN that intends to do business in Korea must always keep in mind the importance of bringing relevant technical expertise to the negotiation table, either as a transactional package or in the form of ongoing sales support.

Many Western multinationals have failed in their Korean ventures because of strong opposition from local companies and the militant unions that believe they do not need foreigners to teach them what they can do by themselves. Foreign companies normally have a hard time persuading the local partner that the foreign partner has more to contribute than technology itself. The constant fight for management control frequently leads to an impasse between the partners. Although the anti-foreign investment sentiment improved substantially after the financial crisis of 1997, one should not underestimate the hidden resentment against foreign-operated manufacturing sites in Korea. Utilizing the services of a local trading firm or taking full control themselves, of course, can make life much easier for foreign investors to do business in Korea.

Others

Of the other cultural groups, the Thais are generally welcoming of foreign import products and in developing working relationships with foreign partners. The Thai government under Prime Minister Thaksin has paid back the IMF loan borrowed during the 1997 financial crisis and put the country back on track to economic prosperity. Thailand is a favored investment destination among Southeast Asian countries because of its pro-business environment, harmonious racial relationships, the diligence of its people and the low cost of living. The unique Thai culture, along with its beautiful land and coastal scenery, has made Thailand a world-class tourist destination.

FACTORS AFFECTING PURCHASING BEHAVIOR

A lifelong quest for enrichment

Even though there is little difference between East and West in the pursuit of a better quality of life, Oriental people perhaps tend to be a little more obvious and a little more predictable in their quest. Besides setting aside substantial sums of money for the education of their children, their typical purchases include an apartment commensurate with their income; a car or two; an overseas family vacation; or a watch, jewelry and electronic gadgets that reflect their social status. The various fulfillments of this lifelong quest are made possible in Asian countries by high savings rates and the strong family bonds that help smooth out any ups and downs encountered in life. The high savings rates in Japan, China,

Hong Kong, Taiwan and Singapore are considered to be a major driving force behind their overall economic success.

Focus on education and the next generation

To most Asians, there are few things more important than getting a higher educational degree. The cultivation of the next generation can start even before the child is born and continues through all phases of schooling. The devotion to education for many Asians derives from culture, tradition, rivalry and family. The advantages that come from an almost-fanatical passion for education are an enduring respect for knowledge and expertise, a constant enhancement of professional knowledge, and a continuous upgrading of working skills.

Recognition of a successful life

As social recognition always receives top priority in the Oriental world, the common measure of success in Asia is the number of brand-name products owned by the individual. While wealthy people in the West may choose to live in whatever way they wish, the average Asian tends to show off their success in materialistic ways. Thus, luxury brands — Mercedes-Benz, BMW, Rolex, Patek Philippe, Louis Vuitton, Chanel, Tiffany, Prada — and membership of prestigious private clubs, no matter how ridiculously expensive, can always command a fair market share in the niche market of Asia. In fact, as more Asians become more wealthy, these brands should be able to increase their market share. Recognizing the preference of the elite group to be socially noticeable, Citibank and HSBC, for example, are making big efforts to offer high-profile, premium, private financial services, and BMW is quickly becoming the most recognizable brand name in China as a result of its aggressive promotion of exciting new models, including the flagship model 760, and the stylish SBU X5.

COMMON BUSINESS TABOOS AND TIPS

It goes without saying that before attending any contract negotiation, opening ceremony or funeral service in Asia, Western business people should always consult with the local sales representative on local customs to avoid committing any errors that are likely to give rise to offense.

As a rule of thumb, it is important to be mindful of the conservative characteristics of most Oriental people and the importance of paying respect to the elderly or to those responsible for organizing any business engagement.

While there is nothing wrong with getting to the point in business negotiations, in Asia it is preferable to take it step by step, consulting with the people responsible for each facet of the business transaction. When all involved are properly covered and convinced in this way, it brings confidence to the building of a long-term business relationship. It is only when such a comfort level is reached that the transaction can move on to the final approval. Therefore, one must bear in mind that haste does make waste in business dealings with Asians. Proper relationships are crucial and to cultivate these it is important that the Western company's local representative maintain frequent contact and social interaction with the proposed partner and, depending on the significance of the deal, high-level personnel from the company too should make visits at appropriate times. For those who are not willing or able to spend enough time in Asia, a rush-in and rush-out visit will not yield much progress. In the mid 1990s, Jack Smith, former CEO of General Motors, made five trips to China in one year to cover all levels of Chinese authorities in central government, city government and JV partner before his company beat Ford Motor for the contract to build a large automotive plant with Shanghai Automotives. This strategy has completely paid off because today the joint venture has become one of GM's most profitable passenger-car businesses, accounting for one-quarter of the profits generated by GM globally in 2003.

NEGOTIATION AS A WAY OF LIFE

While Westerners tend to view each business deal as a separate and discrete entity, Asians are always looking for a good total deal. The same is also true from the standpoint of time. Where Westerners normally treat the negotiation of each project like the beginning of a new baseball or soccer season each year, with past projects having little or no bearing on the current negotiation, this mentality is not necessarily well accepted by Asians, who tend to share success among the partners and their close allies on a continuing basis. Favorable deals are frequently reciprocated and negotiation between Asian partners can be carried out on a continuous basis as long as they consider each other friends. Westerners sometimes find it difficult to break into certain business opportunities that appear, on the surface, to be in their favor but for which they lack the necessary relationships. Asians tend to believe that giving support to each other in business is a natural extension of an enduring friendship.

Westerners who work in an Asian cultural environment must learn to be flexible, but within the legal framework, in dealing with the requests of their Asian customers or partners. Major contract negotiations between WMNs and Asian customers frequently require the Western partner to think differently from their usual way of doing business. For example, Asian customers, particularly those in countries which have low-income levels, consider training or overseas trips as a critical part of their total business deal because it may involve their participation in technology transfer. At the individual level, Asians may also consider that an overseas trip offers a chance to increase their knowledge or raise their social standing. If the representatives of the WMN can use training as a bargaining chip at the right time, it may facilitate the deal or increase the value of the total deal.

HARMONIZING WESTERN BUSINESS PRACTICE IN ASIA

There is no fundamental conflict between Western business practices and the Asian way. Most multinationals with sufficient experience of various Asian countries know that Western business practices can be in perfect harmony with the Asian business environment. What is disturbing and detrimental to the multinationals is the breaching of company regulations by certain employees and executives in order to profiteer beyond their regular compensation package.

For seasoned Western executives, the handling of multinational business in Asia should start from a clear communication of the company's corporate guidelines to ensure that there is no conflict of interest between the WMN and its employees in day-to-day business activities. It is only when corporate guidelines and ethical standards are met in full that business development can be conducted in a sustainable manner. The key personnel involved in setting up, implementing and supervising the Asia business plan must be well trained in the areas of international trade compliance, standards of business conduct, and external communication guidelines. In the long run, the cost of ensuring complete compliance with these fundamental requirements is usually much lower than the cost of non-compliance.

However, training is only a starting point for the entire compliance process. Frontline sales managers, country managers, controllers,

HR managers, purchasing managers and so on must remain alert at all times to ensure compliance by all employees in the country where business is being conducted. Routine audits and verification are essential. These should include regular checks on the background of the shareholders of suppliers and/or distributors and on any relationships between them and the company's employees, particularly in sales and purchasing departments. Any rumors of irregularities should be thoroughly investigated by the authorized legal representative and the compliance officer. It has been proven that multinationals that choose not to pursue irregularities normally turn out to be the losers in the market eventually.

Case Study:

SINGAPORE AIRLINES vs. BRITISH AIRWAYS

Singapore Airlines is the world's leading airline, outperforming its competitors in impeccable service quality both on board and on the ground, availability of routes, state-of-the-art aircraft, competitive fares, frequent-flyer program, and brand name recognition. As a result, its financial performance (with annual sales of US$5.94 billion, a net profit of US$602 million, a return on equity of 9.9% in 2002) has been the envy of the entire airline industry. Despite the setback of the SARS outbreak in 2003, Singapore Airlines continues to be one of the most recognized brand names in the world. Fundamentally, the company's impressive success is attributable to the strong support it receives from the Singapore government through its investment arm, Temasek Holdings Pte. Ever since Singapore Airlines was launched back in 1972, the Singapore government has adopted an entrepreneurship model for Singapore Airlines by appointing board directors from diverse business backgrounds in the private sector around the world, and selecting a member of management as its CEO. Currently, there are three non-Singaporeans on the nine-person board.

What is unique in this success story is that Singapore Airlines is proficient in a business model strongly dependent on three major competencies: providing quality service; managing capital expenditure; and optimizing collaboration with international partners. Singapore Airlines is the pride of every Singaporean and this finds expression in the financial strength of this wealthy city-state. Singapore Airlines constantly shops for the best and the most modern aircraft in order to stay ahead of the competition. The latest addition to the Singapore Airlines fleet will be the Airbus 380, a super-Jumbo which, thanks to its ultra-strong and light-weight composite technology, can accommodate 555 to 800 passengers and offers a generous seating and entertainment environment. The company is expecting to take delivery of the 380 in 2006, ahead of all other global airlines. Singapore Airlines is the industry leader in in-flight entertainment equipment and programs that give its economy-class passengers almost the same service standards as business-class passengers in rival airlines. It is in the area of service quality that the Singaporean discipline and professional training enable it to outshine its competitors by a substantial margin. The fundamental training for Singapore Airlines actually is not much different from other airlines. But the management of Singapore Airlines presents its flight attendants as goodwill ambassadors of their country. They are given much more authority to deal with customers' complaints and concerns than their counterparts in other airlines — a distinct competitive advantage in the service industry. Of course, the strict discipline of the education and training system in Singapore provides good preparation for the demands of the flight attendants' careers with Singapore Airlines.

Collaboration with international partners works to the advantage of Singapore Airlines because any international route exchange is always based on bilateral agreement and mutual exchange. Having established substantial competitive advantages in aircraft and service quality, any collaboration with international partners only reinforces the benefits Singapore Airlines receives from the weakness of its rivals. Coming from the only developed economy in ASEAN and South Asian countries, Singapore Airlines is strategically positioning itself in a market environment that is strongly leaning in its favor because none of the neighboring countries can match the service and aircraft standards it has established.

Among the global airline companies, there are only a few that come close to the financial performance of Singapore Airlines. The majority of the solid performers — Cathay Pacific, All Nippon Airlines and Qantas Airways, for example — are also based in Asia. There are few Western airline companies that can come close to Singapore Airlines in service quality. British Airways and Southwest Airline are two exceptions. Since the latter is predominantly a domestic airline within the US, for the sake of comparison, British Airways has been chosen for this case study. Sharing some of the same service concepts as Singapore Airlines, British Airways is considered to be one of the most service-oriented airlines, with excellent in-flight customer service by well-trained flight attendants, innovative designs in its business class, and an excellent safety record. Of course, British Airways (with 2002 sales of US$12.1 billion and a net profit of US$113 million) suffered as much as the rest of the Western airline industry after the 9/11 terrorist attacks in 2001. However, British Airways was able to implement more successful cost-reduction programs than other Western airline companies and recorded a net profit of US$236 million on a sales turnover of US$13.7 billion in the calendar year ending March 31, 2004.

As a political legacy of Britain's imperial past, British Airways enjoys several profitable and, sometimes, exclusive international routes that would have to be

	British Airways			Singapore Airlines		
Financial Results	2003	2002	2001	2003	2002	2001
1. Revenue (US$ million)	13,719	12,106	11,891	5,773	5,943	5,088
2. Net income (US$ million)	236	113	−202	502	602	343
3. Total assets (US$ million)	22,127	20,177	19,493	9,810	8,834	8,392
4. Return on equity, or ROE (%)	5.9	3.5	−7.0	2.0	2.6	1.5
5. Return on assets, or ROA (%)	1.1	0.6	−1.0	2.6	3.4	2.0
6. EBITDA (US$ million)	1,967	1,530	941	1,100	1,021	1,060
7. EBITDA/Sales (%)	14.3	12.6	7.9	19.1	17.2	20.8
8. Net income/sales (%)	1.7	0.9	−1.7	8.7	10.1	6.7
9. Sales growth (%)	13.3	1.8	−9.1	−2.9	16.8	−5.8

Figure 2.2 British Airways and Singapore Airlines: A comparison of financial performance

negotiated much harder by other competitors. Such route connections usually give British Airways some competitive advantages because most of Britain's former colonies have not been very successful in upgrading their economy or in building their own national carrier. But British Airways has only limited options to improve its profitability because its staff costs are high, its fleet is grossly under-utilized, and its traffic flow is heavily dependent on a mature market. The opportunity to grow its business is constantly challenged by the potential loss of customers to low-cost carriers on its home turf and in its major market, Europe. The difficulties confronting British Airways in many ways are common to all Western airlines. Three years after the attacks on the World Trade Center, most Western airlines are facing rising operating costs due to the high cost of fuel, the need to make additional investments to improve safety features, and excessively high insurance costs, as well as shrinking sales revenues as a result of severe competition from no-frills carriers. Overall, the revenue generated per passenger mile has been reduced by some 30% over the past six years for the entire airline industry, despite the steady improvement in the number of passengers since the terrorist attacks in 2001. The airline industry overall has lost more than US$30.9 billion over the past three years and is not expecting to return to financial health until there is a full recovery in the global economy and a return to reasonable jet fuel costs. Therefore, the prospects for British Airways clearly are not the brightest.

Singapore Airlines, even though it has demonstrated a solid financial performance in the aftermath of SARS in 2003, also faces risks and challenges. The substantial salary cuts imposed on flight crews as a way to battle post-SARS financial pressure were the first of their kind in the company's history. It is not clear whether this type of intervention will adversely affect the service quality on which the company's success is built. Singapore's Minister Mentor Lee Kuan Yew has outlined three principles for Singapore Airlines to stay competitive: do not automatically follow other airlines in terms of pay and other cost benchmarks; loosen work rules so that pilots can fly and earn more; and be flexible about recruitment and do not get locked into rigid systems. Singapore Airlines, known to the world for its unparalleled service, clearly will not be the same if its service quality is compromised.

Meanwhile, Singapore Airlines has started rolling out its own discount airline, Tiger Airways, in a joint venture between the founder of Ryanair and Temasek, designed to combat the increasing presence of low-cost carriers in Asia. Again, this is an untested area in the history of Singapore Airlines and in the Asian aviation industry as a whole. Given its track record of strong leadership there is good reason to believe that Singapore Airlines will continue its outstanding financial performance and maintain its leading brand name in this high-profile industry. After all, as a national symbol, Singapore Airlines is much more than just an airline company to Singaporeans.

Note: This case study was written without input from Singapore Airlines.

CHAPTER 3

ASIA MARKET OPPORTUNITIES

In GDP terms, in 2003 Asia made up 20% of global output. In PPP terms, Asia represents at least 40% of global output today and is projected to climb to 50% within 15 years. Those global giants that do not have an effective business strategy for Asia to deal with these market opportunities and competitive threats may face sudden extinction, just like the dinosaurs 65 million years ago.

MACROSCOPIC MARKET ANALYSIS

GDP-based market analysis

Gross domestic product (GDP), the most commonly used measurement of national wealth, is based on the conversion of various foreign currencies into US dollars and is therefore considered the most useful tool to assess the size of a specific market. It is important to note that, at the time of writing, Japan's GDP (around US$4 trillion) is bigger than the rest of Asia combined. For any company capable of developing differentiated products, Japan is one market on which they should not miss out because Japan, more than any other Asian market, can afford a price premium. On the other hand, there is only limited room for commodity items and non-differentiated products in Japan despite the long-term efforts of many Western companies. For example, US car manufacturers, led by the US government, have been trying to force Japan to open its market and allow access to its comparatively large domestic automotive market. However, despite these efforts the combined market share of GM, Ford and Chrysler remains at a negligible level because US cars in general do not take account of the requirements of the Asian market and offer little differentiation in the eyes of Japanese consumers. However, the Japanese government, bowing to strong political pressure from the US government, eventually lowered import duty and removed certain restrictions on the distribution of foreign products. German car manufacturers such as BMW and Mercedes, perceived as being suppliers of differentiated and superior vehicles by affluent people and the younger generation in Japan, have been reaping the tremendous commercial success that was made possible by the US Government. Another major stumbling block for entry into Japanese markets is the distribution network, which is complicated and inefficient by international standards.

Ranking just behind Japan is China. With a total GDP that has basically quadrupled in the past two decades, China presents the largest potential of all Asia Pacific countries. The latest projection is that the GDP for China, which reached US$1.237 trillion in 2003, will reach US$2.0 trillion by 2008 and surpass Germany as the third-largest economy in the world. The impressive growth in China in the past two decades is matched only by the US after World War II, where massive infrastructure investments, jubilant consumer sentiment and dominant export sales created the biggest economic superpower. As the average per-capita GDP in China remains low, at US$966 in 2003, despite the strong growth over the past two decades, its economic development remains at a relatively modest level. If China continues along the successful path it has been charting, it is generally believed that it may well become a truly awakening dragon, as Napoleon Bonaparte once predicted.

South Korea, Taiwan, Hong Kong and Singapore form the next tier of economic power, typically referred to as NICs or Tiger economies, because each has acquired considerable international trading experience in the manufacturing or service sectors. The number of success stories emanating from the NICs is increasing on the global stage because these countries, after nearly half a century of economic development, have established world-class core competencies in various industry segments. The combined GDP of these four economies is equivalent to another US$1 trillion.

The next major rising opportunity is India, which in 2003 had a GDP of less than US$515 billion. India has enjoyed tremendous economic growth over the past three years, particularly in late 2003 and early 2004. India possesses great business potential as long as the continuing political rivalry between the BJP and the Congress Party does not disrupt the economic roadmap charted by the market reformists. In selected industries such as computer software, India has already demonstrated that it has the capacity to be one of the leading players in the world. In the pharmaceuticals industry and in outsourcing business support, too, India has great potential to be among the global frontrunners. If India succeeds in building these critical industries and removing inappropriate government regulations, there are few limits on how well this country will perform economically. In the process, however, it have to resolve the major domestic challenge of confronting social inequalities while maintaining a market-oriented economy.

ASEAN (excluding Singapore) has a total GDP of around US$510 billion based on 2003 figures. This group of countries has great potential because they have a huge population and abundant natural resources compared to the industrialized Northeast Asia. However, time has proven these countries must improve the efficiency and stability of their political systems before they can position themselves for sustainable economic growth.

Both Australia and New Zealand have abundant natural resources, including iron ore, coal, copper, aluminum, diamonds, and natural gas, and small populations relative to their respective land masses. Australia has the highest levels of natural resources per capita and one of the best living environments in the world. Given its population of under 20 million and its isolated location, Australia is unlikely to become a major economy in the foreseeable future. But both Australia and New Zealand, with a combined GDP of US$468.8 billion in 2003, can certainly benefit from active participation in the dynamic growth of the rest of Asia.

Even though GDP is the most commonly used economic indicator, it can be deceptive as to the true status of the living environment. Its most obvious limitations are its failure to take account of environmental protection or the replenishment of natural resources. Because the majority of Asia Pacific countries do not have sufficient natural resources to compensate for the massive destruction associated with being the global hub of manufacturing activities, it is quite evident that economic development often occurs at the expense of nature and the quality of life. Recently, China published its first "Green GDP" (that is, economic production minus environmental costs) for Shanxi province, its coal-mining heartland. When the costs incurred through environmental degradation and the depletion of natural resources were taken into account, the province's "Green GDP" for 2002 was only 67% of the official GDP figure.

PPP-based market analysis

Parity purchasing power (PPP) is a very different measurement from GDP in the sense that it quantifies the actual purchasing power in different economies. In general, in an economy that has experienced free international trade for years, the GDP and PPP are very similar. In those economies that have been separated from the free-trade bloc, there is normally a major difference between PPP and GDP. A deregulated government policy will eventually close the gap between PPP and GDP as the economy is integrated into the global community through free trade. The gap between GDP and PPP can, however, be used to predict the relative affluent levels of consumers in different countries. If PPP per capita is much higher in one country than in another with the same GDP per capita, it suggests that consumers in the former can afford a lot more purchasing activities than those in the latter. If PPP is substantially smaller than GDP on a per-capita basis, the opposite is true.

The best example to exemplify the gap between GDP and PPP is China, which did not join the global free trade until 1979. During the early days of its Open Door policy, China retained so many of its protectionist policies and unfair trade barriers that its currency, the renminbi, did not reflect its true value in comparison to global standards. In recent years, because of the massive trade gap between China and its trade partners, particularly the US and the EU, the value of the Chinese currency has been under constant scrutiny by the international financial community, which has frequently claimed that the artificial weakness of the Chinese currency must be revised upwards. However, China has many domestic financial problems, including the infamous non-performing loans and the under-funding of the social security scheme, that constantly require the replenishment of fresh capital generated from trade surpluses, inbound foreign investments and government bonds. Without the inflow of fresh capital, the entire Chinese economy would probably be much more vulnerable than the marvelous statistics would otherwise suggest. Therefore, for the foreseeable future China will most likely continue to keep the renminbi pegged to the US dollar while it attempts to resolve its complex financial and fiscal problems. Currently, China is embarking on integration with global financial markets in the areas of insurance and financial services under a very demanding schedule imposed under the agreement for its accession to the WTO.

China's relatively strong PPP vis-à-vis its GDP has a major impact on the market price for a number of items sourced and produced entirely locally. In general, the selling price of these domestically produced items falls way below the selling price of similar products from abroad. Thus, when Western multinationals first entered China it generally came as a great surprise to them to find that their target selling prices for the local market were way above the price range of local products. This is true for most items that China produces locally without having to buy raw materials or import equipment from overseas. Examples of such goods and services include paper, beer, books, basic schooling, medical treatment, trucks, buses, and even satellites. Therefore, Western companies must be mindful of the market price in the selected industry in which they wish to participate.

Another special case is Japan's low PPP relative to GDP. Having a PPP value substantially smaller than its GDP indicates that Japan is falling behind the US (the benchmark) in sharing the benefits of its collective economic success with the general public. For years Japan has been relying on an excessively complicated distribution system under cumbersome laws regulating how products should be distributed by foreign enterprises. Therefore, regardless of the extremely high level of per-capita GDP, the purchasing power of the average Japanese is limited, which is something of a disincentive to foreign companies looking for an opening in Japan's domestic market. The Japanese, especially youngsters, are becoming less patient with the snail's-pace of domestic economic reform and are becoming more receptive to foreign products. Dell Computer is one of the few IT companies that have been successful in distributing computers into Japan through direct sales and now has a PC market share of 10% in Japan. Another potentially big breakthrough will probably come from Wal-Mart in the hypermarket segment after it acquired the Japanese company Sei-Yu. Meanwhile, many Japanese continue traveling overseas to enjoy the full benefit of their purchasing power.

In the past, the PPP for most of the NICs was less than their GDP because of high real-estate costs compared to the US benchmark. However, over the past three years the low interest-rate policy used by the US Federal Reserve to stimulate the US economy has driven up real-estate values in the US, which in turn increases the PPP in the NICs. Today, most NICs, with the exception of Hong Kong, have a higher PPP than GDP, which means that their local purchasing power is more than that of their US counterparts with the same GDP per capita. Benefiting from depreciated real-estate values, low-cost public medical care, low public education costs and low import tariffs, Taiwan now enjoys a per-capita PPP that is almost double its GDP per capita. Both Singapore and South Korea also enjoy a higher PPP than GDP on a per-capita basis because their economies have also gone through similar adjustments but to a lesser degree.

Hong Kong on the other hand, has a lower PPP than GDP because the majority of a Hong Kong citizen's income goes into mortgage payments for living quarters. Even after losing half of their value since early 1997, Hong Kong real-estate prices remain among the highest in the world.

HDI-based market analysis

In the past, personal and social development were rarely considered by most Asians, who were too busy struggling to make ends meet to think about such things. Nowadays, as Asians are becoming better off, matters relating to the quality of life are becoming increasingly important. This is reflected in market trends that indicate a gradual shift away from merely fulfilling basic needs for food, clothing, transportation, education and entertainment towards increased spending on philharmonic tickets, professional sports, postgraduate study programs, overseas family vacations, contributions to charity, support for environmental protection, and so on. This purchasing pattern usually shows up when the average GDP per capita surpasses the threshold of US$6,000 or the average PPP per capita surpasses the threshold of US$10,000. By mastering the HDI-oriented purchasing preference, it is possible to predict the opening of windows of opportunity for certain industry segments, as mentioned above.

Another very crucial factor in determining the onset of HDI-based market opportunities is the cultural element of a specific market study. For those countries that are known to be passionate about extra-curricular knowledge, the combination of HDI preference and the pursuit of lifelong personal development can create a unique demand for certain business opportunities. For example, Club Med was founded by a French company many years ago to promote specialist tourist packages. After a fruitless pursuit of business in Asia in the early years, the company initiated a comprehensive study of consumer behavior in different nationalities and eventually discovered an effective approach to promote their services to customers from different cultural backgrounds. For example, knowing the preference of Japanese consumers for extensive coverage of local cultural history, Club Med hired local specialists who spoke fluent Japanese and arranged cultural events specifically for Japanese tourists. This experience can be very helpful for others who wish to exploit other HDI-oriented market opportunities. The tremendous success of Starbucks across Asia also underscores the common desire for a wider choice of goods than is currently available. Similarly, the concept of HDI-based market analysis can be extended to the incorporation of some special entertainment events into a typical family vacation. The rapid expansion of the scope of business

Countries	Total GDP ($ billion)	GDP per Capita ($ dollar)	Total PPP ($ billion)	PPP per Capita ($ dollar)	HDI
Japan	3,978.8	31,293	3,560.0	28,000	0.938
China	1,237.1	966	6,007.8	4,690	0.745
India	515.0	491	2,966.6	2,830	0.595
Korea, Rep.	476.7	10,006	837.5	17,580	0.888
Australia	410.6	20,969	558.5	28,520	0.946
Taiwan	281.5	12,500	551.7	24,500	–
Indonesia	172.9	817	738.9	3,490	0.692
Thailand	126.4	2,052	426.4	6,920	0.768
Malaysia	95.2	3,915	161.4	6,640	0.793
Singapore	87.0	20,886	112.6	27,030	0.902
Philippines	77.1	964	317.4	3,970	0.753
New Zealand	58.2	15,035	85.8	22,170	0.926
Bangladesh	47.3	349	–	–	0.509
Vietnam	35.1	436	191.6	2,380	0.691
Cambodia	3.7	294	–	–	0.568
Lao PDR	1.7	304	–	–	0.534
Brunei	–	–	–	–	0.867
Myanmar	–	–	–	–	0.551

Figure 3.1 Business opportunities based on GDP, PPP and HDI

Sources: EIU[14]

United Nations[15]

in Las Vegas from gambling into a multi-purpose family destination is another very good example of an HDI-based marketing approach. Both Macau and Singapore are working on a similar business model to build a multi-purpose holiday destination for Asian tourists. In recent years, Thailand and Malaysia have been promoting high value-added tour packages that may include spa, golf, cruising, diving and gourmet dining to attract high-income tourists from all over the world. As leisure and cultural travel become available to more middle-class Asians, it will present one of the biggest business opportunities for many industry segments serving this HDI-based market.

DEFINING MARKET OPPORTUNITIES

Defining opportunities based on organic growth

One simple marketing model is to define the future market size of a particular industry based on current market size, past growth pattern and the projected industrial growth rate in the next five to 10 years. This model is suitable for relatively mature industrial segments such as rice, wheat, paper, poultry, vegetable oils, textiles, steel, coal, gasoline and basic petrochemical products. As the consumption of these commodity items depends largely on the size of the population and, more specifically, on the population of a certain income level within the market, the target market size can be estimated through collecting specific data related to population size, demographic trends and per-capita GDP.

Multinationals, prior to making any decisions on major fixed-asset investments or on setting up a nationwide sales network, must find out the local supply capabilities of their competitors, both current and future. The lack of local market knowledge is one of the most common mistakes committed by WMNs, even for very commodity-oriented industries. While the importance of organic growth is recognized, it is equally important to understand the demographic trends in different marketplaces. For example, Japan is a market with a rapidly ageing population. In such circumstances, the size of the market for many basic commodity items will actually shrink. Similar demographic trends can also be found in almost every Northeast Asian country, Australia, New Zealand and Singapore. Of course, the one-child policy in China is one very special reason why China will quickly encounter this problem while its economy is still in the developing

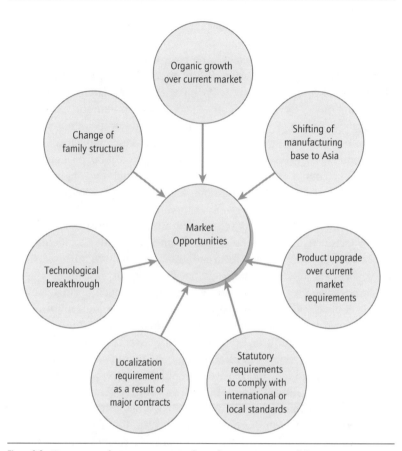

Figure 3.2 Future market opportunities based on various models

stage. In all of these countries, apart from China, the purchasing behavior of the elderly will be similar to that in Western countries because of the relatively high purchasing power.

For the other Asian countries that are still at a relatively low-income level, the demographic trend is not so pessimistic. In the case of India, there is still a major problem to prevent the explosion of her population, in particular those with low incomes and low job skills. Countries such as Indonesia and India that show considerable organic growth potential may not have the income to purchase the promoted items. In the end, even this simple marketing model must incorporate adequate local sales data and key economic statistics.

Defining opportunities based on shifting the manufacturing base

Over the past five to 10 years, some industries, notably the electronics industry, have begun a massive shift of their entire industrial base from the Americas and Europe to the Asia Pacific region. Therefore, the Asia marketing model for such industries should incorporate the Asia market plus a good portion of the current American and European markets. The determination of the size of future Asian markets inevitably must include a comprehensive investigation into the future plans of current customers in the Western market. Some WMNs may opt for high-end applications or quick-turn applications or national security-related applications that clearly are achievable only by those companies with local production sites in the home market. A comprehensive business model should cover the global technical trends, segment by segment, in order to identify the products to be moved in any future migration of manufacturing.

Asia Pacific first became the global manufacturing hub because of its competitive cost position and gradually developed a cluster effect; that is, it developed synergies among relevant component manufacturers that were achieved through close vicinity, short production cycles, joint design, information exchange, and convenience for the buyers. The famous electronics manufacturing belts include northern Taiwan, southern Guangdong and Greater Shanghai. Within a radius of 50 to 100 kilometers, multinational buyers can source a full range of electronics products offered by a number of OEM assembly companies that are engaged in fierce price competition. Multinational buyers naturally enjoy the full benefits of the cluster effect in their total purchasing costs and overall operational efficiency. Some WMNs even situate their regional purchasing headquarters next to these manufacturing clusters.

Similarly, many conventional or labor-intensive manufacturing industries, including textiles, bicycles, shoes, ornaments, candles, auxiliary tools and back-office support services, have already shifted or are shifting to Asia in order to prolong their business vitality by leveraging the favorable cost position and the growing business opportunities in Asia.

Defining opportunities based on product upgrade

During this period of burgeoning economic development, golden opportunities are bound to arise as a result of Asian customers upgrading their purchasing patterns from mere functional goods to comfort or from frugality to luxury. This transition is usually marked by the rise of income levels to a threshold value, the perception of value to customers, and the creation of brand names.

There are many examples of success based on the full capture of product- upgrade opportunities. For example, to Chinese consumers, in the old days, instant noodles meant a pack of dry noodles and some flavoring ingredients that could save kids from starvation until their parents returned from work, or a light dinner for boarding students. Then Chef Kang, a small transplant from Taiwan, completely re-wrote the definition of instant noodles in the China market by incorporating separate packs of sesame oil, specially flavored sauces, and high-grade noodles similar to the noodle soup available only in restaurants. After a smashing entry into market, Chef Kang became an instant commercial success, with annual sales jumping to US$1 billion within five years of the product launch. Many big international players such as Uni-President of Taiwan and Nissin of Japan, having been left in the dust, were still puzzled as to how the management of Chef Kang had been able to see what they could not.

Similarly, Volkswagen of Germany was equally visionary when in 1985, just six years after Communist China had started its unprecedented market reforms, it moved its Quantum production line from Pennsylvania to Shanghai to take advantage of the upgrade opportunities that were becoming available. A new name, Santana, was given to the new identity of the first modern passenger sedan in China. This initiative represented an impressive turnaround for Volkswagen, most of whose previous offshore production plans had failed. More details will be given in the case study at the end of this chapter.

Defining opportunities based on statutory requirement

As various Asian countries gain admission to the WTO, they will have to open up various segments of their own markets while they enjoy the improved trade conditions offered by their counterparts around the world. For example, under the terms of its accession to the WTO China has agreed to completely open up its finance sector to foreign competition by the end of 2006. Multinational banks have been working on this golden opportunity since the early days of China's market reform in the 1980s. HSBC and Citibank are the two most active players in pursuing these new business opportunities in China through acquisitions and direct investment. Simultaneously, Chinese finance and insurance companies are tapping into the international finance markets by making initial public offerings (IPOs) through reputable global companies. The huge success of the recent IPO launched by Citibank and Goldman Sachs on behalf of China Insurance is a shining example of this.

Similarly, India has also had to reduce its excessively high import tariffs — in the order of 20–50% on almost every industrial and consumer product — in order to fulfill its obligations as a member of the WTO. India has opted to start liberalizing its international trade with neighboring countries such as Thailand in order to improve its competitiveness on the global market. Therefore the first wave of business opportunities to enter Indian markets will start from Thailand before full-scale statutory compliance kicks in in the near future.

In addition to the commitments made to reduce taxes and to allow market access as part of the terms and conditions of their entry into the WTO, all WTO members have to endorse certain basic environmental protection standards. For example, the ban on using ozone-depleting chemicals, including fluorinated hydrocarbons, is a mandatory requirement of WTO membership. Thus, the entire fluorinated hydrocarbons industry, including domestic air conditioners or automotive air conditioning systems, has seen massive change since the introduction of these legal requirements. Likewise, the launch of the first fuel-efficiency standards for the automotive industry by the Chinese government will undoubtedly have a major impact on the future competitive environment in China. In order to cope with the rapidly rising demand for oil imports which has made it the second largest oil-importing country in the world, China is ready to impose a fuel-consumption standard that is tougher than those which the United States tried to implement after the oil crises in the 1970s and 1980s. The additional benefit that China is looking for through this new statutory requirement is to increase automotive export opportunities. Those companies that wish to seize such opportunities must be capable of following through with the statutory requirements and incorporating them into their strategic business plans.

Defining opportunities based on localization requirements

Along with any major infrastructure project signed by governments come localization requirements. This is particularly true for major purchases such as power generators, high-speed trains, airplanes and even military equipment. Usually, an Asian government will propose a complex web of local vendors that should be getting a share of the master contract, which should be based on international engineering specifications. Only those local companies that can demonstrate a trustworthy track record and engineering capabilities should be eligible to undertake local production. At the same time, local government will normally request specific technology transfer as part of the terms and conditions of the master contract. Localization requirements are becoming increasingly common because of the intensified competition between WMNs, Japanese corporations and South Korean conglomerates for major infrastructure projects in various Asian countries.

A good example of defining market opportunities based on localization requirements can be seen in the civil aviation industry. As Boeing and Airbus compete for every big order in Asia, more localization projects will arise. To ensure that it maintains its 100% market share in Japan's All Nippon Airways (ANA), Boeing has agreed to allow more localized manufacturing for the launch of its new, energy-saving 7E7 model. Japan will benefit more than any other Asian country from this expansion in the aerospace industry because it has the technological capability to produce high-quality carbon fibers and composite materials, and the heavy industry necessary to cope with the manufacture of airplane components. As a result, it is anticipated that Japan will reinforce its global position as the third-largest player in the aircraft component industry and the third-largest market for aircraft.

Similarly, the increasing demand for a high-speed train network and a modern power-distribution grid in Northeast Asian countries also creates opportunities for localizing several critical components such as train locomotives, high-voltage power-transformation systems, and advanced braking and bridge-reinforcement technology. These new market opportunities are critical for many WMNs that have experienced stagnant or declining demand for major infrastructure projects in their home countries.

Of course, localization can also be mandatory in certain Asian countries which have explicit statutory requirements that prevent foreign companies from owning a majority share in, say, the automotive industry. Here, the foreign partner must implement a localization plan before it is allowed to sell its products to the domestic market. This mandatory localization is, of course, a form of protectionism that will become less acceptable under WTO rules. However, with competition becoming increasingly fierce, it is likely that some players may choose to offer localization as a differentiation tactic or as part of the total sales package. Indeed, it may be very difficult for a WMN not to offer any localization when the race is closely contested.

Defining opportunities based on technological breakthrough

Even though technological advancement in itself is not necessarily a creator of economic value, it usually serves to enhance a business proposition and sustain economic value. Faster CPUs, higher-pixel LCDs, higher-memory-chip digital cameras, camera-equipped mobile phones, more durable clothes, stainless cloth, and radio frequency identification chips (RFID) are all good examples on how technology breakthrough can bring business opportunities. The famous Smiling Curve of value creation (Figure 3.3(a)), originally proposed for hi-tech industries by Stan Shih in 1992,[16] highlights that the value creation, as expressed by the Y-axis, tends to concentrate at both ends of the value chain, as expressed in the X-axis, that is, in R&D as well as sales and marketing. Lower value is created in the middle of the process, which covers such things as repetitive assembly activities.

The technology breakthrough can be derived from research and development in the form of intellectual property rights, while the distribution of finished products is heavily dependent on having a famous brand name and outstanding service quality. Market creation by technology breakthrough is particularly important in Asia because Asian customers are

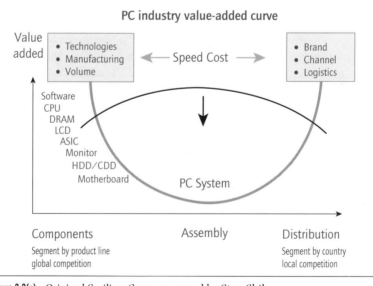

Figure 3.3(a) Original Smiling Curve proposed by Stan Shih

actually more demanding in terms of constant technological advancement and product diversification. Since there is, in general, good manufacturing capability in Asia, the major differentiation factor naturally will rely on the technology.

The basic Smiling Curve concept can also be applied to numerous other industries for an analysis of value creation and business processes. For example, the added value for the digital industry usually concentrates on core technology in semiconductors, software and display, as well as core competency in distributing products through brand management and sales channels. If the same Smiling Curve is applied to the computer software industry (see Figure 3.3(b)), the core technology side normally includes operating systems, middleware, application software and localized software, while the product distribution side normally covers brand name, after-sales support and application knowledge. From the standpoint of the business process, a software company must build a global technological platform for its products that will serve the specific applications needs of its customers in a target local market.

Likewise, the semiconductor foundry industry can also be described by the Smiling Curve (Figure 3.3(c)), with the development of advanced

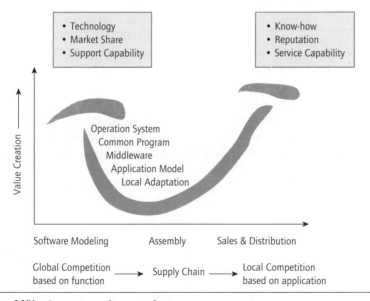

Figure 3.3(b) Computer software industry

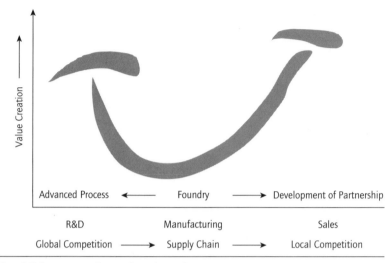

Figure 3.3(c) Semiconductor foundry industry

manufacturing processes as the core competency to create economic value and the development of partnerships with key customers as the product distribution channel.

Even for a seemingly mature industry such as agriculture, it is still possible to re-invent the business by strengthening intellectual property rights and creating new products using new biotechnology (see Figure 3.3(d)). If production can be outsourced in a location close to a big market such as China, it is still possible to achieve substantial economic value. However, the agriculture industry is part of the food industry, which pays a lot of attention to brand name and product quality. Therefore, another critical competency required for this business strategy is the distribution capabilities based on brand name and cost competitiveness.

Another way of creating market opportunities is to use innovative technologies to fulfill future requirements for environmental protection. People are becoming more conscious than ever of the increasing toxicity of our air and water supplies as a result of higher dioxin and furan content in our waterways. These substances are closely linked with the incineration of halogen- containing electronic products, and there is a growing demand to reduce or eliminate our dependence on halogen-based products, or on bromine used in the textile and furniture industries to meet statutory fire-resistance regulations.

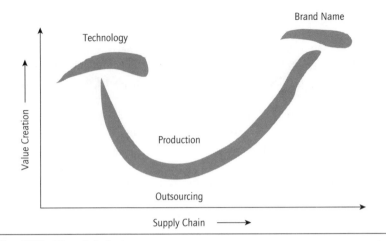

Figure 3.3(d) Biotech industry

One excellent example of progress in this area is the efforts made by several leading resin producers, copper-clad laminators, printed circuit-board companies and consumer-electronics companies to create a halogen-free electronics industry. It is anticipated that following the conversion to halogen-free consumer-electronics products in Japan, scheduled for the end of 2005, there will be a region-wide — or even global — requirement to address this critical environmental issue.

The introduction of the hybrid-cell engine for the automotive industry is another technical breakthrough that can substantially reduce environmental pollution. The broad acceptance of the hybrid engine in Toyota's Prius model around the world underscores the gigantic market potential for such a good cause provided that the technology-related increase in purchase cost is not prohibitive and can be offset by a reduction in fuel consumption. Answering the loud call for solutions to environmental problems, Toyota has announced that it will introduce the Prius into China, too.

Defining opportunities based on change of family structure

Only 30 years ago the concept of the traditional family to Asians was fairly straightforward: it consisted of a working father, a care-taker-for-all mother, several children, and grandparents. However, the rapid spread of Western values through the mass media has had far-reaching effects on Oriental society over recent years. While the percentage decline in the number of traditional families in Western populations has been steady, to around 50%, most Asian societies have witnessed a sharp decline to a record low. Meanwhile, there are more and more people, in particular well-educated young people, who choose to stay single much longer than ever. In Asia, divorce rates in nearly every country have risen dramatically in recent years. For example, in Shanghai and Taipei, the divorce rate has reached one-third, which is not very far below the average American or European figure of around 50%. Since China removed the need for government approval for any divorce application only five years ago, the pace of change is nothing short of phenomenal. These changes in family structure have wide-reaching implications for the structure of society, for consumer behavior and, hence, for market opportunities.

The changing family structure in Asia means that greater business focus should be given to small families, female decision-makers, and even single householders. For those consumers that are classified as individual economic entities, the concept of HDI is becoming increasingly important. The quality of products and services will carry a much higher weight than the price itself. In higher-income countries, for example, the ownership of pets and their care will no doubt become a major business opportunity. Knowledge-based travel, health spas, music appreciation, gourmet dining, wine tasting and convenience stores will also receive special attention from these consumers.

CURRENT AND FUTURE MARKET SHARE IN VARIOUS ASIA PACIFIC INDUSTRIES

Figure 3.4 sets out the estimated current and future market share of various Asia Pacific industries based on sales revenues. Essentially, all industries in the region will grow at a much faster pace than those in the US and the EU. Industries such as automotive, construction, computer hardware, computer software, consumer goods, energy, food and beverage, insurance, luxury goods, merchandising and so on will experience even stronger growth because they are closely linked to the rapidly growing middle-class and the unique Asian culture.

Industry	Asia Market Share in 2003	Asia Market Share in 2020
Aerospace	25%	40%
Automotive	33%	50%
Auto Parts	40%	50%
Banking	15%	30%
Business Service	10%	25%
Capital Goods	50%	60%
Chemicals	40%	50%
Computer Hardware	30%	60%
Computer Software	15%	40%
Construction	40%	60%
Consumer Goods	30%	50%
Energy	30%	50%
Financial Services	15%	30%
Food & Beverage	20%	40%
Healthcare	25%	35%
Insurance	15%	35%
Luxury Goods	35%	50%
Media & Entertainment	40%	55%
Merchandising	25%	45%
Metals	35%	50%
Telecom Service	35%	50%
Travel & Transportation	35%	50%
Asia Population	52%	60%
Asia GDP	20%	35%
Asia PPP	40%	50%
Asia HDI	Medium	Medium

Figure 3.4 Current and future market share of Asia Pacific industries as a percentage of the global market

MARKET SEGMENTATION

Pyramid-shaped market segmentation

In a typical income-distribution curve, the X-axis usually represents the percentage of population while the Y-axis indicates their disposable income levels. In general, most growing market segments in Asia in their infancy can be viewed as being pyramid-shaped because the high-income group makes up only a small percentage of the total population, the middle-income class is gradually taking shape, and the low-income earners still comprise the absolute majority of the population. As the poor in large nations such as China, India and Indonesia actually make up the largest percentage of the market, these countries fit the description of "pyramid-shaped". While the elite group at the top of the pyramid enjoys the same wealthy lifestyle as the very rich in a developed economy, the majority of the population can barely afford their basic needs. In such a society (as shown in Figure 3.5), the top 20% of the population can earn more than 15 times the income of the bottom 20%.

The daunting reality for a pyramid market shape is that any society that has a huge disparity in income distribution is prone to social instability. Such societies must work harder to narrow the income gap by

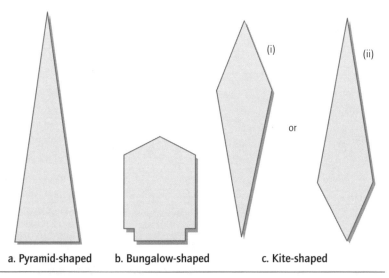

a. Pyramid-shaped   b. Bungalow-shaped   c. Kite-shaped

Figure 3.5 Three models of market segmentation

Note: X-axis: Percentage of population   Y-axis: Consolidated income after tax

enabling the low-income earners to advance to the middle-class while instituting fair competition rules for all players. Essentially, the success or otherwise of this will determine whether social stability can be sustained. The establishment of an effective and fair legal system will determine how the country can support future economic development in both public and private sectors.

Bungalow-shaped market segmentation

As the net income distribution for the citizens in certain countries is kept to a small range, the shape of the income-distribution curve looks like a bungalow, with very few low-income people (as a percentage of the total population) sitting as the foundation of the building supporting the large majority of the population, which has a small income spread. High-income Scandinavian countries, certain Western European countries and Japan are typical examples of this type of market segmentation. In this category, the wealth normally is fairly uniformly distributed across the overall population, either as a result of a narrow income range offered by employers or of extremely high incremental income tax imposed by the government. The common characteristics of this type of market segmentation are generally high education levels and dominant socialism within a free-economy system. Except for the few that live in poverty, the average citizen enjoys a fairly high income.

This type of market segmentation is usually characterized by a sound social security net that covers many basic medical, educational, food and transportation needs. Nevertheless, high-end purchase items are within the reach of the richer people. The consumers in this typically well-educated society tend to behave in a very environmentally responsible manner. In this category, there is more emphasis on human development than on pure GDP figures, and general consumer behavior typically reflects higher spiritual and moral concerns than are evident in a typical capitalist society.

Kite-shaped market segmentation

With a small high-income group sitting on top, a large middle-income population forming the middle section, and a relatively small low-income group lying on the bottom, the shape of the income-distribution curve, when placed in an upright centralized position, looks like a conventional kite. If a country does not address its income distribution problems, the high-income earners tend to derive more of the benefits of the economic growth than the rest of the population. In such a scenario, the shape of the income-distribution curve will change from Figure 3.5c(i) to Figure 3.5c(ii), with middle-income earners suffering the most. This market segmentation reflects a typical capitalist society such as the United States or developing countries such as the NICs after their initial success in accumulating and distributing wealth. The common characteristic for this market segmentation is that the average middle-class consumer actually has substantial purchasing power, which in turn is one of the main driving forces of the consumer market. However, the income gap between rich and poor can be disturbingly high. In the pro-business environment that prevails, the rich are encouraged to take necessary investment risks in pursuing financial returns and a kite-shaped society has a considerable capacity for creating entrepreneurs. However, the big trade-off is that there is a general lack of social security systems, particularly in the area of pension plans to take care of older citizens.

The elite of this society, as the true champions of entrepreneurship, lead the world of the free economy in innovation and wealth creation. Some of these very wealthy people are perfectly capable of improving the productivity of current business processes. More importantly, they are the creators of brand new business ideas and inventors of marvelous products and services. The majority of wealth-building breakthroughs in human society come from this type of market structure because successful risk-takers are generously rewarded without too much sharing of the wealth they have created with the less fortunate or the less skilled. Naturally, the winners in the free economy are the most opulent consumers because they are what capitalism is all about. However, this society in general is making little headway in narrowing the gap between rich and poor. What makes this type of society productive and innovative also makes it ineffective in dealing with poverty and ignorance. The purchasing behavior of those at the very bottom end of this kite-shaped market segmentation, be they in Asia or in the US, can best be described as hand-to-mouth.

VALUE-CHAIN ANALYSIS

A typical value-chain analysis, in particular for technically oriented products or knowledge-based services, can best be described by Stan Shih's Smiling Curve (see Figure 3.3(a)). The majority of the business value is normally hidden at the two ends of the supply chain. The leading end of this curve represents the creation of the value proposition while the trailing end represents the realization of the value appreciation. The former is normally referred to as innovation in a value-possessing product or service, while the latter is best described as product distribution.

It is important to bear in mind such basic value-chain concepts in developing a business strategy for Asia because value appreciation is heavily linked to culture, market segmentation, income distribution and the existence of a potential business opportunity. As a prelude to preparing a business strategy, it is vital that a value-chain analysis is conducted on a target market within a specific country or the entire region. The focus of this study should be based on where the fundamental value can be released and sustained for a targeted group of customers with a certain income level in a market-specific cultural environment. Only when these basic parameters for a specific market opportunity are properly understood and, preferably, quantified over a foreseeable period can the market potential be captured for further analysis. For example, many companies are interested in exploring the potential new environmental protection business opportunities that may arise as a result of the 2008 Beijing Olympic Games. The Chinese government has made a commitment to the International Olympic Committee to reduce the emission of CO, CO_2 and NOx before the Games. It makes sense, therefore, for a company that specializes in providing clean-fuel technology for massive transportation requirements to target the upgrade of the large number of buses in Beijing still using diesel technology developed in the late 1960s. As a starting point, the business plan must clearly identify how many such buses there are on the road today and over the next four years, taking into account the usage of public transportation of different types, the potential new owners of passenger cars and demographic trends. At the same time, the business model must compare the proposed replacement — such as the Compressed Natural Gas (CNG) tank or the new hybrid technology — with the current diesel engine system and be able to justify the value creation and the sustainability of the proposed solution. The next step is to assess the current bus companies to determine if they are capable of making the necessary improvements without resorting to foreign technology and, most importantly, to see if they are able to pay for upgrading the emission technology. Only when all these parameters are properly examined can a business model be established for further fine-tuning. Whenever applicable, specific value-chain data must be entered into each step of the flowchart and from one value chain into another; which usually means from the raw-material supplier to the end customer, one step at a time. By undertaking such a detailed exercise, the strategic planning team can then understand the full value chain of the proposed business. Depending on how much influence the company has with the decision-makers in the chosen industry vis-à-vis its competitors and how much value is hidden in the target industry segment within the entire value chain, the potential business turnover and its economic value can be determined both qualitatively and quantitatively. (This subject will be examined in more detail in Chapter 7.) It is estimated that there will be as much as US$10 billion-worth of infrastructure-upgrade projects, such as the clean-fuel bus project, available in Beijing City alone for the 2008 Olympic Games.

BRAND NAME AND PERCEIVED VALUE

Brand-name management

There is no doubt that a brand name carries a commercial value and is an important asset for doing business in Asia. The globally famous brands frequently listed in the top 100 brands by *BusinessWeek* have little problem being recognized and appreciated by the average Asian customer, thanks to the powerful mass media and smart advertising campaigns. But brand name is much more than advertising. It incorporates the familiarity and favor of customers, built through continuous efforts to create a unique image, that is indicative of its success in creating desirable products and services. This familiarity and favor allows the brand both price premium and volume preference over its competitors. Therefore, brand name actually carries substantial market value that can help a company survive a short-term economic downturn and demand a premium on stock value. A good long-term regional business strategy must include a branding strategy. Typical topics for the regional branding strategy are how to capitalize on the asset of a global brand name, how to design an effective local advertising campaign, where to focus the brand name promotion, and how to protect the brand name in a high-risk market where counterfeits may jeopardize the globally recognizable standard.

In the rapidly growing Asian market, with its vastly different culture, a brand name can be created with proper business planning. Equally, it can be destroyed by poor brand management. Samsung, for example, is probably one of the best examples of creating a successful brand name in recent times. In addition to its highly visible advertising campaigns in popular global sports events, major international airports, metropolitan downtown districts and in the news media, Samsung has built up a reputation in the electronics industry as a strong innovator in product design and as a market leader. At the 2004 international Industrial Design Excellence Awards, Samsung was one of two major winners from Asia (BenQ being the other). In fact, Samsung Electronics has been among the top 10 companies in the world receiving patents for at least the last five years and always ranks in the top three in the world in any business segment in which it participates. There is an undeniable link between brand name, innovation, market share and profitability. In this regard, Samsung falls behind only Toyota and Sony in the global branding rankings of all Asia-based companies and may surpass Sony within three to five years if it can maintain its current momentum. (A case study on Samsung is included in Chapter 5.)

Creating a brand name for market penetration

Another major issue related to brand-name strategy is whether having a local brand name increases the chances of a product range broadening its market access. After some fruitless years spent in trying to expand the market reach of its well-known brands, Coca-Cola created two specifically Asian brand names to appeal to customers who would prefer a beverage with an Asian name. The juice drink "Qoo" picks up on the quality image associated with a Japanese name. The other product range, which carries the brand name "Sunshine" in Chinese, includes chrysanthemum tea, peach tea and soybean milk. The name creation, if successfully executed, can open up new market opportunities, increase total market share and create additional niche markets.

Creating new brand names for the Asian market is a major decision for multinationals and one that must involve experts in languages, culture, advertising, business operations, sales and marketing. Normally the process begins by forming a brand-name committee that might include the CEO, the global and regional heads of strategic business units, branding specialists, customer-service specialists and production associates. The committee should start by identifying its core values, image, competencies, and vision, followed by a thorough review of how the company has performed so far in penetrating the target market. Only when it can be shown that all possible means of extracting commercial value out of the current brand names have been exhausted is it time to search for a new brand name for the target customer group in the selected market. It is vital to make a clear distinction between the new brand name and the existing famous brand name. Only when such detailed planning is done properly can creating a new brand truly add market value to the company.

While WMNs have cause to celebrate the success of their famous brand names in penetrating Asian markets, it is important that they recognize that Asian players are catching up in this area. For major Asian players such as Samsung or Acer, who already enjoy global standing, or for those Asian companies with a vast potential domestic market, the next 10 years will prove crucial to their global aspirations. The Olympics in Beijing will no doubt provide a stage for China to showcase its economic achievements as well as its top brands. China's top computer maker, Lenovo (formerly Legend), is already leading the charge by becoming the official computer equipment and service provider for the 2006 Winter Olympic Games in Turin, Italy, as well as for the Beijing Games. Likewise, other major Chinese or Indian players will also promote their brand names aggressively because their economies of scale will enable them to justify such market activities. It is likely, therefore, that several Chinese and Indian brands will become internationally known in the next 10 years.

TIMELY ACCESS TO A MARKET

Easy though it may sound, achieving timely access to a market is one of the ultimate challenges for seasoned business executives. Timing is all, because it can lead to total success or complete failure, depending on how the market is shaping up, how the customers change their purchasing behavior, and how much capital expenditure is needed. The smashing successes of Nintendo's Game Boy, Mattel's Barbie Doll, Sony's Walkman, Pfizer's Viagra, BMW's Mini-Cooper, Apple's iPod, Yahoo's website, Google's search engine, Starbucks' coffee-focused cafés and TSMC's entry into the wafer market are excellent examples of timely access to an emerging market. Timely entry to the Asia market can be critical because of its past success in attracting many foreign investors and its burgeoning ability to make its own investments. The best time to enter a particular market segment will vary from industry to industry. For example, Volkswagen had an early lead in China's automotive market because few other automobile manufacturers in the early 1980s noticed that China had the potential to become the largest auto market in the world by 2020. Since investment in automobile manufacturing is normally in the order of US$1 billion and above, a decision of this magnitude will obviously have a major impact on the financial health of any multinational.

The problem for second-wave investors who enter a market late revolves around the limited bargaining power they have in dealing with local governments and major distributors. The later-comers to China's automotive market usually need to settle for a less attractive partner in a remote market location. Ultimately, the less favorable market conditions may have a long-term impact on the return on investment.

Having first access to a market by no means guarantees the success of a business, however. During the early days of opening up the Chinese market to foreign investors, the French PSA Group was able to put Peugeot into the market shortly after the arrival of Volkswagen. But the first Peugeot sedan introduced to the market used the same artistic design as in France and was perceived by most Chinese consumers as being unconventional and something of an eyesore. Worse still, from the outset Peugeot struggled with quality problems, cost issues and serious infighting with its local partners. Finally, the PSA Group decided to abandon the Guangzhou Peugeot project and to focus on a separate investment in Hubei, with China Second Automotive. The PSA Group based this new venture on its Citroën XZA model, but almost made the same mistake by offering its European-designed hatchback model, which again did not appeal to Chinese consumers. Only after expanding its product range to include the traditional family sedan did Citroën begin to do better. Meanwhile, its sister company, Peugeot in Guangzhou, had to be sold to Honda to bring the painful investment experience to an end. Learning from this experience, Honda encountered few problems in launching the right product into the market. With sales constantly hitting new records in China, Honda will soon start exporting its products made in Guangdong to the global market.

It is important to keep in mind, therefore, that while timely access to a market is a critical factor it is not the only prerequisite to achieving business success. Any multinational with an ambitious business plan and deep pockets must also have a solid understanding of the target market to determine when to be the first-mover and how best to execute its business plans.

PROJECTING NEW MAJOR TECHNOLOGICAL OPPORTUNITIES

The proliferation of manufacturing facilities and technological know-how that has resulted from deregulation and free trade over the past quarter of a century has clearly narrowed the gap between the West and the East, even in hi-tech segments such as information technology and genetic engineering. Western executives who are searching for growth opportunities in the Asia Pacific region must recognize that the fundamental strength of the Western economy is embedded in the ability to be innovative in creating marketing ideas, business processes and product designs. Only those companies with the necessary management expertise to capitalize on their tangible and intangible assets can formulate a successful and sustainable business plan. Detailed discussion on innovation will follow in Chapter 5.

BusinessWeek, Fortune and *Newsweek*[17] recently predicted that virtual companies such as Amazon or eBay will eventually figure out how to transact business virtually, on any scale and at any time, using wireless communication devices. Companies that can develop the necessary technology to facilitate this and protect the security of virtual transactions will be the winners in this emerging market opportunity.

As the earth's reserves of fossil fuels become increasingly depleted to the point where they will soon be unable to sustain continuous economic expansion, the need for an alternative, sustainable energy source becomes ever more demanding. Fuel-cell technology will be the next big thing for the transportation industry and the companies that will lead the hybrid-engine technology are most likely to come from Japan. Toyota, or other companies that have strategic partnerships with the technological leaders, are capable of making a revolutionary breakthrough in this field.

The next big innovation may then be in the field of molecular biology and genetics. Only those countries that are willing to embrace the emerging opportunities can possibly take the lead in this revolutionary, if controversial, technology, which will inevitably give rise to a great deal of ethical debate over the kinds of biotechnology or genetic engineering that are acceptable for commercialization.

Another way of reaping business opportunities in Asia is to harness the power of brand names, such as Mercedes-Benz and Louis Vuitton, in a growing market. Even though Mercedes-Benz no longer achieves the high scores in product-quality surveys that it once did, it is still a powerful brand name and a symbol of social status in Oriental society. Building a brand name is a very delicate process over a prolonged period of time. This requires consistent and high-quality advertising campaigns, a thorough understanding of customers' purchasing behavior, links to well-respected celebrities and, above all, a commitment to providing top-quality service at all times. Servicing a prestige-market segment requires a substantial investment in fixed assets, information systems and service expertise because converting a name brand into business success requires much more than simply selling a highly desirable product. Companies that are fortunate enough to have a valuable brand name must define their value chain precisely and deliver impeccable service consistently to protect the core value of their business. Highly effective management information systems and communication skills are vital for managing this type of high-end business.

Business opportunities will undoubtedly present themselves, too, in the emerging field of nano-technology, which is already being used commercially in the textile-coating and catalyst industries. Further advances in nano-technology may come from restructuring at a molecular level so that basic materials can be transformed into more complex and potentially more powerful applications as yet unseen and undreamed of. Such hi-tech developments may lead to a dramatic scaling down in the size of manufacturing facilities or electronic appliances if the technology can reach the commercialization stage.

Case Study:

VOLKSWAGEN vs. TOYOTA

In global rankings, Toyota is an ambitious number two, with aspirations to take a 15% global market share by 2020 and to overtake General Motors at the top of the world rankings in the next three to five years. Volkswagen holds fifth spot in the global rankings, with its strength concentrated largely in Europe and in China. Toyota is no longer purely an Asian-based producer because, in 2003, for the first time, Toyota produced more cars and SUVs in the US than it did in Japan. As a matter of fact, Toyota is probably one of the most successful global companies in the world in profitability, quality, customer satisfaction, innovation capabilities and sales split between the US, Europe and Asia. But, despite the fact that its headquarters is only a two-hour plane journey away, Toyota missed an early opportunity to make a major investment in China and is now having to play an aggressive catch-up game. Volkswagen, on the other hand, has not been very successful in overseas investments outside Europe, except in China. Thanks to its timely move into the market and a successful business plan to bring its parts suppliers into China, Volkswagen achieved total sales of 697,000 vehicles in 2003, a market share of more than 36% — a figure it could not even achieve in Germany.

Toyota's strengths go far beyond those associated with the Japan Inc. phenomenon of the 1980s. Most notable is the culture of total quality control (TQC) that sustains a continuous quality-improvement program designed to cultivate customer loyalty. Toyota has been able to perform much better than the other Japanese companies because it is unencumbered by the complicated cross-ownership relationships with which many of the big Japanese conglomerates are burdened. As a result, Toyota is free to make its own business decisions and, consequently, must be prudent in making its investments pay off. The company

	Volkswagen			Toyota		
Financial Results	2003	2002	2001	2003	2002	2001
1. Revenue (US$ million)	108,322	90,756	77,915	162,571	134,856	113,297
2. Net income (US$ million)	1,361	2,697	2,565	10,924	7,935	4,619
3. Total assets (US$ million)	148,074	113,666	91,893	207,178	174,236	149,167
4. Return on equity, or ROE (%)	4.6	10.5	11.3	14.2	12.7	8.4
5. Return on assets, or ROA (%)	0.9	2.4	2.8	5.3	4.6	3.1
6. EBITDA (US$ million)	12,650	12,590	10,563	24,792	18,610	14,457
7. EBITDA/Sales (%)	11.7	13.9	13.6	15.3	13.8	12.8
8. Net income/sales (%)	1.3	3.0	3.3	6.7	5.9	4.1
9. Sales growth (%)	19.4	16.5	−3.0	20.6	19.0	6.8

Figure 3.6   Volkswagen and Toyota: A comparison of financial performance

Sources: Mergent Online database[18] and authors' research

enjoys excellent financial management and, through constant and specific cost-reduction programs covering every component, is the cost-cutting leader of the global auto industry. The company's operating profits for 2002 were at least three times more than those of GM and Ford combined and, in 2003, exceeded US$10 billion. Toyota also enjoys a total market capitalization that is more than the combined total of its top three competitors.

What is marvelous in Toyota's accomplishment is how transparent it has been in driving its business success while most other automakers clearly have problems keeping their heads above water. Inherited with the culture for pursuing excellence (*kaizen*) is a core competency that separates Toyota from its competitors. Employees are rewarded both with formal recognition and financial rewards for eliminating quality defects from the management system. Toyota's management teams religiously practice PDCA (Plan, Do, Check, Act), rather than the Six-Sigma methodology that is more favored by others in their pursuit of continuous improvement. In order to address the communication issues that can frequently stifle production during the complex car-assembly process, Toyota uses face-to-face discussions or brainstorming sessions (*obeya*) to search for the best solution from the entire workforce. This practice has been extended to include the cooperative program with its suppliers. Every year, Toyota rates each of its suppliers according to how many new ideas the supplier contributes to the company's designs and new models. Toyota maintains a very close joint-development program with its suppliers from the standpoint of both design excellence and cost control. From knowing the value of every component it purchases, Toyota has developed a unique competitive advantage over its competitors. Since a typical automobile consists of up to 10,000 parts, the prevention of human or systematic mistakes during the assembly process is one of the most critical competencies for automobile makers. Like most good Japanese manufacturers, Toyota allocates considerable resources to *pokayoke*, a foolproof management system that incorporates the use of electronic sensors and crosschecks between machines and people. When a production line is stopped because a problem has been detected, the operator is rewarded and complimented. The entire team will then work together to fix the problem rather than leaving it to the repair department to patch up.

Toyota is also an industry leader in managing global platforms by using the same basic car bodies or body shells around the world, even though the models may have different names in different markets. This essentially eliminates the duplication of heavy capital investment in creating complex product lines and excessive inventory. Brilliant design ideas are frequently exchanged among design teams based on different continents and among selected suppliers. As a result, Toyota's product range, including the high-end Lexus division, is considered the most comprehensive in the entire automotive industry. In order to keep its products appealing to the younger generation and to attract female customers, Toyota's marketing team in Japan holds costume parties and raffles, with DVDs as prizes. In California, Toyota launched a marketing campaign to link its two low-end models with the younger generation by holding video-game contests and offering hip-hop CDs. The successful promotion in California is being expanded into other states in the US.

Despite registering almost-perfect scores in almost every performance category, Toyota faces two major challenges: a lack of success in the European high-end market segment, and its relatively small market share in China. To address the former, Toyota has been working hard to improve its image as one of the leading technical providers in the automotive industry through its participation in motor sports. Since the mid 1990s, the company has been an active participant in Formula One racing and has set up its own design center in Europe to attract the best talent to work on the design of sexy products that reflect the aspirations of buyers. There is growing evidence that Toyota will become more competitive in Formula One in the years ahead. But, success in motor racing does not necessarily guarantee an increase in market share for such high-end automotive products in Europe because for Europeans the image of prestigious cars incorporates unique heritage as well as technological advances. Toyota clearly needs to refine its business strategy in this regard. The decision to set up a European automotive design center in Nice, France, should help to improve Toyota's appeal to European customers. The robust sales growth in Europe in early 2004 seemed to confirm again that Toyota is on the right track to meet its ambitious goal to grab an 8% market share in Europe by 2010.

In China, Toyota is working hard to make up lost ground on Volkswagen and GM. After signing an agreement with First Automotive Work (FAW) to make the Crown, Corolla and Land Cruiser models, Toyota is aiming to increase its market share in China from 1.5% to 10% by 2010. Through its participation in building Japan's first BOT (build, operate and transfer) airport at Nagoya, near the company's headquarters, Toyota now has much easier links to many key markets, including direct flights to major cities in China. Given the company's track record in achieving a leading market share in various Asian countries, few people doubt the success of the ambitious expansion plan laid out by the Toyota management team.

As for Volkswagen, its enormous success in China and its traditional strong presence in German-speaking countries give the company a strong base for remaining a key global player, regardless of its weak product line-up and average product quality. As one of the high-cost producers in the automobile industry, Volkswagen is always attempting to upgrade its products into the luxury-car segment through, for example, co-producing an SUV with Porsche's Cayenne, or through entering the V-8 or V-12 luxury-sedan market by acquiring Bentley. However, Volkswagen has a strategic misalignment issue that it must address, and sooner rather than later. This involves its equity investment in Audi, another high-end producer, which will be the first to suffer from any success Volkswagen has in upgrading its own product range. In addition, with two dominant luxury-car producers, BMW and Mercedes-Benz, also located in Germany, the chances of Volkswagen penetrating the high-end market are not very promising. The recent financial results for the first quarter of 2004 confirmed that Volkswagen's high-end investments are far from being successful. Meanwhile, the company will have to focus on its fundamental strength in middle-range automobiles by reinforcing its cost-saving initiatives and the brand-name strategy associated with German car technology. It must also leverage its dominant position in China for further expansion into other automotive segments in China as well as other emerging Asian markets.

PART II

A MICROSCOPIC VIEW OF THE ASIA PACIFIC REGION

CHAPTER 4

ANALYZING THE COMPETITION

If a genius like Albert Einstein recognized the benefits of looking over other people's shoulders, are we so smart that we don't have to do so?

GLOBAL PLAYERS

We saw from Figure 3.4 where some of the future business opportunities in the Asia Pacific region might lie. The next step is to analyze the potential competition, and a good place to start is by assessing the rankings of major multinationals within the selected industry sector. This information is readily available in business publications such as *BusinessWeek*, *Fortune* and *Forbes*, and on the websites of industry associations and the multinationals themselves. From these sources it is possible to find relevant financial and sales information, as well as details of the product range and specifications of whoever your major competitors might be.

However, few multinationals will be able to achieve the market-share figures shown in Figure 3.4. The majority will fail, for a number of reasons: they will lack a significant presence in the region; they will mistime their entry into the market; their product range will be inadequate; their costs will make them uncompetitive; or they will lack local supply and service capabilities. As a rule of thumb, a WMN is considered well positioned in Asia if its market share is more than half of its home market share for a specific industry segment. As we saw in Chapter 3, market segmentation in most Asia Pacific countries normally mimics one of the three models — pyramid-, kite-, or bungalow-shaped — for both consumer-oriented and enterprise-oriented industries. In the pyramid-shaped market segmentation, the accessible customer base is quite small because of the WMN's strategic weakness in coping with the business opportunities in the region. In the kite-shaped market, the lower portion of consumers still lack purchasing power. Only the middle-income level of the population can afford substantial purchases and are thus the target group for most marketing studies. Even for a bungalow-shaped market, which has a higher average income, there are challenging issues such as parity purchasing power, local supply and service capabilities, or customized products for the local market that can yield less satisfactory results. Therefore, a good business strategy must start by focusing on understanding the customers' requirements and analyzing the competitive conditions among all major players. The company must then identify its own fundamental weaknesses and work to overcome them by making adequate plans to create competitive advantages within the region. A systematic way to develop strategies and plans appropriate for the Asia Pacific are given in Part III of this book.

It is critical for a WMN to have a thorough understanding of its competitors from the US or Europe. WMNs generally share similarities in their management philosophy, technological focus, cost structures and human resources policy. In Michael Porter's terms,[19] the five forces for determining the competitive position of a firm — entry barriers, industry rivalry, threat by substitution, the bargaining power of suppliers, and the bargaining power of buyers — provide a great deal of common ground for most WMNs in the Asia Pacific region. Most of all, in the eyes of Asian customers, top WMNs are perceived to have similar values and are normally categorized in the same price range. In principle, when key core competencies are at similar levels, WMNs tend to compete more with other WMNs in Asia than with the local players. However, different WMNs may have different commitments to the Asia market, different business development strategies and different historical experiences in the region. As a result, the rules of the competition in Asia may be completely different from those in their traditional markets. When two Western multinationals compete with each other in Asia, the deciding factor frequently rests on their local capabilities, including supply capacity, service levels, cost position, and their management team on the ground. Those multinationals that do not have a regional strategy can find themselves constantly changing direction, aggressively pursuing sales volume one day and price increases the next. One day, they may opt for an expensive expatriate for a position that can be localized, and then the next day pull out all their expatriate staff as being a deadweight to the company. When a multinational cannot run its business according to a well-defined business strategy, inconsistency of business decisions can create confusion and confrontation among its various functional teams and business units. Adding to these woes can be a regional team that is not fully committed or properly directed to the cause because they feel victimized or neglected in the corporate political battles, making it much difficult to conduct business than it is on the company's home turf.

On the other hand, successful global players tend to have a long-term commitment to the Asia Pacific market, even though they may also realign their product portfolio or restructure their Asian organization. Most successful WMNs entered the Asian market with an ambition to excel and they learned to define their unique competitive strategy based on a thorough understanding of the market and the weaknesses of their competitors. Coca-Cola provides an excellent example of this. Riding on its unparalleled brand name, Coca-Cola's business strategy covers every single geographic location in the region, including reformed communist countries, Muslim-dominated Central Asian countries, remote island states in the South Pacific, and so on. Even in the harsh environments of many pyramid-shaped markets, it has succeeded by adopting effective local practices such as delivering the product via bicycle or tricycle. It is worthwhile noting that Coca-Cola implemented this comprehensive business strategy while its rivals were still contemplating how to enter some of the key markets. As a result, Coca-Cola draws roughly 28% of its sales revenue from the Asia Pacific region and is achieving higher margins and cash flows from its Asian sales because it has outsourced its bottling operations — a traditional cost-prohibitive problem for Western food and beverage companies.

Another shining example of success is LVMH, the parent company of Louis Vuitton, which draws more than 40% of its revenue from the Asia Pacific region. In addition to its highly recognizable brand name, Louis Vuitton has done an excellent job in consistently presenting the superior image of its products in major Asian metropolitan cities by setting up elegant flagship stores, introducing attractive products, creating eye-catching advertisements and providing impeccable customer service. In one advertising campaign (though not one conducted by LV itself), the LV bag was shown to have remained intact after more than 70 years in the ocean depths with the Titanic. What could be more appealing than a product that combines mystery, romance and the durability of superior quality? LVMH has outperformed its competitors by creating a unique product image and selling a dream of perfection to its customers. Such a strategy is invaluable in Asia, particularly for the high-end consumer market.

REGIONAL POWERHOUSES

In general, major regional players enjoy certain home-court advantages over the WMNs. These include a better understanding of local market requirements; better connections to the key local decision-makers; more influence on government policy; better access to local suppliers; more bargaining power with local suppliers; and greater access to local talent — all of which give them a competitive edge over their rivals from abroad. For WMNs the best competitive strategy, at least in the early stages, is to leverage their global competitive advantages — brand-name recognition, their leading market position in advanced economies, superior technological capabilities, global account approval, and global purchasing agreements for both raw materials and finished goods. Since these basic tactics are generally known to most WMNs, there is a need to develop specific business plans to implement each of these competitive advantages. For example, identifying the local market leader and its followers in a specific industry is vital before a company can concentrate on promoting its image as a qualified supplier. The success of such a promotional campaign has to be measured numerically — in market share or profitability — against the anticipated timeframe of the business plan. Whenever a deviation from the target is detected, a backup plan must be implemented.

Once a WMN establishes a beachhead, it should move into the next phase, which is building key local competencies in manufacturing, purchasing, development, technical services and human resources. The extent to which it can harness these competencies will eventually determine how successful the company will be in achieving its goals.

Another key element for multinationals in building a business in Asia is the ability to utilize their regional strengths, which most Asian regional players are still struggling to do because of the vast territory and diversified cultures. For example, most South Korean *chaebols* have only recently begun to make major investments in China as a whole because traditionally their participation in Chinese markets was limited to northern or northeastern China. The Japanese conglomerates, too, have been late arrivers in China. Western multinationals that have built successful businesses in Taiwan or Singapore or Hong Kong tend to have a better chance of entering China smoothly because they are able to draw on the resources and past experiences of their regional organizations. They can leverage their product-development capabilities in Japan to create Asia-specific products against their regional competitors. A good example of this is Ford's decision to use the Mazda Design Center to create motor vehicles specifically for Asia, saving Ford hundreds of millions of dollars. Xerox, too, employed a similar strategy in having Fuji-Xerox develop a copy-machine for the Asian market, which has proved successful despite the fact that Xerox USA has been struggling in its home market. WMNs can also move members of their regional management teams into key management posts at a start-up site without having to go through the cycle of hiring, training and retaining. Using experienced personnel in this way is estimated to cost a fraction of what it would take to utilize resources of purely Western origin. This flexibility of movement is an obvious advantage for a WMN that has established a pool of human resources in the region.

An effective Asia business strategy should capitalize on regional resources and competencies and adapt them to global business requirements. WMNs should establish key performance indicators (KPI) that will have a major impact on their short- and long-term success. The benchmark or best practice for each KPI within the company should be established and shared throughout the different branches of the company. The topic of utilizing regional human resources is discussed further in Chapter 10.

Western multinationals need to understand that many Asian regional players are getting bigger in terms of sales revenue and stronger in terms of core competency. In the 11 case studies used in this book, three Asian players are bigger than the well-known Western counterparts, and five of the 11 Asian companies looked at are more profitable than their Western counterparts. In addition to the Japanese conglomerates, the sales revenues of South Korea's *chaebols* are also big by global standards. For example, Samsung Electronics has an annual turnover of US$54 billion per annum; Posco's is now more than US$10 billion; and the top 30 *chaebols* contribute more than 75% of the country's total GDP, or US$357 billion.

Some of the leading Taiwanese companies too are, after years of ambitious expansion into electronics and petrochemicals, listed among the heavyweights on the world stage. For example, Quanta, the leading ODM for the notebook industry, achieved annual sales of US$10 billion in 2003. The Acer Group had annual sales of US$16 billion in 2003 and this figure is expected to exceed US$20 billion in 2004. The Formosa

Plastics Group had total sales exceeding US$26 billion in 2003 and is poised to reach US$33 billion in 2004. This rapid growth is giving these regional powerhouses enough muscle to enter the global arena. Nine of the world's top 10 notebook companies rely on Quanta to design and produce various notebooks for them. As the leading producer of notebooks and mobile phones, the only area in which Quanta has yet to demonstrate its supremacy is in sales and marketing capability. Should it decide to meet this challenge, it could prove to be a nightmare for the Western multinationals. Similar examples can be found in the shoe industry, which sources more than 75% of its total requirements from a handful of Asian companies with production bases in China and Vietnam. These Asian players are a vital part of the global supply chain but fall short of entering into direct competition with their name-brand customers in the market place. But, in some cases, certain WMNs such as Nike have achieved tremendous success by cooperating with their regional partners in entering the Chinese market together. Nike's partnership with Pao-Chen, a Taiwan-based company that has numerous production facilities in China and Southeast Asia, provides a good example of this. With Nike concentrating on advertising and product promotion, Pao-Chen helps produce and distribute Nike sports shoes in big cities and small villages all over China. This is a win-win strategy that enables both companies to enjoy the leading position in the market, and one which points up the importance to any good regional strategy of developing alliances and partnerships.

FRAGMENTED LOCAL MARKETS

Within the Asian market, there are many fragmented small players in various industries. They owe their existence to the past protectionist policies adopted by their governments. As most of the key Asian countries are now members of the WTO, these protective measures are being systematically removed. On the surface, the options available to these small local players seem to be limited to merging with a bigger player, entering a specialized segment or closing down. Indeed, some of these players have found a specialized niche, while others have found ways to reduce their cost base and continue to thrive at the forefront of ferocious price wars. Many WMNs have found it difficult to comprehend how certain local players can sell at a price level at which even a company with world-class economies of scale cannot deliver profitability. The reality for these survivors varies by industry and by company, but they seem to find ways to compete by taking advantage of low costs of labor, materials, equipment, management and finance, or less-stringent environmental regulations. WMNs must therefore have a solid understanding of the selling price and cost structure of the market they wish to engage in. Certain mature industries or products in the Western world may not have any real market opportunities in Asia if there is no additional value created during the investment process. This is particularly true in those countries in which the PPP is much bigger than the GDP. During the early 1990s, for example, many global paper companies poured large sums of money into the paper industry in China in anticipation of capturing the high growth potential by wiping out small local players. Once they had learned the market reality that only products with extremely low prices were acceptable to most local customers, the foreign investors had little option but to bow out. During this painful process, even the mighty Asia Pulp and Paper Company was unable to make its world-class facilities cost-competitive against local small players and its US$13.9 billion investment quickly became a non-performing loan. Likewise, many global beer companies invested heavily in China in the 1990s based on statistics that China ranked second in total consumption of beer while individual consumption was still one of the lowest in the world. Many foreign investors assumed that China's domestic market could provide economies of scale for them to produce high-quality beer at a globally competitive price. Unfortunately, there were at least 400 local beer companies — almost one brewery for each large city — that competed on extremely low prices and few, if any, economies of scale. What surprised the multinationals was that the average Chinese consumer did not have the same expectations regarding packaging and storage conditions as their Western counterparts. The majority of Chinese customers could see no value in cold, glass-bottled, beer because they were used to beer at room temperature in very inexpensive packaging. By eliminating two of the most expensive components in delivering the product to customers, the local beer companies were able to defeat these high-profile multinationals and forced many of them to pack up and retreat after accumulating heavy financial losses. Of course, market environments can change. Once consumers become more affluent, quality standards rise. This is why more multinational beer companies have now begun to return to China, despite the terrible failures of the 1990s. In 2004, for example, Anheuser-Busch, the king of beer in the US, having already spent US$1 billion and 10 years trying to enter the China market without major success, outbid its rival, Miller, for 29.4% of the Harbin Brewery in Northeast China, paying US$139 million at an astonishing P/E ratio of 49.3 times the 2003 earnings.

DEFINING KEY COMPETITIVE FACTORS

Given the uniqueness of the Asian market, it is important that business strategists pay special attention to local attributes in defining key competitive factors beyond their traditional analysis. The competitive threat can come from the Western world as well as from within the region. A study of old foes from similar backgrounds offers a starting point for the WMN to position itself. However, a thorough understanding of local market requirements and local players is absolutely critical in the business planning process.

The large number of participants in the Asia market and the vast differences in cost structure between global players, regional players and small local players mean that competition will be much more intense than in other parts of the world.

While global technical trends apply in Asia as well as anywhere else, there tends to be more product substitution on offer here than in the US or Europe because there is a wide range of expectations to be met, from customers at the top end (who tend to be followers of global trends) to customers at the low end (who have unique local demands). Therefore, while a WMN works on the global trend on substitution, attention must be given to define the special requirements imposed by Asian customers. For example, most beverage companies are now spending a lot of money on defining the next big thing following the tremendous success of Starbucks' diversified coffee options. WMNs must keep in mind that herbal tea or Oriental tea remains the preferred beverage of many Asians. The idea of creating a substitute can be a fad or the product of technical hype or a cultural event or a combination of these, but only genuine innovators can create this core competency. A comprehensive study of Asian consumer behavior and the current business environment in any chosen sector must be part of this evaluation process.

In dealing with suppliers, a multinational must be able to leverage its global and regional purchasing power to develop the competitive advantages necessary to engage in long-term competition in Asia, where fierce competition tends to drag down the selling price.

A multinational will also need to make full use of its global coverage of a specific industry by sharing relevant marketing information and experience gained in different parts of the world in order to keep the preferred supply position in the specific market in which it is seeking to compete. At the same time, it must improve its competency in gathering local market information and in building credibility with key decision-makers in that market.

SELECTING BENCHMARKING CRITERIA

Identifying the market leader and its winning formula

For any WMN wishing to participate in any industry, it is vital to study how the current market leader achieved its leadership position. If the market leader is where it is mostly as a result of having low costs, the entrant must assess whether it can achieve the same level of competency based on the scope of the investment. If it can't, it will have to concentrate on a specific segment of the industry where it is able to create value perceived by the target customers.

If the market leader specializes in the distribution of average-quality products, the entrant must understand the cost structure for a newcomer to deliver the products effectively to the target customers. The distribution of imports or locally sourced products may be subject to heavy government regulation in emerging markets such that the multinational is not allowed to distribute imported products. Where products are approved for local sale, the selection of a cost-effective distributor becomes a vital part of the business strategy. Fortunately, there are some well-established distributors in emerging countries, but the multinational must possess sufficient market intelligence to enable it to select the right partner. As WTO rules are implemented over the agreed period, some of these restrictions for retail and distribution will be abandoned. For example, the Chinese government has allowed foreign companies to distribute products not made by themselves in China since the end of 2004. However, the importance of conducting benchmark studies of the entire value chain remains the same.

Identifying best practice

Contrary to the beliefs of certain Western executives, Asian companies actually have several best practices in management. According to a study conducted in the 1990s by the Boston Consulting Group, an American printing manufacturer in Singapore had 30% higher productivity, 50–100% faster time to market, 10–15% better quality, and up to three times as many models than an equivalent plant in the United States.[20] Similar results can be found in most of the WMNs when the productivity is compared across their plants located in different regions. It is important for WMNs to recognize that certain best practices for their business may already exist within their own operation or in that of their competitors in the Asia Pacific region. As Asian culture tends to nurture a disciplined workforce, it is not unusual that productivity or quality in Asia is better, provided that management systems are set up properly from the outset. A WMN must learn to be humble when making judgments on its regional or local competitors. There have been many business failures that can be attributed to the WMN simply ignoring its regional competitors, as if customers were just desperate for salvation courtesy of the WMN. This type of catastrophic failure happens more often than not to WMNs with a dominant position in their home market who march into Asia, normally under the blunt direction of top executives expecting to duplicate that success overseas. Where there is not a complete understanding of the local competitive environment, haste almost inevitably makes for waste.

From a management perspective, the identification of best practice should cover every major competency needed to compete in the Asia Pacific region. However, practically no company is able to be the best in every competency category. The best way to describe the winning formula is the best-in-class business model based on the decathlon competition. Typically, the Olympic decathlon winner will win two or three events, be among the top five in six to eight events, and never fall out of the top 10 in any remaining events. Simplistic as it may sound, this analogy has correctly described how business strategists must focus on creating dominance in two or three core competencies while maintaining operational excellence in all other areas. There is never room for mediocrity in a winning company. Among the main responsibilities of the senior executive committee is how to define these competencies against those of their competitors.

SEARCHING FOR COMPETITIVE ADVANTAGE

In an emerging industry

An emerging industry normally offers the innovator an advantage over its competitors because the value created by the new product far exceeds other key competitive factors such as cost, availability and customer service. Sometimes, too, an innovative product can replace more than one product and can, therefore, command a premium price, just as Nintendo's Game Boy was able to do by superceding the cumbersome TV monitor and computer system that preceded it.

However, if the driving force for the emerging industry is not based on free-market principles, it can be a trap for investors. For example, government regulators in Asia, most noticeably in China, have been trying to create a brand-new code-division multiple-access (CDMA) mobile-phone system, called the TD-SCDMA, to compete with the current CDMA used by Motorola or the wideband W-CDMA that is the backbone of Nokia's dominant system. Wireless software companies such as Qualcomm must therefore position themselves in all these emerging technologies through joint design programs because China is already the largest mobile-phone market in the world. To miss the boat at a critical time may mean the total loss of future business in a major marketplace.

Another critical factor in assessing the feasibility of introducing a brand-new technology is to measure it against local or national standards. Recently, China's government has imposed a requirement that all Wi-Fi gears for wireless communication equipment sold in China must incorporate a locally developed data-encryption technology which, so far, only local Chinese companies have access to. As this encryption technology has not been made known to foreign players, companies such as Intel, which depends on China as its second-largest market behind the US, is having a hard time realigning its business strategy. Having invested nearly US$1 billion in two Chinese chip factories, Intel has to find a way to resolve the impasse with the Chinese government. Following recent high-level discussions between China's vice premier, Wu Yi, and her US counterparts, the deadline for implementing the new encryption code has been postponed indefinitely.

Another potential problem faced by emerging industries is that new technology can sometimes leapfrog existing technology in such a way as to render an emerging or existing industry obsolete. For example, wireless communication is quickly becoming the dominant form of communication worldwide and advances in wireless technology have the potential to make obsolete the entire US$1 trillion-worth of fixed-line, cable-based networks globally. However, this may work in favor of the latecomers to emerging economies such as India and China where the fixed-line cable network is not yet as extensive as elsewhere, in that they will not be faced with having to duplicate investments in something that may soon have to be replaced.

In a specialized industry

In highly specialized industries such as biotechnology, specialty chemicals and machinery or, indeed, in the premium segment of any industry, the core competency frequently revolves around highly specialized technology that is protected by patents or confidential know-how. Because this type of industry normally does not have a large market, a WMN with global coverage for a specialized industry must focus on how to maintain its technical supremacy as well as on how to control the total operational costs within a specific marketplace. If this is done well, the return on investment can be lucrative.

The major risk for such industries is that, with the proliferation of advanced technology and the expiry of patents, specialized products can quickly become commodity products. A WMN that chooses to operate in the Asia Pacific region must ensure that its patents are recognized and valid in the countries in which the company is seeking to operate. Often, a multinational would not have registered its patents in every Asian country because it failed to foresee the market potential and the competitive nature of the marketplace. There will be further discussion on this topic in Chapter 5.

In a fragmented industry

Where there is no dominant leader in an industry, this implies that the industry does not require increasing economies of scale for survival or that a larger investment does not necessarily guarantee a substantial increase in market share or a greater return on investment. Such industries — advertising, books, cosmetics, construction, hotels, legal, music, printing, restaurants, retail stores, spas, real estate, interior decoration, to name but a few — can be highly fragmented. What the players in these industries must have is a differentiation strategy because a company does need to capture a selected group of customers.

Western multinationals wishing to engage in these industries must clearly identify their target customers and examine how realistic a prospect it is that the target customers will buy the product or service being offered. It used to be very easy for the Big Four accounting firms — Deloitte, Ernst & Young, KPMG and PriceWaterhouseCoopers — to choose where they should participate in a local market because their global clients usually invited them to join at different stages of business expansion.

Likewise, big international law firms followed their global clients around the world. But, as WMNs tighten their belts, the selection of a global service provider is no longer guaranteed if either service quality or cost fails to meet expectations. In a way, the widely available low-cost alternatives in the Asia Pacific region are changing the business scope of many global service companies. For example, outsourcing financial services to another WMN such as Accenture used to be a great cost-saving idea for multinationals operating in the US or Europe. But this is no longer the case now that they have learned how inexpensively Asian service providers can provide the same service. Sometimes WMNs may choose to develop a shared services center from their own Asian operations.

However, cost is not necessarily the most important consideration in fragmented industries. In most cases, differentiated products or specialized services are perceived by clients as having the highest value. Therefore, a WMN participating in the service industry must pay special attention to the cultural details of the chosen market. For example, feng-shui, or geomancy, is an important factor that should be considered by all service providers in Asia.

In a maturing industry

In a traditional maturing industry, players are obliged to cut their costs aggressively if they wish to stay in the game. In broader terms, there is no difference between East and West in this. However, as the overall Asian business scope may not be as broad as in the West, there is a fair chance that even a maturing industry in the East may possess some potential for upgrade or expansion by a WMN.

In general, there is little incentive for a WMN to enter a maturing industry in Asia unless there is a hidden value to be released. There are a few exceptions to this, the banking industry being one of them. As a result of tight regulatory control and a narrow definition of banking services, the banking industry is frequently considered to be still maturing in many Asian countries. Overall profit margins for the industry over the past five years have been on the decline, while those in the West have been rising. There is, however, a potentially very large market for all kinds of financial services in Asia, particularly in China and India where the banking industry is heavily guarded by government agencies. The case study at the end of this chapter focuses on how well Citicorp and HSBC have positioned themselves in this burgeoning industry.

ANALYZING CORE COMPETENCIES

Ability to deliver lowest possible cost

Since Asia is generally considered to be the hub of global manufacturing largely because of the ability of regional players to deliver the lowest possible total cost, WMNs need to learn from their regional counterparts about total-cost management. In a highly competitive industry such as consumer electronics, for example, the policy of many Asian companies is to get a new quotation from all suppliers for every purchase order. Because there is generally a surplus supply capacity in this industry, suppliers are subject to intense and constant competition to reduce their prices.

Such procurement practices have been adopted by several famous hyper-chain stores, including Wal-Mart, whose direct annual purchases from China alone amount to more than US$10 billion, to drive down the cost of every purchase item. Because of their enormous purchasing power, such companies are in a position to invite an ever-growing number of new participants to join in the supply-chain activities. Other ways to reduce the total costs will be discussed in Chapter 6.

Ability to create differentiated products and services

The second core competency in creating market dominance is the ability to create differentiated products that are perceived by customers as creating value. Western multinationals have had a clear advantage over Asian players in this regard because of the modern technologies available to them as they seek to improve product performance.

But, in recent years, Asian players have made tremendous progress in product development and manufacturing excellence and there have been many instances of commercial success for Asian players who have managed to extract incremental value out of a differentiated product originally created by a WMN. For example, a number of innovative ideas in advanced electronics — display, memory chips, wafers, and so on — originating in the US research laboratories of companies such as Bell or Motorola have only been able to blossom fully in Asia because Asian players tend to commercialize new products much quicker and are more willing to take risks in making major new capital investments. A Western multinational, therefore, needs to assess whether it is capable of outperforming Asian players in this critical competency.

Ability to focus

The ability to focus comes generally from the collective strength of a management team that prioritizes a specific business strategy and supports that priority with reinforced resources. Western multinationals often lack specific knowledge of the Asian market, which hinders them in formulating an effective business strategy for Asia. They have to be able to discern the subtle differences between their global strategy, based on their long-term exposure and hands-on experience, and their Asia strategy, which can often be based on limited market knowledge and incomplete sales experience.

The safest way for a WMN to proceed is to focus on what it is good at vis-à-vis the needs of the local market, as revealed by the intensive research it has undertaken in advance of entering that market. However, the ability to focus is to a great extent dependent on the strengths of the local business team and the local management organization. This topic is discussed further in Chapters 9 and 10.

Ability to make improvements via Six-Sigma methodology

The nature of competition is such that to succeed in a dynamic business environment requires that a participant be capable of defining its customers' requirements, of measuring and analyzing its own performance against its own targets and against its competitors, of improving its performance, and of controlling the improved conditions it has achieved. This evolving methodology is what has become known as the "Six-Sigma Way".[21] The advantage of adopting this approach comes from aligning all business units and functions under the same business objectives. The work of each member of each business team and each member of each functional team will be better coordinated when the common company objectives are clearly delineated.

While Six-Sigma has become firmly embedded in the management practices of many leading WMNs in recent years, its successful implementation is very much dependent on the commitment of the management team, on how it is built into the company's key performance indicators and, most of all, whether it is carried out precisely. The Six-Sigma methodology, sound though it undoubtedly is, does not in itself guarantee that company objectives can be achieved without concerted effort. Any company, Western or Asian, can develop the required competencies as long as there is a commitment by the leadership team and the results justify the cost of setting up the Six-Sigma Way.

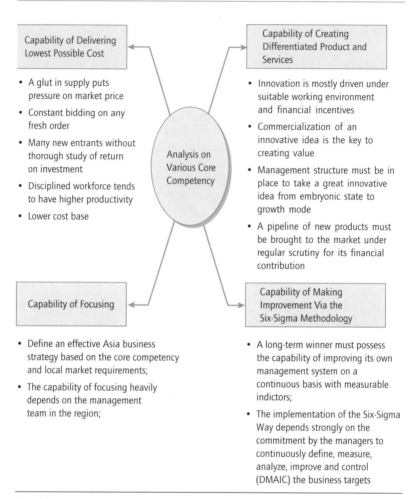

Figure 4.1 Analysis on various core competencies

CITIGROUP vs. HSBC

Citicorp is a 100%-owned US company and led the global banking industry in total profitability (US$15.3 billion) and market capitalization (US$211 billion) in 2002.

HSBC (formerly, the Hongkong and Shanghai Banking Corporation) started its business in Hong Kong and eventually made London its headquarters prior to the handover of Hong Kong to China in 1997. Today HSBC shares are traded on the Hong Kong, London, Paris and New York stock exchanges. As a legal entity, HSBC is a British company. However, its current strength (total net profits of US$6.2 billion and a market capitalization of US$126 billion in 2002) is built on a long history of success in Asia, which gives a clear demonstration of how quickly national borders can disappear in the global banking industry.

As the global industry leader, Citigroup bestrides Asia like a giant in the commercial banking services segment, which includes derivatives, foreign exchange, debt through project finance, cash management and transactional services. The successful integration of Salomon Smith Barney into its global banking branches in 2002 has undoubtedly given it even greater creditability. Many high profile initial public offerings, including the highly successful China Life launch in 2003, simply serve to reinforce the view that Citigroup is the dominant player in this key banking segment. Citigroup is also highly rated in the equity market because it has a wide platform encompassing big privatizations, innovative offerings, accelerated placements, ADR, convertibles and exchangeables. Through leveraging its high visibility, it has proven itself the pre-eminent leader of syndicated loans in Asia (excluding Japan) by completing a total of 55 deals, valued at US$5.4 billion, in 2002. Citigroup also leads Asia's banking industry in project finance as the region continues moving away from traditional infrastructure financing. Using its abundant experience, it is able to try new models and new techniques for its clients in financing major projects. Its recent issuing of credit cards in China through a local partner in Shanghai was another watershed event that demonstrates how aggressively Citigroup is tackling the huge Asia consumer market. In June 2004, it was one of four banks to receive a derivatives license from the China Banking Regulation Commission, the first such licenses issued since the banning of the derivatives business in China following a number of price-rigging scandals in 1995. In a nutshell, as the Citigroup slogan says, "Citi never sleeps", and it will undoubtedly continue to launch ambitious business initiatives around the world, keeping all of its competitors on their toes.

HSBC, too, is expanding rapidly from its Hong Kong stronghold to mainland China and other Asian locations by offering diversified financial and advisory services under the slogan "The World's Local Bank". Though trailing Citigroup in commercial banking services, HSBC is leading many other important segments in Asia. For example, it is the market leader in issuing international bonds because it has been able to establish strong ties with many important clients in the region and extend its market coverage in the United States by buying several international banks. In addition, it is pushing aggressively into the local-currency bond market in several Asian countries. HSBC is also rated by *Finance Asia Magazine* as the market leader for cash management, trade finance, and as sub-custodian for institutional mandates. HSBC is trying to leverage its considerable local experience, particularly in Asia, by promoting itself as the world's

Financial Results	Citigroup			HSBC		
	2003	2002	2001	2003	2002	2001
1. Revenue (US$ million)*	94,713	92,556	112,022	39,968	28,595	35,261
2. Net income (US$ million)	17,853	15,276	14,126	8,774	6,239	5,406
3. Total assets (US$ million)	1,264,032	1,097,190	1,051,450	1,034,216	759,246	695,877
4. Return on equity, or ROE (%)	18.2	17.6	17.4	11.8	11.9	11.8
5. Return on assets, or ROA (%)	1.4	1.4	1.3	0.8	0.8	0.8
6. EBITDA (US$ million)	29,180	22,581	23,830	15,144	11,079	9,086
7. EBITDA/Sales (%)*	30.8	24.4	21.3	37.9	38.7	25.8
8. Net income/sales (%)*	18.8	16.5	12.6	22.0	21.8	15.4
9. Sales growth (%)*	2.3	-17.4	0.2	39.8	-18.9	-6.6

Figure 4.2 Citigroup and HSBC: A comparison of financial performance

Sources: Mergent Online database[22] and authors' research

*Revenue (or sales): Figures are net of Internet expenses

local expert. HSBC's differentiation strategy has proven to be very effective in an environment in which most banks, regional or global, are beginning to look increasingly similar.

Given the tremendous growth potential in several emerging countries, particularly China, both Citigroup and HSBC are acquiring banks in China in anticipation of the deadline (the end of 2006) by which China must completely open up its financial markets to outside corporations. In December 2002, for example, Citigroup purchased a 4.62% equity in Pudong Development Bank in Shanghai for US$72 million, while HSBC has spent a total of US$80 million for equity participation in Shanghai Bank and Fujiang Asia Bank. More recently, in June 2004, the Bank of Communications, the fifth-largest commercial bank in China, agreed to sell 19.9% of its shares to HSBC — the biggest foreign investment to date in China's banking sector. The deal, valued at US$1.75 billion, gives HSBC a major presence in the nation's financial services market ahead of any of its rivals. However, the finance sector has been a weak spot for China's economy since market reforms began. For example, the unusual protest, against the loss of US$10.4 million, by a group of small investors in front of the main branch of the Bank of Communications in Shanghai in July 2004 underlines the dilemma confronting the trust segment, which has been something of a regulatory gray area.

On the other hand, both Citigroup and HSBC have been approved by the People's Bank of China to provide limited local-currency loans in China. This unprecedented authorization can be seen as preparing the big four banks in China for future competition. Towards the end of 2003, the Chinese government further announced that it would inject US$45 billion from foreign-trade reserves to offset the notorious non-performing loans, which are estimated to account for as much as 25% of total outstanding loans owned by China's four giant banks. The China market presents tremendous opportunities for both Citigroup and HSBC, enabling one to seal its leadership in the market or the other to narrow the gap over the next 10 years.

CHAPTER 5

THE TECHNOLOGY FACTOR

Innovation can come and go depending on whether or not the environment is conducive to creative ideas.

INNOVATION VERSUS INVENTION

Sources of innovation

The fundamental strength of Western-style management is based on three pillars: its relentless pursuit of sustainable profit; its adoption of the two-way, "democratic", communication process; and, most important, its ability to innovate. Innovation, in our terms, refers to the creation of a new product, a new manufacturing process, a new business process, or a combination of these. It is much more than invention or insight or ingenuity or intuition individually. Rather, it is the product of all these that comes through the application of managerial skills. Since the Industrial Revolution, most of the important scientific inventions have taken place in the Western world because its culture has tended to embrace and encourage technological advancement. This innovative culture, along with a free economy that can reward risk-takers, is the main driving force behind the remarkable economic accomplishments by Western industrial countries and corporations. A successful WMN will constantly be examining itself to see if an innovative culture is still part of its management philosophy and practice. Unlike other tangible assets owned by a successful company, the ability to innovate can vary with changes in the company's culture and in the environment in which it operates.

With globalization has come a replication of Western-style management structures and its innovative culture that can be found in some successful Asian companies in Japan, Korea and Taiwan. As the technological gaps between East and West narrow, the ability to innovate becomes increasingly important. Nowadays, most advanced economies are heavily dependent on the service sector, including IT, finance, education, design and medical care, which can only flourish in the right environment and when their people are properly empowered. In a highly competitive market such as Asia, the ability to innovate has proven crucial to success.

On the other hand, when an industry no longer values innovation or when innovation can no longer create competitive advantages, it normally means the industry has reached a commodity status or a state of maturity, in which the surviving players have to rely on operational excellence in, say, cost reduction or organizational restructuring to squeeze out any redundant costs. If a company sees itself falling into such a position, it must begin to analyze how this decline has come about and challenge its overall strategic direction, giving serious consideration to any possible business strategy or option to expand outside the box it finds itself in. Re-engineering the future direction of a company in itself can be an important innovative process. The most effective way for a company to create economic value is to fully capitalize on its competitive advantages in a more attractive industry segment than its current segment.

USING SUPERIOR TECHNOLOGY TO CREATE COMPETITIVE ADVANTAGE

Technological competency is the most important competitive advantage that a WMN can have for engaging in business development in Asian markets. In many instances, multinationals dominate in a selected industry as a result of having a well-established or patented technology. In the aerospace industry, Boeing and Airbus dominate the global market for mid-range and long-range commercial jets because this industry was, from the outset, built on the dominant technology of the West. Since the re-qualification of the key components in such a safety-oriented industry can be prohibitively expensive and time-consuming, it is extremely difficult for new players to gain entry into the parts-supply industry. The extremely high capital requirements for entering the aircraft industry mean that strong financial support from government also plays a pivotal role in transforming a great technology into a successful business. Similarly, in the pharmaceuticals industry Western multinationals enjoy a clear advantage over their rivals in the East. In the global top 20 pharmaceuticals companies, only one spot is occupied by a company from the East — the Japanese company Takeda, in 19th position. In an industry that requires combined strengths in R&D and global marketing backed by huge long-term financial commitments, the leading multinationals have a clear advantage. The vibrant venture-capital market in Western countries also gives them an extra competitive edge.

Whenever technological advantages can be preserved through the application of patents, the industry will continue to enjoy satisfactory profit margins. In an industry such as pharmaceuticals, in which there is a common dependency on patented innovations, the structure of the industry is normally conducive to all of its players earning reasonable returns. It is important, therefore, that a WMN gears its business strategy towards building an innovative product portfolio and leveraging its broad-based technical strengths as a global player. Those who cannot create a unique competitive position through technological strength usually end up less successful in Asia than on their home turf simply because the Asia market tends to drive all commodity players into cut-throat competition arising from a glut in supply. This is probably at its most serious in Northeast Asia, with its heavy concentration of ambitious players in Korea, China and Taiwan.

THE DOWNSIDE OF OVER-RELIANCE ON TECHNOLOGY

Predicting technical trends in Asia

While developed Western countries generally enjoy technical supremacy over their Asian counterparts, it is important not to lose sight of the different market requirements in East and West. In Asia, for example, limited living space often dictates that household appliances or cars are both compact and multi-functional. As a result, engineering or product design in Asia must give greater attention to ergonomics, energy efficiency and durability — a differentiating factor that seems to be more appreciated in Europe than in the US.

In Japan, a greater sensitivity to environmental protection has become the main driver for numerous green technologies, including the hybrid engine for cars and halogen-free electronics products. While a great many technologies in this area were pioneered in the West, Japan has become the leader in their applications and it is vital for Western companies not to overestimate their own understanding of these markets simply because they hold the patents. Because of the vertical integration commonly adopted in Japanese industry, some crucial innovative environmental protection technologies were developed and commercialized in Japan a long time before their introduction into the global market. For example, environmentally friendly electronics products such as the notebook and the mobile phone had been available commercially in Japan for nearly three years before Western countries even started to debate the viability of such technology. A technical leader can easily become a market follower as a result of neglecting a rising market opportunity or being incapable of delivering a commercial success. In the contest for converting fledgling technology into business opportunities, a sense of self-congratulatory technical supremacy often becomes a company's worst enemy.

The use of proprietary equipment as a package deal

Some Western companies have great success in their home marketplace by providing proprietary production or processing equipment to complement products with a specialized application. For example, Kodak successfully promoted traditional film, film-development chemicals and film enlargement based on special developing equipment designed and produced in Europe. However, the traditional film-development industry is now under extreme pressure from digital camera technology and high-quality home printers. Kodak is also under pressure on another front. Fast turnaround for film development is dependent on having highly reliable processing equipment and Kodak is experiencing fierce competition from Fuji's in-house machine which, surveys show, is subject to less downtime than Kodak's processing facilities. Worse still, Kodak did not have full control over the maintenance of its developing machines and is in constant dispute with some major distributors over this issue. Failure to maintain complete control over package deals with distributors can, as the Kodak example makes clear, lead to continuous uphill battles — despite the considerable advantages that a widely respected brand name carries.

In this area of package-deal competition in Asia, the Western multinationals appear to be losing out, largely because they prefer to stay focused on a particular market opportunity rather than pursue the integration, be it vertical or horizontal, favored by Asian players. As international competition intensifies, the winners will be those that can deliver full, problem-free, value to their customers. For those companies that have to rely on the supply of complementary equipment to achieve key value for customers, it is important to ensure that they are capable of delivering the consistent performance that such package deals require. When the complementary equipment is outsourced, they must benchmark themselves against their leading competitor and discover the root causes of any performance gaps. It is only through such an analysis that the company will be able to propose countermeasures to close the gap and create performance advantages of its own.

RISKS OF LOSING TECHNOLOGY IN ASIA

From fake watches to cloned cars

Frequent business travelers to developing Asian countries will be very familiar with a range of counterfeit products on offer: from the latest music CDs and Hollywood movies to golf equipment, classic shirts, brand-name luggage and diamond-decorated designer watches. While the availability may no longer surprise the seasoned traveler, what continues to amaze is the quality of the counterfeits. Such has been the improvement in quality that it is becoming increasingly difficult to distinguish between the counterfeit and the locally licensed version. It is instructive to see how this has come about, and the case of CDs or DVDs provides a clear example.

Many international entertainment companies have accepted the disparity in purchasing power between their home markets and those in Asia and, in an effort to encourage greater respect for copyrights, have been selling their products at a lower price in certain Asian countries, hoping to take advantage of potentially high sales volumes and the improved margins that come from lower local production costs. However, the control of licensees has proved to be much more difficult than anticipated. After receiving the licensed product from the copyright holders, many licensees quickly copy the original CD or DVD and send it to a web of satellite factories. While the licensee still keeps track of what it should legally pay to the licensor, there are many more copies sold through different channels without any royalties being paid. In some cases, these counterfeits are even exported back to the country of origin.

The basic reasons for this rampant piracy, of course, are greed and a lack of law enforcement. But there also seems to be a lack of cohesive effort on the part of the global entertainment industry to invent counter-duplication technology and to pursue serious offenders. Because of the rapid proliferation of counterfeits, the industry is facing the worst recession in its history — which runs directly counter to the rosy projections of a home entertainment boom. Similarly, high-end luxury goods and computer software companies claim losses of billions of dollars through the infringement of intellectual property rights (IPR). Adding to the difficulties in prosecuting offenders is the fact that often the counterfeiters are in league with local government officers, who also benefit from the offenses.

What is happening in the automobile industry is even more alarming to foreign investors. Conventional wisdom had it that, given how capital- and technology-intensive the business was, it would be impossible to clone a complete vehicle. In fact, this was exactly the line of thinking adopted by Martin Poste, president of Volkswagen China, in 1996 when he categorically ruled out such a possibility.[23] But, however improbable the scenario may seem, it is now a reality. There are cloned vehicles of the old Audi 5000 (now called Red Flag, after Audi's license technology expired and was sold to China First Automotive at a nominal value); of popular Toyota models, including the Camry and Corolla (which are being replicated by Zhejiang Geely), and of Volkswagen's Jetta (which is replicated by an Anhui producer, Chery, who bought the design and an obsolete plant in Mexico from Volkswagen's Seat division). By far the biggest surprise, however, is the latest cloned vehicle, the Chery QQ, which was introduced to the Chinese market even before the model on which it is based, GM's Spark, was officially launched on the global market. With cloned products generally selling at 20% to 30% lower than the authorized products coming out of joint-venture plants in China, they are capturing market share in China much faster than the big JVs because they are of almost-comparable quality, though they may lack some of the more sophisticated options offered by the originals. Furthermore, these local producers are not content to restrict their activities to the China market. In June 2004, Geely announced plans to sell 5,000 vehicles to the Middle East and South America in 2004, compared to just a few hundred the previous year. For 2005, Geely has set a target to sell up to 6,000 vehicles in the largest vehicle market in the world, the US. In 2003, Chery sold 1,200 cars overseas, a figure it hopes to increase to 10,000 in 2004.

While the cloning strategy commonly used by many local partners in China is upsetting most foreign investors, Chinese entrepreneurs are able to exploit these gray areas opened up by national economic development plans which require that local producers have at least a 50% market share in this so-called pillar industry. And there is certainly no shortage of global players rushing to get a piece of the action in what is potentially the largest automotive market in the world.

While multi-billion dollar investments continue to pour into China, the Western multinationals must develop a business strategy that keeps their core technology within the company. Robust business growth must never be allowed to disguise the very real possibility of losing hard-earned technological advantages. Eventually, even well-established Chinese companies will also need the protection of intellectual property rights in order to sustain their business growth. Once the value of a brand name is jeopardized, copycats can be detrimental to foreign players and local players alike. As China starts pushing its own brand-name products into the global arena on a massive scale, it is vital for the government to take concrete action to drive counterfeits or cloned products out of business. Towards the end of 2004, China's Supreme People's Court and national prosecutor's office jointly issued an interpretation of its IPR law by lowering the threshold for the prosecution of piracy infringements to US$6,000 in sales and broadening the definition of unauthorized use.[24]

Means of obtaining proprietary technology

Technology licensing is common in the international business community to transfer a proprietary technology into a production base in Asia. Indeed, every equity investment in Asia involving proprietary technology normally comes with a license agreement between the owner of the technology and the local legal entity. When a business is able to return satisfactory financial results to all equity holders, a technology license is an effective bond for all partners. But if there are problems in reaching the target for return on investment, the license fee and expatriate costs are normally the two most contentious issues in running a successful joint venture. Once the honeymoon period of the partnership is over, it is not unusual for unforeseen difficulties to arise. Where different perceptions exist about the value of intellectual property rights, it is not uncommon for confrontations between the partners to escalate to the point where they put their individual interests above those of the JV.

Many WMNs take pride in sharing confidential information with their employees because they believe the free flow of information is a key strategy in developing management consensus. In compliance with legal obligations that apply in various developed countries, Western multinationals often publish comprehensive technical data on such things as material safety. Sometimes this involves a full disclosure of all material components and their respective ratios within the product. These, of course, can be easily reconstructed into a production recipe, which can prove dangerous in those Asian countries that are famous for "entrepreneurship". Therefore, to minimize any unnecessary exposure of their proprietary information, WMNs need to adjust their minimum reporting requirements in accordance with the local statutory regulations rather than those that pertain in their home markets.

There are many opportunities for WMNs to lose control of their technologies in Asia. For example, original equipment manufacturer (OEM) contractors and their sub-contractors are supposed to keep their specialist know-how under license agreement. But, as soon as the OEM contractor starts to produce the highly specialized goods, he needs to have full access to the technological base in order to deal with any issues regarding quality that may arise and to upgrade product performance. As the WMN gives its Asian OEM contractor more design responsibilities, this too requires a full disclosure of technology from time to time. Once this process has started, it is hard to backtrack. Given the availability of highly skilled engineers and scientists in Asia, any technology can be absorbed and modified by local players to suit the specific needs of the market. Sometimes, certain OEM contractors purposely report higher defect rates so that they can keep some products for their own sales channels. After they have built sufficient product experience through these private channels, they then introduce their own modified products based on the cloned technology. Because the Asian OEM contractor is much closer to the local market than its WMN partner, there is a much greater chance of the contractor developing a successful parallel market, particularly where the market does not require other competitive advantages such as economies of scale or brand name.

In most industrial segments, job-hopping is another common source for the leaking of confidential information, either accidentally or by design. The relentless downsizing and restructuring policies of the WMNs are themselves partly responsible for creating an environment in which managers and engineers are constantly on the move between companies. The less secure employees feel, the greater are the chances of the pirating of confidential technology taking place.

PROTECTING INTELLECTUAL PROPERTY RIGHTS

Advances in the field of information technology have made it necessary to rethink the whole system for protecting confidential business data such that protection always stays at least one step ahead of those who would seek to exploit the intellectual property of others. Some companies choose to replace the CD-ROM facility in their personal computers with a centralized storage platform. Unfortunately, duplication technology is now so advanced that seemingly innocent electronic gadgets, such as portable hard drives, can easily store up to one gigabyte of information, the equivalent of two CD-ROMs. A personal digital assistant (PDA) can be equipped with wireless capability to tap into a company network. Certain software programs can record every keystroke entered by a targeted individual.

From an IT security standpoint, a firm must lay out a comprehensive system that can provide convenience for its employees and yet safeguard critical management information. A typical IT security policy usually starts from a high-level authorization that defines a user profile based on the individual's job function. The next step is to identify valuable commercial or technical data which, if it fell into the wrong hands, could become the core competency for a competitor. A good IT security management system is one which builds adequate compartments into these valuable data banks into which only authorized personnel are allowed access.

It goes without saying that companies should select their OEM contractor or distributor very carefully, choosing only those who believe in honesty and long-term partnerships. Partnerships must be seen to be of benefit to all parties so that the chances of pirating intellectual property by undisciplined or disgruntled employees is kept to a minimum. Whenever supervision is lax or communication is poor, the chances of losing both technology and market to a dishonest employee increase. There is no way that management can withhold access to the technology base to every employee in the course of normal business. The question is, rather, the extent to which each employee requires such access in order to fulfill business objectives. This is a very fine line and seasoned executives in Asia must be prudent in their decisions. The generally accepted way is to dissect the technology into several parts (normally a maximum of four in the entire value chain) that are sequentially connected but not all open for access by any one individual. To do otherwise may become counterproductive to the effective functioning of the organization.

The Western multinational must also provide its frontline business managers with adequate legal training and provide dedicated legal support within the region. The availability of responsive legal counseling for frontline managers is critical to maintaining the consistency of the company's position in dealing with the highly complicated requirements of the Asia market. Once appropriately qualified general legal counsel has been chosen, a network of professional support in the form of an IP lawyer, a litigation lawyer, an international-trade compliance lawyer and a patent officer must also be put in place for consultation. Once a legal position is established at corporate level, the company's legal representatives must ensure strict compliance with it within the region through active participation in its enforcement. IPR protection can be effective only if it is enforced rigorously.

Employment contracts, too, can be used as an extra level of protection against the abuse of intellectual property rights. When, as inevitably happens, an employee leaves, the company must ensure that it has made sufficient legal provision to restrict that individual from being able to use confidential information in the service of a potential competitor for a reasonable period of time. Where such confidentiality agreements appear to have been breached, the company will require solid evidence verified by litigation lawyers before it has any chance of pursuing the case and obtaining redress. In nearly all disputes related to confidentiality agreements, the biggest problem for the company is to prove the case with hard evidence and to validate the commercial loss. Frequently, when confidential information is not properly classified or recorded against open literature, the company cannot even begin to build a case. When an illegal disclosure is proven, the next critical step is to prove that material damage to the business — a deteriorating commercial position or aggravated market conditions — has resulted. Unfortunately, in the business world, particularly in Asia, few customers will want to cooperate in providing the hard evidence that is needed to prove a commercial loss. This reluctance often arises from wanting to avoid the potentially troublesome litigation process and possible counter-suits. Company executives must handle such delicate situations with diplomacy and skill. Seasoned executives should, however, be equipped to handle these problems before they arise by dealing with customer relations with sensitivity and by being aware of potential morale problems with current employees, and to mitigate the actions of certain unscrupulous former employees before they can inflict further damage on the company.

CONVERTING INGENUITY AND ECONOMIES OF SCALE INTO INNOVATIVE VALUE

Many ingenious prototype products created by university and corporate scientists in the US in the 1960s and 1980s that failed to generate full-scale commercial success have found fresh legs in Asia thanks to the critical consolidation of global manufacturing facilities in the hands of a few big Asian players. The liquid crystal display (LCD) is just one example of this. Back in the 1960s, US scientists discovered the special properties of liquid crystal which, under certain conditions and when placed precisely between glass, can form the basic mechanism for displaying an image. Unfortunately, brilliant though the idea was, it enjoyed only limited success in very specialized avionics and military applications. A number of major WMNs, including IBM, after spending many millions of dollars in R&D, were unable to achieve any real commercial success, mainly because of the excessively high cost to the consumers.

However, since the global electronics industry started its unstoppable migration to a few Asian destinations, the LCD industry has achieved true economies of scale in Korea, Japan and Taiwan. By 2000, Korea and Taiwan had entered into a fierce contest to capitalize on this technology, making major capital investments for its use in notebook computers, while Japan focused selectively on specialized applications such as the mobile-phone screen. In 2000, the combined total capital invested by this industry was US$6.7 billion and will reach US$11 billion in 2004. With the scale of production expanding at such a rapid rate, unit costs naturally fell substantially and, as a result, the industry has been experiencing tremendous growth in replacing conventional TV tube and computer monitor displays. In 2004, the total turnover for the LCD industry is projected to reach US$60 billion — an increase of 40% over the previous year. Like the semiconductor, the LCD is a key design component in the electronics industry. The leading companies in the LCD industry, such as Samsung, LG and AU, will certainly enjoy the innovation value that is made possible by combining ingenuity and economies of scale.

OPTIMIZING TECHNICAL CAPABILITIES

To meet the demands of Asian customers for speedy, knowledge-based technical support, WMNs must decide on when best to set up a technical center to support business development. Usually the best time to do this is after initial market testing has proved the market's acceptance of the product and the product differentiation strategy has been activated. At this stage, modifications or improvements to the original product may be necessary to align the product portfolio with the evolving needs of the marketplace. If a company is not able or prepared to make the adjustments necessary to capture such incremental opportunities, it risks losing its competitive market position to those who are, thus jeopardizing its overall business objectives.

The fact that Asia is now the hub of most global hi-tech developments makes it even more important for Western companies to establish a technical center here so that they do not miss out on emerging business opportunities. The nature of hi-tech competition is such that it requires continuous innovation in R&D and rapid conversion into commercial products. Only those companies that are committed to devoting the necessary technical resources in the region will keep abreast of technological trends and remain competitive.

The allocation of technical resources by the strategic business unit should be based on their expected economic returns, normally expressed in five- to ten-year net present value (NPV). Before a business plan is officially approved, it is subjected to close scrutiny and a series of rigorous technical and market tests, feasibility studies and cost analyses. The details of how to formulate such a business implementation plan are described in Chapter 7.

Ideally a technical center should be situated within the main production site to ensure close communication between operational and technical staff at every stage of the production process. The center should be led by a business-oriented technical manager who, in turn, reports to the regional business manager. The business unit is responsible for ensuring that market feedback is properly incorporated into product design to serve the needs of the market.

While technical centers are critical to business development, this does not necessarily mean that there should one in every key market location. As with any other core competency, it is more important to have a technical center with high-caliber staff in one or a few locations than to have many sites. Many WMNs have demonstrated that business value can be unlocked by a market-oriented technical center. Those that have tried to centralize product development in the US or Europe frequently find themselves left behind simply because providing remote technical services to Asian customers hardly ever works. Asian producers across a range of industries have long proven themselves to be much faster than their Western counterparts in introducing new products. In the case of automobiles, for example, leading Japanese companies have reduced the product-development cycle of a new model — from design to launch — from four years to 1.5 years, while most of their Western counterparts are still struggling to bring it down to three. In the IT industry, companies such as Samsung have reduced the development cycle for a new mobile phone to as little as six months. Western companies could not hope to keep up with this pace without mobilizing their resources in Asia.

CREATING VALUE BY DEFINING TECHNICAL STANDARDS

The pursuit of technical excellence has long been accepted as one of the defining characteristics of Japanese manufacturers. Japanese companies have laid the ground rules for the creation and upgrade of technical standards across a range of industries worldwide.

Frequently, Japanese manufacturers, through their participation in specification review committees, are able to introduce unique product designs that are available only from very specialized material specifications used in Japan. A good example of this is in the area of civil engineering. Through the superior performance of such companies as Toray, Mitsubishi Rayon and Toho, the Japanese established a dominant position in the global supply of carbon fibers for use in several civil engineering applications where high-tensile strength is critical. Through strategic alliances with carbon fiber and resin producers, Japanese companies have been able to set standards across a number of areas from high-strength reinforcement to low-temperature applications. A country that adopts these standards as its own can automatically lock itself into a very small pool of suppliers. The aerospace industry provides another good example of this. Toray, the largest carbon fiber producer in the world, has created unique material specifications for the Boeing 7E7 that offer superior structural strength and ultra-low weight at a competitive cost. As a result of its relationship with Boeing, Toray is in a powerful position vis-à-vis other well-established composites companies, which have to negotiate for a license to use the approved technology in order to gain access to new market opportunities.

Such examples can be found in many industry sectors. Setting new technical standards can be critical to a company's ability to create value. Many companies fall behind the competition simply through failing to maintain solid contacts with influential certification agencies such as Underwriters Laboratories, ASTM or DIN that may have a great influence on national or international standards and thus on the future of their business.

TECHNICAL SUPPORT AS A VALUE-ADDED SERVICE

Typical technical-support activities that can be tailored for a selected audience may include general technological reviews, industry updates, objective-based product design or special formulation activities, and trouble-shooting for a performance problem. Since technical support may extend

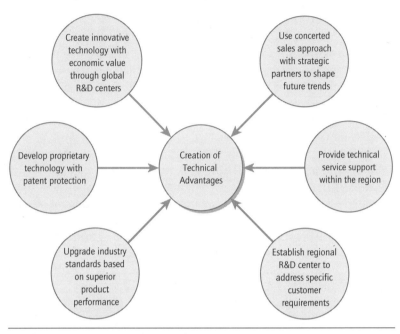

Figure 5.1 Means of creating technical advantages

across product design, manufacturing, market trends and networking, it is vital that expertise in this area is built and maintained over an extended period to ensure reliability of products and services for customers. Traditional notions that technical support is confined to the production area are no longer sufficient to meet the needs of Asian customers, who are becoming increasingly specific and sophisticated in their technical requirements of suppliers.

Some WMNs are very good at utilizing technical support to achieve their goals, gearing their services to the specific needs of the customer in such a way that the customer becomes reliant on their specialized assistance. Once this reliance is established, the seeds have been sown for a loyal and long-term business relationship.

DEFINE THE VITALITY INDEX AND LIVE WITH IT

A vitality index is a means of measuring how successful a company has been in introducing new, value-creating products and services into a target market on a continuous basis. As shown in Figure 5.2, a typical vitality index might be the turnover, profit margin or cash flow derived from the sales of new products launched over a specified period of time. Some companies define it specifically as the sales of new products launched over a five-year period as a percentage of total sales revenue for the current year. This model, however, tends to be oversimplified and can be misleading when it comes to allocating business resources because the sales revenue being tracked is only the top line of a financial statement. Focusing on revenue generation based on a pipeline of new products can, in fact, be one of the most dangerous business plans because it can drive the entire company in frantic pursuit of new business opportunities that may not resonate well with its current competencies. In many cases, top-line growth may require excessive new capital investment or is achieved at the expense of the bottom-line results.

The pursuit of profit margin, too, can lead to similar abuse in guiding company resources into a brand-new area that may require large capital investment or may bear no relation to the company's current strengths. The worst scenario here is that the company may eventually consist of many small independent business units that cannot compete on a global scale or cannot weather the cyclical ups and downs of the particular industry sector.

The use of cash flow as an overall measure of success appears to make more sense because it takes into account amortization on investment and is discounted based on the actual interest rate the company is paying to support the business. NPV is, therefore, probably the most reliable indicator of business vitality because it represents the net current economic value based on the interest rate used by the company to finance all of its investment activities. NPV is equivalent to the sales revenue over the next five years minus all costs, including the annualized capital investment, and is discounted against the time over which the revenue will be generated at a selected interest rate. Put simply, NPV is the closest approximation to the cash generated by a business proposition within the business environment in which the firm is operating.

Regardless of the simplicity of using NPV as a vitality index, it should be noted that it does not provide a strategic view on positioning, sustainability, valuation and flexibility that are all vital for the implementation of a successful business strategy. Formulating a successful business strategy requires a comprehensive approach, as we shall see in Chapter 7.

	Year 1	Year 2	Year 3	Year 4	Year 5	Year 6
Volume (PCS or MT)	0	50	200	600	2,000	5,000
Sales (US$1,000)		250	1,000	3,000	9,000	20,000
Direct Cost (US$1,000)		100	400	1,200	3,600	7,000
Sales Margin (US$6,000)		150	600	1,800	5,400	13,000
Indirect Cost (US$1,000)		25	100	300	900	2,000
SGA (US$1,000)		15	60	180	540	1,000
R&D (US$1,000)		10	40	120	360	800
Adjustment Related to Operation (US$1,000)		0	0	0	0	0
Operating Profit (US$1,000)		100	400	1,200	3,600	9,200
+Depreciation (US$1,000)		10	40	120	360	800
EBITDA (US$1,000)		110	440	1,320	3,960	10,000
Tax (@25%) (US$6,000)		-28	-110	-330	-990	-2,500
Working Capital (US$1,000)		-50	-150	-450	-1,350	-2,650
Capital Expenditure (US$1,000)		-500	0	0	-1,000	-1,000
Net Cash Flow (US$1,000)		-468	180	540	620	3,850
NPV (US$1,000)	+3,266					

(a) Revenue = US$33,250,000

(b) Sales Margin = US$20,950,000

(c) Net Present Value (NPV) = US$3,266,000

Figure 5.2 Tracking vitality index by (a) revenue (b) sales margin & and (c) net present value

Note: *Discount rate at 8%

Case Study:

MOTOROLA vs. SAMSUNG ELECTRONICS

Motorola has been an icon of the global electronics industry since the early 1970s, when it launched numerous groundbreaking gadgets that heralded the onset of the information age. The fundamental strength of Motorola came from the vision of its legendary founder, Paul V. Galvin, and an uncompromising commitment to technological leadership. Under the guidance of strong leaders, Motorola transformed the electronics industry by launching innovative technology that brought one industrial breakthrough after another. During those boom years, Motorola was one of the few American hi-tech companies to invest heavily in emerging markets, including China.

Unfortunately, confident of its technological supremacy, Motorola made the major mistake of ignoring the market trend towards digital phones, allowing its main competitor, Nokia, which embraced the rising technology in the mid 1990s, to take the lead in mobile-phone technology. In addition, Motorola failed to pay sufficient attention to implementing innovative manufacturing concepts — including its own Six-Sigma model. The rapid proliferation of its product lines by different design teams around the globe became such a production nightmare that its production costs were higher than the industry average and the time to market lagged behind more nimble competitors such as Nokia and Samsung. In particular, Motorola seemed to underestimate the competitive nature of the hi-tech market and, until recently, consistently overpriced its products. Meanwhile, the company was distracted by the conflicting demands of its mobile phone, global positioning system (GPS), semiconductor, wireless network, broadband communication and smart electronics interests. Subsequently, Motorola has had to undergo a major restructuring, from the top down to every operational level, in order to stay afloat after the worst financial performance in its entire history in 2001/2002.

Samsung started its ascent to the global IT arena as a shining star because, unlike Motorola, it was capable of following and, indeed, setting market-oriented technological trends, and it had nimble R&D design capability and manufacturing excellence. Samsung began its pursuit of global leadership in the DRAM chip sector — the heart of electronics — and demonstrated an unsurpassed ability to manage in a highly competitive industry. Today, Samsung is the largest player in this sector in both sales revenues and net profits. Samsung truly believes it is capable of thriving in the business of low-margin consumer electronics. It also believes its focus on hardware, rather than software and content, will enable it to overtake long-time rivals such as SONY and Matsushita.

Once it had built up confidence in running a successful global memory-chip business under the leadership of its chairman, Lee Kun Hee, and its president, Yun Jong Yong, the company initiated an ambitious business strategy to be the

	Motorola			Samsung Electronics		
Financial Results	2003	2002	2001	2003	2002	2001
1. Revenue (US$ million)	27,058	26,679	30,004	54,114	49,641	36,025
2. Net income (US$ million)	893	−2,485	−3,937	4,978	5,877	2,304
3. Total assets (US$ million)	32,098	31,152	33,398	32,751	28,711	21,055
4. Return on equity, or ROE (%)	7.0	−22.1	−28.8	20.3	27.7	15.0
5. Return on assets, or ROA (%)	2.8	−8.0	−11.8	15.2	20.5	10.6
6. EBITDA (US$ million)	2,751	295	−3,251	9,105	8,883	4,144
7. EBITDA/Sales (%)	10.2	1.1	−10.8	16.9	17.9	11.5
8. Net income/sales (%)	3.3	−9.3	−13.1	9.2	11.8	6.4
9. Sales growth (%)	1.4	−11.1	−20.2	9.0	37.8	4.2

Figure 5.3 Motorola and Samsung Electronics: A comparison of financial performance

Sources: Mergent Online database[25] and authors' research

leader in all industry sectors in which it chose to participate. Currently, of the eight sectors in which it participates – DRAM chips; big-screen television; DVD players; flash memory; LCD display; microwave ovens; mobile phones; and MP3 players – it is the global leader in the first four and is among the top three in the others. Samsung's triumph, however, is much more than simply market share. During 2002, a dismal year for all other global electronics giants, Samsung earned US$5.9 billion net profits on sales of US$49.6 billion, profits that exceeded the top 10 Japanese electronics companies combined.

Considering that Samsung Electronics, the flagship of the colossal Samsung Group, had been saddled with heavy debt following the Asian financial crisis, what it has demonstrated is the implementation of a marvelous business strategy based on its unique competitive advantages. Defying Western management dogma, Samsung relies on vertical integration and perfecting it in several critical components, including chips and LCD displays, that can account for between 60% and 90% of the cost structure of some digital devices. While most WMNs abandoned the idea of being everywhere in the electronics industry value chain, Samsung not only invested heavily in the manufacture of these core components but also utilized them as its unique competitive strength in the market. Samsung, as the global leader for DRAM chips, also leads in static random-access memory and controls more than half of NAND flash-chip market for storing large music and color-image files. Samsung's leadership position in LCD displays also gives it a competitive edge over all its competitors when thin-film LCD is the preferred choice for PCs, TVs and mobile devices.

Instead of acting as an OEM or EMS for big Western companies, as most of Taiwan's electronics companies have done, Samsung had sufficient confidence in its innovative products to compete directly with its overseas rivals. It was also one of the early pioneers in the Chinese market and achieved respectable business results, recording sales of US$5 billion in 2003. Samsung attributes its success in China to moving part of its development and design functions to China to improve its core competencies in the local market. Samsung's innovation capabilities can be traced back to a tech-savvy Korean culture that seems to have an unlimited appetite for new gadgets. While many Western countries are still pondering the arrival of the 3G, Koreans have been using their mobile phones to watch TV or video-on-demand and to handle their bank transactions on a routine basis since October 2000. Korea has the highest broadband subscription rate, at 70% of all households, in the world. As of June 2004, Korea also leads the world in subscriptions to 3G mobile phones, with 29.7 million users. This compares with 20 million US users and 2.8 million users in Western European countries. It is no coincidence that such a hi-tech atmosphere encourages innovation and innovators. Samsung took full advantage of the creative ideas generated by its own domestic experiments and polished those products before it brought them to the international market. In doing so, it was also able to achieve manufacturing excellence by constantly benchmarking its quality standards against its Japanese peers and keep its cost base comparable with the lowest in the industry, normally found in Taiwan or China. Samsung only allows its own upstream plants to supply half of its demand in order to ensure its component producers are always competitive in both quality and cost. Whenever it can, it customizes its products for niche markets. Even in the commodity segment, which includes the memory chip, Samsung is much more profitable than its competitors because it prefers building specialized chips for global giants such as Dell and Microsoft. On top of all these competitive advantages, Samsung has made full use of its vertical integration to establish a reputation within the industry as one of the fastest in bringing innovative products to the market. In the ferociously competitive world of the electronics industry, Samsung has defined a unique business strategy and demonstrated its credibility in achieving its goals.

For Motorola, enormous challenges lie ahead if new CEO Ed Zander is to turn the company's fortunes around. A well-known marketing and operations expert, Zander has already divested the company of non-compatible business units such as semiconductors and is in the process of turning around its largest division, mobile phones, by introducing innovative products that can excite customers. Motorola is already well positioned in China, the largest mobile-phone market in the world, and other emerging markets thanks to its early investment during the boom days. As the leading foreign brand in a highly saturated mobile-phone market that boasts no fewer than 37 local players, Motorola must improve the attractiveness of its designs, its quality image, and the lead-time to the market within an acceptable cost structure. The battle in China is set to be a litmus test for both Motorola and Samsung in their fight for the leading position in the global mobile-phone market. Eventually, probably within the next five years, digital wireless home appliances and their integration systems will be the most important market opportunity for all electronics companies. Those companies that aspire to lead in their chosen sectors must learn from the success of Samsung and define their own unique competitive strategies in this highly competitive industry.

CHAPTER 6

THE COST FACTOR

The legendary basketball player Michael Jordan excelled not only in his magical offensive moves but also in his tenacious defensive responsiveness. The combination of these two seemingly incompatible skills and his commitment to teamwork make Jordan an all-time icon in this sport.

UNDERSTANDING THE NATURE OF A COMPETITIVE COST POSITION

The reputation as fierce price-cutters that Asian competitors have established over the years is based primarily on a favorable cost position achieved through having a lower cost base or higher productivity than their Western competitors. Equally important, Asian players tend to opt for this approach because, in reality, most have few other competitive advantages. Asian competitors lower their selling price in order to secure business because they set lower margin targets than their Western counterparts, who tend to set a floor price and are not willing to lose money, either in the short term or the long term. Asian players normally find such financial discipline to their advantage in cut-throat competition against their Western competitors. Whenever a market faces stagnation, competitive pricing frequently becomes the decisive factor in the awarding of a business contract. The electronics industry is known to be a killing field for companies that can't differentiate themselves by product or by services and are forced to mark down their prices on a continuous basis if they wish to stay in the market. The same trend can be found in numerous commodity industries that supply to mega-stores such as Wal-Mart and, to some degree, in certain commodity segments of many industries, such as the subcompact car category of the automobile industry.

Having abandoned their internal manufacturing capabilities in the face of Asian competition, many Western companies choose to concentrate on trading and distribution and might intentionally develop more suppliers than their demand might justify in order to keep the suppliers busy competing amongst themselves in Asia. The upside of such purchasing strategies for Asian players is that they become experts in cost reduction and expenditure control. In a free economy, such a vicious cycle eventually intensifies competition along the entire value chain. Whenever there is a substantially uneven distribution of profit in the value chain, the less fortunate will constantly improve their competitive competency in order to capture the remaining value left in the value chain. WMNs need to understand that there is a limit on every measure to bring down the cost. Once cost-cutting measures have been replicated by most competitors, market forces automatically level the playing field and eventually bring the competitive environment back to the same starting point until the next entrepreneur dares to take on the challenge to explore a new business initiative. Therefore, from a strategic viewpoint, the key point in choosing the option to reduce costs is that it must be considered as a complementary measure — rather than as the only means — to reinforce the company's overall competitive position.

Direct costs

Most Asian countries, except Japan, Hong Kong and Singapore, enjoy certain cost advantages as a manufacturing base. In the case of China and India, such cost advantages can be very substantial if a company is able to release hidden cost benefits. As shown in Figure 1.3, China's PPP is 4.9 times its GDP, while India's is 5.8 times. What this implies is that a WMN must seriously identify where these potential cost savings can be realized when they do business in either of these countries. Frequently expatriate production or project managers, under intense pressure to build a local team within a demanding timeframe, make the common mistake of headhunting experienced talent, regardless of the specific nature of the position, by offering two or three times the market salary rate. At the outset, this may seem very affordable. But under the right conditions, in China an experienced local engineer or accountant with good foreign language skills can hop between jobs as many as 10 times, with a substantial increase in salary each time, before finally settling into a long-term job. Job-hopping is such an epidemic that it can easily become the company culture and is therefore highly inimical to building an effective organization. Employers who poach in this way will always face the uncertainty of never knowing how long the employee will stay or whether this will be just another stop along the road to somewhere else.

Regardless of debatable cost areas such as the cost of borrowing, Asian players overall enjoy favorable indirect cost benefits. The production labor cost in China has been very flat for many years, mainly because of the abundant supply of unskilled labor. Even with the tremendous growth in the coastal cities over the past 25 years, migrant workers from the hinterland can still support the labor market for a long time to come, as the static direct labor costs tend to show. Alternatively, labor-intensive industries may also relocate their factories inland every few years to take advantage of the low labor costs that only exist in less-developed areas.

As to other key direct costs such as raw materials, both China and India are highly competent in providing a full range of manufactured goods mainly because each has had a long history of economic self-reliance and an abundant supply of qualified scientists and engineers. The options for exploring possible cost reductions on raw materials will be discussed later in the chapter.

Western executives are frequently amazed by the basic engineering capability that exists in China and India to manufacture very specialized products, ranging from unique pharmaceutical products to high-end military products that are normally only found in advanced Western countries. Of course, there is still a substantial gap between the Asian giants and the West in quality-assurance management and advanced integrated computerized control. Western purchasing agents are frequently surprised to discover that the "state-of-the-art" products that are supposed to be coming out of their own expensive R&D programs can already be found in numerous research institutes in China and India. Many Chinese academic institutions require their scientists to take part in commercial ventures so that they can become self-supporting financially. This mandate has given tremendous impetus to every advanced research institute to create specialized products for the end-users — a far cry from the days of the sleepy socialist economy. However, under this unconventional product-supply model the cost structure is often far from transparent. Many academy-based suppliers, under pressure to prove the financial viability of their products, do not necessarily include fixed-asset investments and operating costs in their cost calculations and frequently offer very attractive quotations to Western companies in order to secure major supply agreements for highly specialized products, particularly in pharmaceuticals and fine chemicals. Also under tremendous pressure to improve their profitability, WMNs usually find it hard to resist such offers and begin providing technical assistance to help these willing producers upgrade their supply capability, making the suppliers more competitive than ever. Similar partnerships between local supply and foreign demand are also found in India, but there the local partners tend to be specialist companies rather than academy-based or government-related suppliers.

Indirect costs

One of the major problems with the cost position of Asian players is a lack of transparency in indirect costs, particularly those related to the true investment cost or operating cost or financial expenses, which arises as a result of complicated cross-ownership arrangements between suppliers and customers. In recent years, the offering of stock options to employees in hi-tech industries in Asia, as well as in Silicon Valley, has become a controversial issue in the dispute over anti-dumping cases because if the cost of such high equity ownership were to be included in the production cost, this could make a significant difference to the total cost of the product.

In the US and Europe, the average indirect personnel costs, including medical expenses and pensions, typically runs at between 20% and 40% of the already high level of direct personnel costs. In the automotive industry, for example, which has a long history of union disputes in Western countries, the management of indirect costs, which can be as much as US$1,500 per vehicle, has become a decisive factor for the survival of entire companies such as GM. Faced with industrial relations problems, a company will naturally contemplate shifting at least part of its manufacturing base to Asia in order to improve its long-term viability. The indirect personnel cost in Asia, with the exception of Japan, is very low in absolute terms. In fact, during the early stages of attracting foreign investment, some Asian countries excluded certain critical components related to social security programs while redundancy costs were kept at an absolute minimum. The indirect personnel costs in Hong Kong and Singapore as a percentage of total personnel compensation costs are among the lowest in the world. China and India tend to have very complicated indirect personnel cost structures and a high percentage (in the range of 50% to 80%) of indirect personnel costs vis-à-vis direct personnel costs. A typical pay slip for an Indian employee can have up to 20 itemized calculations related to indirect benefits. The complexity of Indian-style management is undoubtedly related to the long history of government interference in business and economic affairs. Even today, some of these compensation-related terms and conditions are still the subject of frequent debates in parliament. In China, too, there is still uncertainty over how the government intends to fix the grossly under-funded social security scheme. However, in both countries, the net impact of these indirect personnel costs on investors remains insignificant.

Other indirect cost benefits in an emerging economy may come from the initial investment, such as land purchases and certain major capital expenditures. Whether an investor can enjoy such cost benefits depends to a great extent on the thoroughness of the initial market survey and the subsequent negotiations. In general, an investor should investigate at least three possible sites. The best way to secure the best possible land lease is to cross-check what price a local investor or an investor from Taiwan or Hong Kong pays for land nearby. The meager local knowledge possessed by most foreigners is usually the primary reason for their being in an unfavorable cost position from the outset in countries like China, Korea and India where transparency on investment costs can be a major problem.

Marketing and sales

The costs of marketing and sales (M&S) are usually another major weakness for foreign players because of the constant struggle to strike a balance between management control and cost-effectiveness. Knowledge of the local market is a critical core competency that any WMN must possess to be successful. The sheer size of the Asia Pacific region makes it virtually impossible to have a presence in every market location and cost-prohibitive to set up many sales offices and warehouse facilities. As a rule of thumb, each WMN needs to determine its top five or 10 territories in which to locate its Asian business units, depending on the specific nature of the industry. Frequently, the selection of the top four is quite straightforward and is usually China, Japan, Korea and India, as evidenced by their GDP or PPP. The next tier usually involves ASEAN, Australia/New Zealand and Taiwan.

For the purposes of controlling M&S costs, where the company is servicing industrial customers, it is always valuable to locate the sales team close to the production site. The concept of the home office for a sales team is not well accepted in Asia because of the cultural reasons explained in Chapter 2. Companies that have implemented this concept normally experience lower productivity, more resentment, and a higher turnover of staff during an economic upturn. Companies that have enjoyed success with the concept on their home turf may wish to consider renting a smaller office to be shared by sales and business support personnel as an alternative solution.

Having a reliable distributor as a business partner to supplement the direct sales to key accounts is crucial, given the massive territories in the region to be covered by different business units. Depending on the size and profitability of a business unit, an experienced distributor, properly selected to match the strengths and weaknesses of that unit, can play a vital role in both sales coverage and ongoing after-sales support. An ideal distributor must have broad-based market coverage and an in-depth knowledge of the various applications of the product range owned by the unit. Finding a good distributor is a very important marketing exercise and comparable to the selection of a joint-venture partner. Normally the selection process must start with a comprehensive market study, followed by a thorough procedure designed to match the strengths and weaknesses of the two companies before a trial contract is granted for a specific period. The consequences of not selecting a suitable distributor can sometimes be more devastating than hiring the wrong sales manager. This is because a distributor is a quasi-company which, when it has acquired all the necessary competencies to be an independent player in the same industry, may compete in the same market. It is not uncommon for Asian distributors to set up parallel product lines during the course of a valid contract. Equally important is to ensure that control over the distributors is exercised by a sales manager and overseen by a supervisor who know the ins and outs of the business. These checks and balances are vital because many distributors try to corrupt the sales manager who is directly responsible for managing the profitability of distributors. A corrupt sales manager, who in some cases may turn out to be the hidden owner of the distributor, can cost a business unit dearly because the company may eventually lose its entire business in this sales territory and face a competitor who knows crucial details of the company's operations. On the other hand, a good distributor will treasure the long-term partnership and compensate for any weaknesses the company may have in joint sales efforts. When a distribution agreement is reached, the costs are best controlled by the distributor, while the company should remain focused on implementing its overall business plan.

The costs of not getting the right arrangements in place for this critical area undoubtedly outweigh the cost of implementing a proper management system.

Research and development

In controlling R&D costs, the pivotal decision revolves around how much technology and how many experienced expatriates are needed to support the business unit. The SBU must first make an assessment of the technical competency requirements against the expected results, such as the introduction of new products and technical support, over the period defined in the business plan. In the area of R&D, having a small team staffed with competent personnel is normally what it takes to build an impressive product portfolio and a pipeline of value-added products. Given the high priority to keep vital technology within the company, it is vitally important to bring in certain expatriate technical experts who can truly contribute to the unit's future business development.

A good technical team usually consists of diverse talent drawn from various scientific disciplines and cultural backgrounds in order to serve the industry's needs across what is a diverse region. Striking a balance between local and expatriate, experienced and young, talent is an important HR decision because this balance will help develop a sustainable business plan. In this regard, it is important to have HR planning in place on a continuous basis in order to prevent unexpected replacement costs that are usually excessive and can be very detrimental to the development of new business opportunities.

Corporate allocation

Of all cost elements that have to be considered, corporate allocation (the administration costs generated by corporate headquarters) is usually either the most political, if it is handled in a controversial way, or the most strategic, if it is handled in a way that promotes the company's long-term competitive position. It is important that a cost-effective global organization gives responsibility for every single cost element, such as IT, financial services, administration, HR and so on, to a manager, who must be accountable for the services provided at a competitive market rate. A good WMN should always benchmark its corporate costs against the best practice in the same industry or one with similar service requirements.

For example, the generally accepted ideal target for IT costs ought to be between 0.5% and 1.0% of sales revenue, while financial services costs should be between 0.8% and 1.2% of sales revenue.

IDENTIFYING CRITICAL COST ELEMENTS IN THE VALUE CHAIN

Product design

This is an area in which Asian producers are quickly establishing themselves as cost leaders because it is necessary for their own survival that they extract every possible penny from the value chain. For most manufactured goods, product design is normally the first target for substantial cost savings. In the IT industry, Asian players frequently use vertical integration and production alliances to shorten the design time as well as to cut the total cost.

Normally the business process begins with an agreement between the participants in the project on the target market price of the end product, before each component is assigned a target cost. The contractors participating in the project must then either commit to meeting these costs or be replaced by another vendor. Since there is generally a glut of suppliers, an alternative partner can usually be found to drive down the cost. Each participant will focus on its respective specialized area in order to meet the target cost on a timely basis. This model has been proven to be very competitive in both cost and time by comparison with the model favored by many WMNs that tends to rely on many independent companies and many individual meetings in a very lengthy supply-chain process. Not too long ago, many WMNs thought Asian players were simply experts in reverse engineering; that is, in dissecting, analyzing and copying whatever advanced products became available from the West. Now, however, the business model for the IT industry is that the WMNs mainly contribute the fundamental design ideas or marketing concepts, while the Asian players carry out the rest of the tasks along the entire value chain, apart from the interface with customers at the beginning and end of the process.

Purchasing

Commodity suppliers

This classification is important in the sense that a commodity is not differentiated and must be constantly subjected to dynamic market conditions to keep it competitive. In this category, successful purchasing primarily comes from having up-to-date market knowledge and superior bargaining power. This means that a firm must devote sufficient resources to collecting and auditing market prices within a specific country to ensure that its purchases are always in line with market conditions and consistent with its own purchasing power. A free exchange of pricing information within a global purchasing organization is vital if the company is to reap the benefits of getting the best price from different geographic locations. Given proper coordination, the Asian purchasing team should have a good opportunity to bring the best cost to the global purchasing team because of the traditionally high parity purchasing power in China and India.

Specialty suppliers

The definition of a specialty supplier is normally related to the degree to which its product is subject to entry barriers or where its initial fixed-cost investment is prohibitive. In dealing with specialty suppliers, a strategic partnership is essential for long-term success because, by definition, specialty suppliers offer a unique product or service in the value-creation process. A company must assess if a specialty supplier is capable of assisting it in the long term through creating innovation beyond its current specialty product range. If a specialty supplier lacks the ability to upgrade its products, this inevitably leads to major confrontations when current price premiums can no longer be justified under the pressures of the commoditization process. A WMN must therefore evaluate whether a specialty supplier is indeed able to bring value through both price concession and product update. The latter is vitally important in Asia because the creation of a superior product image helps sustain the competitive position in the marketplace. Securing an exclusive offer from a specialty supplier for a highly differentiated product is another way that a company can create value.

Tolling partners

Tolling, by definition, is a contractual production service rendered by a third party and is used by the company to avoid having to expend its own capital resources. An effective way of managing the purchase of proprietary raw materials without incurring capital investment costs by looking for a tolling partner that has either free capacity or an aspiration to do business with a WMN. A typical Asian tolling partner with an established business enjoys a favorable cost position in comparison to a typical WMN's cost structure. Another advantage of working with an Asian tolling partner is the speed with which a product can be brought to market. However, this tolling arrangement can be strategically successful only when the company is in full control of the intellectual property rights and has specialist market knowledge. In determining the suitability of a potential tolling partner, the WMN will need to review the candidate's track record in a similar industry, its competitive cost position against other Asian players and its compatibility with the company's strategic goals. Most Asian tolling partners accept volume-based pricing, which can be very advantageous to the company, and most are willing to work on a long-term relationship provided that the benefits are mutual.

Sales and operational planning

The downsizing of sales and operational planning within an organization through consolidating office locations can generate substantial savings, particularly in high-cost countries. The current trend towards moving customer-service centers to China or India confirms the increasing recognition by WMNs that utilizing these low-cost bases can improve their overall cost position. Providing such services are also being seen by the Chinese and Indian governments as a new way to attract foreign investment. In most cases, these governments welcome the setting up of outsourcing service centers and are willing to revise their business licenses to accommodate this. The Shanghai government, for example, offers tax incentives for foreign investors to move their regional head-quarters into the city.

However, the biggest challenge for this type of service center is to build a competent service team on a sustainable basis. This task can be daunting and success should not be taken for granted. Even for experienced customer-service staff from China, it may require as much as one year of on-the-job training in a well-established customer-service center in order to bring them to the level of competency typically available in a regional hub such as Hong Kong or Singapore. The best way to ensure that this happens smoothly is to mobilize a regional team at both the implementation and steering levels, with the former focusing on processing orders and the latter on the internal coordination of business and functional support activities. A joint change-management committee must follow each stage of the mapping process closely until consistently satisfactory feedback from the affected customers is confirmed.

In general, the biggest potential cost savings from the sales and operational planning function come from the reduction in working capital that results from centralized stock planning and control. In this, the minimization of stock entry points plays a vital role and is a joint decision by the management of the SBU and the support function. Having an order entry based on a three- to six-month rolling forecast is another effective way to reduce stock levels but is heavily dependent on market realities and the discipline of the sales team. Keeping raw materials on consignment is another means of achieving significant reductions in working capital. Unfortunately, there is a trade-off in most of these cost-reduction efforts because competitors will soon detect the weakness in the market and find a wedge to work against the company if these management decisions cannot be implemented smoothly. In many commodity segments, a WMN will find it more difficult to realize these cost savings because of the general availability of competitive stocks and the very short lead-times required by most Asian customers. In certain electronics segments, the lead-time requirement is as short as four hours from the time of placing an order to receiving the goods. For specialty segments, it is more likely that savings from the change of supply logistics can be achieved because of the bargaining power that the company has in supplying a differentiated product. Wherever a local or regional manufacturing site exists, the savings in working capital can be even more substantial than sourcing from a distant supply point in the US or Europe.

Operational excellence

The benefits to be had from a consolidation or "rationalization" of manufacturing sites should be weighed against the total cost of providing multiple sources of supply based on a comprehensive financial analysis of the product range to be offered to customers. Provided that it can be supported by an analysis of its net present value, the sales team and the customers, the consolidation of multiple manufacturing sites into fewer sites or a single site normally represents one of the most significant cost savings of all the support functions. In a typical manufacturing industry, production costs can represent between 10% and 30% of the selling price. When a company is facing a declining market share or the increasing commoditization of its product line, the consolidation of multiple sites can be a very powerful strategy to reap the cost benefits. Asia Pacific plants located in the low-cost countries tend to offer the best long-term option. There is an increasing acceptance of conventional or hi-tech products made in China, even by quality-conscious customers in Japan or Northern Europe. In 2002, China became the second-largest exporter of electronics products in the world and is aiming to take a greater market share in the near future.

Many critical operational cost elements can actually be reduced significantly because of the high parity purchasing power in China and India. Civil engineering costs related to building a factory, for example, can be as little as 25% of the total cost of an equivalent job in a Western country. For commodity products such as basic inorganic chemicals that are highly dependent on the depreciation cost of assets on the ground, making as many fixed-asset purchases as possible in China can have a significant effect.

Logistics

The transcontinental freight transportation business, whether overland or by air, is a highly competitive business that is often saturated with competent players. Participants in this market normally quote within one or two percent of the final acceptable price, which is heavily reliant on volume discount. Therefore, it is highly desirable to leverage on the combined volume from different affiliates and sister companies to get the best deal from the transportation companies with similar geographic coverage in the market. Keeping close track of the market freight cost is one of the most useful ways of keeping this factor under control because companies may become complacent when the delivery of products is running smoothly.

What can make a big difference in the logistics cost is the management of the distribution network within a sales territory, particularly in an emerging market. In India, for example, even though several highway infrastructure projects have been started, the nationwide transportation network will remain quite primitive for the next five years because of the costs involved. The high costs involved in setting up a business in Japan or the import restrictions imposed by local governments in China and India can also make the cost of doing business in Asia prohibitive for many companies. For small and medium-sized sales volumes, the cost of distribution by a local distributor can be substantially less than that when a WMN undertakes its own distribution function. However, as business volume grows, it is possible that the company will need to improve the key account support that is available from its own distribution. At different stages of its growth, therefore, the WMN will be forced to reassess how best to meet its distribution requirements.

OUTSOURCING OR INTERNAL SOLUTIONS?

During the boom years of the late 1990s, personnel costs in the US, particularly for health care, were rising rapidly, and it was not uncommon for WMNs to opt for outsourcing as a solution to this problem. Normally when a WMN makes a decision to outsource financial services, a global contract is signed across different geographic locations in order to maintain consistency in the overall financial records for the purposes of future consolidation or for external audit. Unfortunately, the cost benefits or cost-neutral position that this brought in the Western world frequently diminished when the high costs involved in outsourcing similar services in Asia were taken into account. The high cost of outsourcing in Asia can arise from having to deal with a variety of languages, from high software license expenses, from excessive back-office support, and the eventual costs of terminating these outsourcing arrangements. Consequently, an increasing number of Western companies are starting to set up their own finance or business service centers in low-cost countries such as India and China. The potential savings to be made from finding in-house solutions can be substantial. In India, for example, WMNs can achieve cost savings of up to 40% by simply transferring their existing in-house services. If the same concept can be implemented for various business units across many different developed countries, there is no doubt that the total cost savings can be tremendous.

In the face of powerful technological developments and the blurring of borders between countries under the unstoppable march of globalization, companies will always have to find productivity gains through innovative means. Those that can't will find that their competitive position will be compromised.

COPING WITH COST STRUCTURES IN THE REAL WORLD

In many foreign-investment hot spots, such as Shanghai or Mumbai, the cost of setting up a business has risen outrageously since the mid 1990s. For example, the office rental for a Grade A building in downtown Shanghai is now more expensive than for a similar building in most of Hong Kong. If the current trend of foreign investments in China continues, Shanghai may surpass Hong Kong and, indeed, Tokyo as the most expensive city in the region for foreigners to do business. This type of sharp rise in indirect cost again underlines the dilemma for certain WMNs that rush into an investment hotbed for cost benefits. Faced with rising local personnel costs, high expatriate costs, congested traffic, and less-experienced local staff, some WMNs will be questioning whether Shanghai is indeed the best location for a regional hub.

A strategic alternative for regional headquarters could be to use Hong Kong, which is second to none in infrastructure, as the financial and management hub while moving most back-office and operational support services to the Pearl River Delta in southern China. A commercial office or business support branch could be located in the key metropolitan cities of Tokyo, Shanghai, Seoul, Singapore, Mumbai or Melbourne. The experience of several WMNs is that such a model can deliver satisfactory cost-performance benefits. However, because of the tremendous market potential in China, Shanghai, being geographically superior to all other Chinese cities, is still regarded as the future regional center for WMNs in Asia.

Managing project costs for a critical start-up

The start-up period of any business always requires strong corporate support ranging from engineering assessments and safety improvements to recruitment and IT installation. It is estimated that 85% of WMNs overrun their start-up budget in Asia, as opposed to 30% on their home turf. The fact that start-up costs generally overrun is indicative of a lack of control over a wide range of variables related to a start-up project, but in Asia the cost overrun can also be attributable to insufficient local knowledge, inadequate planning, cumbersome import procedures and poor global coordination. Given the high probability of cost overruns in Asia, the appointment of an experienced project manager with a strong track record is highly desirable. Local experience is important but not necessarily a prerequisite. Whenever possible, an assistant with a good engineering and purchasing background is always helpful to bridge the gap between project expectations and local realities. However, most WMNs still have problems finding the right project manager to run their projects in non-English-speaking Asian countries. If the WMN has plans for long-term operational expansion in Asia, it is imperative that it has a pool of qualified engineering managers who stay abreast of ongoing operational issues within the region. Frequent contact with the regional engineering team certainly ensures that adequate local knowledge is maintained in the corporate planning department. At the same time, some talented personnel must be kept within the region to keep the knowledge base current in order to handle the frequent technology transfers and hardware improvements associated with new business development.

There is no easy way for a company to have full cost control until all project activities are captured on a master chart which lists such information as project owner, specific tasks, reliable sources of supply, accurate delivery dates, clear accountability and a precise completion schedule. Frequently, companies build their implementation schedules around previous experience in similar projects in Western countries. But, the methodology, manpower, equipment and legal requirements for executing an agreed engineering work can be vastly different in Asia. In general, there are more government regulations, albeit not necessarily transparent, in Asia than in Western countries. However, Asian contractors tend to be more flexible than their Western counterparts even though the alternative solutions available to them frequently are not based on the same engineering principles commonly used in the West. Instead, many Asian contractors tend to look to Japan's standards as the benchmark. As Asian contractors tend to be results-oriented, it is generally acceptable to include a penalty clause in the contract to cover any failure to meet a challenging schedule. Asian civil engineering contractors frequently exceed the expectations of WMNs regarding completion times, even with relatively low levels of automated support at their disposal. If a project team with a balance of local and foreign engineers can be assembled, this is a good starting point for implementing the project. Through precise and routine follow-up at each step defined in the master chart, the project team can normally avoid the expensive delays that frequently hamper access to a business opportunity. If the project is an important one, senior executives in the region must be made fully accountable for its success.

CONTINUOUS IMPROVEMENT OF COST POSITION

The cost leader in any market is, by definition, the one that has the best programs in place to maintain its cost supremacy over its competitors when it comes to head-to-head price-cutting. This can only work if the cost leader can cultivate a cost-conscious culture throughout the entire organization, from the CEO down to new hires. If cost competency is what it takes to maintain or improve a competitive position, CEOs must then ask how they themselves can contribute to this objective.

The importance of the CEO's contribution should never be underestimated, as the experience of Stanley Gault clearly shows. Gault, who ran neck-to-neck in the final contest with Jack Welch for the top job at GE and was later nominated on several occasions by *Fortune* and *BusinessWeek* as the best CEO for his outstanding achievements in managing plastic-goods manufacturer Rubbermaid, again proved his worth when he came out of retirement to energize the Goodyear Tire & Rubber Company. In 1990, Goodyear had experienced the first financial loss in its entire corporate history and Gault embarked on a rescue mission. A marketing whiz and an exceptional team-builder, Gault orchestrated one of the most impressive turnarounds in US corporate history in his first 60 days on the job. In order to correct a confusing marketing strategy that had plagued the company, he energized the team by promoting a series of breakthrough products such as Aqua-tread to highlight the company's safety image. He also launched the Intrepid tire from the US carrier Intrepid and he committed the firm to Formula One racing to present an image of technical leadership. At that time, the tire industry was infamous for its poor cost structures and Gault turned himself into something of a role model when he brought light bulbs from home and dimmed the lights of the entire executive floor. He gave the lead in the company's cost-reduction initiatives and provided the momentum that ensured that these programs were shared and maintained by all employees, including a traditionally powerful labor union. As a result, Goodyear went on to record improved financial performances for nine consecutive quarters. After Gault officially went into his second retirement, Goodyear returned to its old ways, with Gault's successor relying too much on acquisitions and losing focus on developing a value-added business strategy.

Another important characteristic of competition by cost is the inevitable limitations of such competition, as can be seen from developments in the mega-store industry. In its battles with arch-rivals K-Mart and Sears in the United States, Wal-Mart — under the slogan "Everyday Low Prices" — clearly understood that maximizing the genuine purchasing power of US households would be the decisive factor. Neither K-Mart nor Sears was able to keep up with Wal-Mart's best practices in keeping down costs in areas such as purchasing, logistics, store construction, shelf leasing, and merchandising finance. Once it had captured the consumers with such policies, Wal-Mart went on to dominate the segment around the country and is now the largest company in the world, with an annual turnover at US$258 billion in 2003. However, using low cost as the key competitive strategy has its limit when a player enters a brand-new market. For example, Wal-Mart has not been able to deliver the same impressive business growth in China, where it faces many low-cost local players. Without the local sourcing expertise and cultural knowledge that are essential to meet local customer demands, Wal-Mart has been lagging behind some local competitors.

BRINGING ASIAN COST STRUCTURES TO GLOBAL ORGANIZATION

In addition to making use of the well-known skills of software engineers from India, and the exceptionally good production capabilities in Taiwan, Korea and China, WMNs are also beginning to shift their entire business-support centers, their shared financial-services centers and R&D centers to China and India. Are they really abandoning their home countries for short-term benefits? The answer is more intriguing than might appear at first glance. In the heated race of global competition, the basic principles of the free economy require that all resources should be freed up in order to gain maximum efficiencies. The tough reality is that this migration of traditional jobs will be irreversible unless major innovations such as Internet technology can be used to change business processes or to enable users to enjoy even higher productivity than those who provide the products or services. Therefore, it is important for WMNs to accept this fact and start bringing the best Asian cost structures to their global organizations.

In general, a successful Asian organization must start with market-driven business processes. A company must have a well-defined market position in all the major business segments it is serving. For example, a company can have four SBUs serving various industrial segments, with some being the technical leader and some the cost leader within their respective segments. Each SBU must determine its cost position on an ongoing basis in order to sustain its market position. For SBUs that operate within a cost-driven industry segment, every single function must have a benchmark cost position aligned with current technological trends. As technology evolves, the cost position must also be updated to remain competitive. What this means is that the company must have a series of cost realignment programs tailored to any possible technological advances. Each time the market changes by an incremental step, the company should always be ready to meet the challenge before it actually arrives. A WMN with a strong team in Asia can help bring this core competency into the global organization.

Certain skilled labor, particularly in the engineering repairs and maintenance department, can be another important asset to WMNs in developing countries. Because of the broad base of training available through apprenticeship programs, China actually has a pool of maintenance talent that is sometimes comparable with their technically advanced counterparts in Germany. The potential impact of Chinese engineering talent is very similar to that of India's software engineers. With appropriate language training, these maintenance specialists can also make a substantial contribution to reducing a WMN's operational costs.

ANTI-DUMPING ISSUES

Of the anti-dumping cases raised by WTO members up to the end of 2003, Asia Pacific countries made up around 60%. Leading the list within Asia were India, with 67%, and China, with 27%. The heavy concentration of anti-dumping cases in India and China underscores the tendency by these countries, both late entrants, to use their accession to the WTO as a weapon to battle international competition or to use this privilege as a tit-for-tat tactic when they are accused of dumping various products. These figures also highlight the tremendous litigation skills possessed by Indian lawyers. In general, India has weak manufacturing capabilities compared to the big economic powers in Northeast Asia. When foreign competition intensifies in these two emerging economies, more often than any other countries they resort to the protective measures allowed under WTO rules. Quite correctly, these anti-dumping regulations have become a highly effective tool for them to use in seeking punitive compensation or, simply, as a pre-emptive measure to send advance warning to potential rivals in similar industries. China's use of anti-dumping lawsuits against her Western trade partners also reflects the Chinese government's frustration that it is subject to an unfair trade condition, Market Economy Status (MES), imposed by the EU and the US. Under MES conditions, instead of conducting a detailed cost analysis on a Chinese producer that is alleged to have dumped its product on an overseas market, the US or the EU simply has to find a "reference" market as the basis for cost calculations for Chinese producers. The argument used by the EU and the US during the WTO accession negotiations was that China did not have a "reliable" cost or price structure. However, China's government insists that market reform in China has gone much further than most Western countries would like to admit. According to China's official statistics, by the end of 2003, 98% of the products sold in China were priced according to the market mechanism. In order to avoid unnecessary international trade friction, it is prudent for both China and her trade partners to quickly resolve this artificial trade restriction.

For companies engaged in trading with India and China, the frontline sales team and logistics personnel must fully understand the legal definition of a dumping claim because anti-dumping charges do create commercial and strategic damage for an SBU and the company. The domestic industry that files a petition only needs to prove one single case of violation in order for the dumping claim to be accepted by the government. In the course of litigation, the crucial points for a petitioner to prove are the normal value of the product in the home country of the company accused of dumping the product and the exact economic damage inflicted on the domestic industry in loss of revenue, salaries, pre-tax profits and cash flow. Sales managers must know their true production costs before they engage in any price competition in these emerging markets.

Case Study:

DOW CHEMICALS vs. FORMOSA PLASTICS GROUP

Just bear in mind that the American chemicals industry, as a sector, was the biggest contributor to US exports only 20 years ago. Globally well-known companies such as Du Pont, Dow, Monsanto, Rohm & Haas, and Union Carbide were considered to be both technology leaders and low-cost producers because there were few other industries that depended so much on economies of scale. As time went on, Du Pont and Rohm & Hass became highly specialized in certain segments such as fiber reinforcement, electronics and engineering materials. Monsanto transformed itself into a life-science company. Dow Chemicals, on the other hand, has stuck largely with manufacturing excellence by investing heavily in vertical integration for the production of chemicals and petrochemicals of all kinds. Dow has also made several very aggressive acquisitions recently (including Union Carbide, with its annual sales turnover of around US$5 billion) in anticipation of being able to leverage economies of scale from its mammoth global platform. In the process of developing such a cost competency, Dow Chemicals has become one of the most productive chemicals companies, with sales revenue per employee reaching nearly US$700,000.

This is a remarkable achievement by the operational standards of the chemicals industry, and one that was, in the past, only achievable in the oil industry and the international trading sector. However, a close look at the major reorganizations that Dow Chemicals has undertaken over the past three years after rare consecutive financial losses in 2001 and 2002, shows that the chemicals industry has changed dramatically on a global scale. First of all, the era of cheap oil will probably not come back again because OPEC and non-OPEC oil producers are now having difficulty keeping up with demand for petroleum around the world. Secondly, all the oil-producing countries and oil companies, reckoning the benefits of keeping oil prices high, are less eager to invest in major explorations after the humiliating collapse of oil prices in 1998 that saw the oil price dip to US$9.4 per barrel against OPEC's target of US$22 to $28 per barrel. Thirdly, the incremental investment cost to develop new sources of oil may be substantially higher than was required in the past. Fourthly, there are alternative supplies of nearly all commodity chemicals from producers in Asia and the Middle East. The rise of the Formosa Plastics Group of Taiwan exemplifies how this industry, once dominated by WMNs, is now undergoing the largest consolidation restructuring in its entire history. The profitability of the chemicals industry had been inexorably depressed over a three-year period until the strong industry-wide recovery of 2004 that was driven by a shortage of certain critical raw materials. The commodity chemicals industry nevertheless is still highly cyclical because of a global glut in supply, particularly in Asia.

	Dow			Formosa Plastics Group		
Financial Results	2003	2002	2001	2003	2002	2001
1. Revenue (US$ million)	32,632	27,609	27,805	26,014	20,131	16,756
2. Net income (US$ million)	1,730	−338	−385	2,671	2,046	407
3. Total assets (US$ million)	41,891	39,562	35,515	47,424	42,837	40,657
4. Return on equity, or ROE (%)	19.0	−4.4	−3.9	21.7	19.3	3.9
5. Return on assets, or ROA (%)	4.1	−0.9	−1.1	5.6	4.8	1.0
6. EBITDA (US$ million)	3,922	1,911	1,850	4,162	3,221	2,178
7. EBITDA/Sales (%)	12.0	6.9	6.7	16.0	16.0	13.0
8. Net income/sales (%)	5.3	−1.2	−1.4	10.3	10.2	2.4
9. Sales Growth (%)	18.2	−0.7	20.8	29.4	20.1	9.5

Figure 6.1 Dow Chemicals and Formosa Plastics Group: A comparison of financial performance

Sources: Mergent Online database[26] and authors' research

Led by the legendary management icon Y.C. Wang and his brother, Y.T. Wang, the Formosa Plastics Group, with a combined annual turnover of more than US$26 billion in 2003, can trace its origins back to a humble start-up PVC plant in southern Taiwan around 50 years ago. The Group's initial growth coincided with the golden age of the US chemicals industry, which churned out revolutionary products such as nylon for women's pantyhose, Teflon for non-stick cooking pans, Kevlar fiber for use in soldier's helmets and polycarbonates for bulletproof windows. Formosa Plastics, which had just opened up its first production site, was wondering how it could compete with an output of 4 MT per day in a market dominated by gigantic US, European and Japanese players. Y.C Wang made probably the first crucial business decision of his life by going for an immediate expansion of capacity based on an incremental fixed-asset investment so that the factory could lower its unit cost base that would enable it to compete in overseas markets. Nevertheless, the competition from Japan was so intense that Formosa's tiny plant was driven into financial distress. Y.C. Wang was convinced that the only way to survive was to expand to take advantage of economies of scale – a strategy he followed throughout his career. Fortunately, this was also a boom time for Taiwanese export-oriented industries such as textile goods and plasticware because the Taiwan government had just embarked on an ambitious economic development plan for import-substitution as well as for export-processing industries.

Formosa Plastics Group went one step ahead of its competitors by vertically integrating into PVC processing areas such as upholstery, piping, construction, and so on. Whenever there was a need for more participants to establish economies of scale, Formosa Plastics Group was willing to accept the coexistence of small local competitors and helped all downstream players to prosper, even potential competitors, in order to grow the entire domestic chemicals segment closer to the global scale. This strategy turned out to be pivotal to the Group's attempts to establish a strong foothold in the commodity chemicals industry. Because of this strong alliance, Formosa.Plastics was able to ride out several stormy economic downturns, including the 1974 Oil Crisis, the post-Tiananmen Square period in 1989, the financial meltdown in Asia in 1997, and the post-IT bubble period of 2001. Y.C. Wang attributed his success to a long-term alliance based on word of honor – in other words, to traditional Chinese/ Taiwanese culture. Y.C. Wang's frugality was also at the heart of the Group's success. His early fortune was built around retail sales of processed rice, in which he threw in home deliveries and cleaning storage bins as extras at the same price as his competitors. He insisted on simplicity and rationalization in all business activities, including his own travel: he traveled economy class until he was 75 years old. Naturally, the key members of his management team, mostly old pals and close relatives, shared his vision and management philosophy and were religious about driving down cost in every facet of its operations. Formosa Plastics Group reckons that 95% of its profits are achieved through the continuous improvement of its production processes and cost structures. Today the Group enjoys tremendous cost benefits from a completely integrated petroleum complex. In this regard, it is even stronger than Dow Chemicals, because it has its own fleet, its own harbors, its own power plant — all close to the main growing market. It even has its own man-made island to house one of the largest petroleum compounds in the world. All these investments were initially valued at US$10 billion but the output is now rated to be around twice the scope of the original investment. Again, Mr. Wang is using his favorite game, economies of scale, to keep his competitors on their toes because his company is now among the cost leaders in most commodity chemicals.

Naturally, an excessively high oil price over a prolonged period will have an adverse effect on all industries in the long term. But Formosa Plastics has a wide product portfolio that includes oil refineries, petrochemicals, fibers, basic chemicals and many downstream industry segments. The fact that it is more diversified than most typical chemical or oil companies gives it a cushion to absorb high oil prices through its participation in various industries with different economic cycles. However, the diversified portfolio also makes effective management more complex. Formosa Plastics has a backward integration for its electronics materials division, from epoxy resin, glass fiber, copper foil, copper-clad laminate, to printed circuit board division, semiconductor chips division, flat-screen display division, and even chip design alliance. This vertical integration benefited the Group during the boom years of the IT era when economic value was created for all individual business units throughout the entire value chain. During downturns such as that experienced in 2001, the Group, of course, suffered a lot but was nevertheless able to keep its capacity running at around the industry average simply because of its supply to internal users and strategic alliance partners.

Clearly both Dow Chemicals and Formosa Plastics are facing challenges in a rapidly evolving market environment. Dow Chemicals had struggled with financial difficulties for almost three years until the former CEO, William Stavropoulos, came out of retirement to steer the company out of its depression by instituting comprehensive cost-reduction measures and by driving substantial price increases. He is also currently in the process of divesting the company of some non-core business units in order to maintain the long company tradition of paying dividends even during an economic downturn. The upbeat economic sentiment of early 2004 clearly worked in favor of Dow Chemicals because its stock price at one point reached a nine-year high regardless of the high oil price. Dow Chemicals is currently undergoing another round of realignment programs designed to reduce its cost base in line with high oil prices. Its efforts to enter more specialty chemicals businesses may prove to be more challenging because fundamentally Dow's management structure was set up for the commodity chemicals business. The specialty chemicals business offers better financial returns on investment but normally requires a very responsive team to handle product development, technical services, and customer service. Above all, it does not depend as much on economies of scale as the commodity business in which Dow Chemicals is truly one of the world's leaders. It is imperative that the company does well in China, where it has long had major expansion plans, including a naphtha-cracking plant in northern China, but has only recently started some second-tier projects with a view to building sufficient business and customer base to justify the billion-dollar naphtha project.

Meanwhile, Dow Chemicals' main competitor in Asia, Formosa Plastics Group, has just announced further expansion that will put it in head-to-head competition with Dow. With close access to the China market from an offshore petroleum complex in Mai-Liao, Taiwan, Formosa Plastics Group has positioned itself as one of the main challengers to the major multinationals, including Shell, BP and BASF, which have already embarked on major capital investment in China. While the Taiwanese government still imposes certain investment restrictions in China on Taiwan's blue-chip companies, Formosa Plastics Group has already established an early market presence and gained local market knowledge. It is only a matter of time before the Group makes major direct investment in China. Its biggest problem ironically lies in one of its greatest strengths — the exceptional leadership of Y.C. Wang. Y.C. Wang is about to turn 90 years old and the question of succession is becoming ever more pressing. Apart from his younger brother, who is also in his 80s, there is no one in the Group who comes close to having the authority with which he has held this complicated company structure together. With members of the next generation of the Wang family already running individual companies within the Group, it remains to be seen whether these affiliates and subsidiaries will be able to work together towards a common goal that until now has been defined solely by the vision and ambition of Y.C. Wang.

PART III

FORMULATING AND IMPLEMENTING A STRATEGY FOR GROWTH

CHAPTER 7

FORMULATING A SUCCESSFUL BUSINESS STRATEGY

"The five essential elements of the Rules of War are:
1) measurement of territory; 2) estimation of resources; 3) calculation of
manpower; 4) comparison of relative strength; and 5) assessment of proba-
bility of victory."

(Master Sunzi, 500 BC)

DEFINING THE MARKET

Simplistic though it may sound, an effective business strategy must start
from a precise definition of what the company is engaged in and what it
is not. In a manufacturing-related business, this definition appears to be
relatively straightforward. But once it starts to get involved in technology
licensing and providing services through different strategic options, this
market definition can become increasingly complicated. In the healthcare and banking industries, for instance, it is not unusual for revenue to
change once the market definition is altered.

The market definition for a specialty chemicals company can include
providing specially formulated high-performance, thermal-set chemical
solutions used in conjunction with fiber reinforcement, as well as specialized building blocks for automotive, aerospace, electronics, engineering and industrial applications. If its basic chemistry — say, polyester,
polyurethane or epoxy — is also included, the market can be expanded
accordingly.

In the automotive industry, a basic market definition would revolve around designing and assembling vehicles used in passenger transportation and would thus normally include the passenger sedan, sports coupe, van, and sports utility vehicle (SUV). In fact, this definition would be suitable for approximately 90% of the automotive companies in the world. A highly specialized segment such as the luxury-car market, however, would have a very different definition — to provide the best-in-class sedan, with exceptional comfort, impeccable craftsmanship and sensational power, for example. Such different market definitions clearly serve a very different customer base and accordingly should have very different marketing plans. It is clear, though, that there could be substantial synergies for certain companies from serving in both markets. This is illustrated by Mercedes-Benz's ownership of Maybach, or BMW's ownership of Rolls-Royce. Figure 7.1 shows how market descriptions can be broken down into even more distinct classifications and provides a template for related business planning.

(1) By industry type

In this example, the company's current market is in Industry I, Industry II and Industry III. But, with the competencies at its disposal, it can immediately tap into a similar industry, Industry IV, which will become the target for future expansion. If the company is able to expand its current competencies through acquisition or strategic alliance, it is possible for it to enter other potential markets in Industry V and Industry VI. Honda Automotive Company provides a good example of this pattern. Honda was a highly successful motorcycle company before it moved into the passenger vehicle industry and became one of the major players there. Using its core competency in engine technology, it has recently expanded its market into the company-jet industry.

(2) By product range

Usually this is an inward-looking way of defining the market based on many years of commercial experience or a pattern within a specific industry. A company may define its current market segments as, say, Product A, Product B and Product C, with these products serving several different industries or customer bases. With a little fine-tuning of its production technology and greater marketing effort, it could introduce other products, Product D and Product E, to the market for immediate expansion.

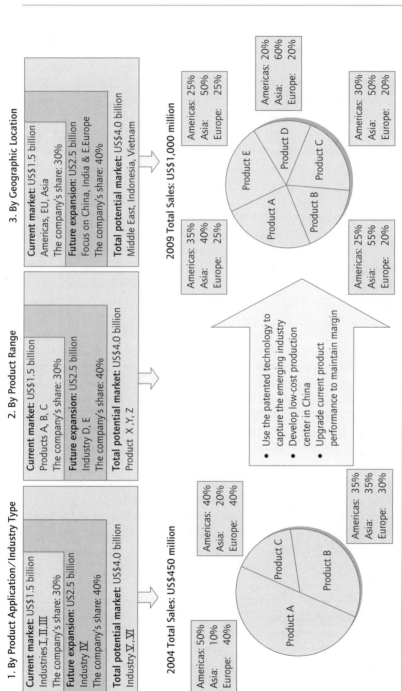

Figure 7.1 Defining the market for buisness planning

If the company sees the value of branching out into another product technology, it may go after another market opportunity by introducing Product X, Product Y and Product Z. The pharmaceuticals industry is one that defines and grows its business based on product range. Since most pharmaceuticals companies have ample financial and marketing resources to promote a product once it is protected by patent and Food and Drug Administration (FDA) approval, they normally align their marketing activities and resources to the launch of a new product.

(3) By geographic location

A firm can break down its market segments by geographic location, such as the Americas, the European Union (EU) and Asia. The broad-based definition of the EU normally includes countries located in Europe, Africa and the Middle East and is often referred to as "EAME". The old way of defining markets adopted by most WMNs showed North America, South America, Europe, and the Rest of the World because this was how most WMNs expanded their business from their traditional home turf. Over time, however, most have accepted Asia as part of their current market and give it the same prominence as the Americas and the EU. But, as Asia is a very large area, there is value in defining the immediate expansion opportunities in China or India or Eastern Europe. If a company is successful in developing its markets in China, India and Eastern Europe, the next wave of opportunities will naturally fall in Indonesia, Vietnam and the Middle East because of their respective population sizes.

As Figure 7.1 illustrates, these three market classifications can be consolidated into a pie chart showing product types and geographic breakdown. It also shows the company's current global sales and market share (2004) broken down by region and product segment.

Figure 7.1 also illustrates how the company might map out its vision of where it wants to be in five years (2009), using the same breakdown of key market information. The company clearly anticipates growth for all product groups in Asia; for Product D and Product E; and in total revenue.

It has also identified the main thrusts for potential business development, these being the use of its patented technology to capture the emerging industry; establishing a low-cost production center in China; and upgrading its current product performance to maintain sales margins.

Of course, this basic planning cannot be done without adequate knowledge of the competitive environment and the attractiveness of the industry; that is, without basic market intelligence.

BASIC MARKET INTELLIGENCE

Once a market has been defined, the next step is to survey the range of competing products, their respective performance and their acceptance by customers in the targeted market segment. For example, for an environmentally friendly electronics market segment, we may have the following competitive product range:

Company	Product name	Performance	Market acceptance
Japan A	M	Top	Best, high price
Japan B	MAT	Good	OK, less costly
Japan C	KK	Good	None, less costly
Taiwan A	B	Good	OK, competitive price
Taiwan B	EM	Good	Licensed by Japan A
Taiwan C	T	Top	Best, competitive price
China A	Y	Marginal	None, competitive price
China B	Z	Top	Under development
Thailand A	TA	Top	Japanese transplants
WMN A	G	Marginal	Limited, high price
WMN B	AR	Good	Limited, high price
WMN C	GG	Top	Limited, high price

This basic survey data will be used in the subsequent analysis of market attractiveness and comparative competitiveness that will eventually define how the company should be positioning itself for emerging business opportunities.

FORMULATING A BUSINESS STRATEGY

All good business planning starts with a clearly defined corporate mission statement that includes business scope, product range, geographic coverage, and the competencies on which it intends to build. Once the mission statement has been agreed upon, the company must scrutinize its current competitiveness in the selected market and assess how it can improve on this. It should also examine external factors such as the industry attractiveness (which we will look at in greater detail later in the chapter) and the strengths and weaknesses of its competitors. It must also anticipate if and how these factors might change during the lifespan of the business plan.

Once this has been done, the company needs to verify whether these observations are supported by market realities. It is essential to cross-examine a business plan using external reference points such as a customer, a supplier or an industry analyst. This is particularly important for Asia, where a lack of local market expertise may lead to failure. The company will need to assess the value chain of the industry and determine the critical customer value (CCV). In assessing CCV, the company will be giving close consideration to such things as product performance, technical support, quality and price, and the relative priority that different target customers accord to each. With a clear understanding of the value it needs to deliver, it can then plan the main business activities required to fulfill its objectives. To help the company come to a strategic view, a business strength matrix (BSM) is needed. A BSM plots industry attractiveness against relative competitiveness, and will be explained in more detail later in this chapter.

The necessary construction of individual BSMs from the present state to the future state is called a strategic directional matrix (SDM). Such projections must be based on the firm's core competency, market trends, customer feedback and competitors' activities. Once a preliminary business plan has been established, a gap analysis is needed to assess any possible variables that may have adverse effects on the final business outcome. At the same time, the resource requirements of individual business units and support teams should be addressed to ensure the plan's feasibility. Once this preliminary strategic programming is complete, the next step is to merge the five-year business plan into the normal budgeting and activity tracking process. The whole process of formulating a business strategy is summarized in Figure 7.2.

ASSESSING CURRENT MARKET SITUATION

An effective business plan can only start from having a thorough understanding of the company's current market position based on a systematic review of all the key market forces. Of these, industry rivalry, product substitution, the bargaining power of suppliers and customers, and entry barriers are the dominant factors, as Michael Porter pointed out in 1985.[27] Figures 7.3 and 7.4 illustrate how Porter's five-force model can be used to assess the value chain for the aircraft and electronics industries, respectively. For a number of years, the aircraft industry has been dominated by two major players — Boeing and

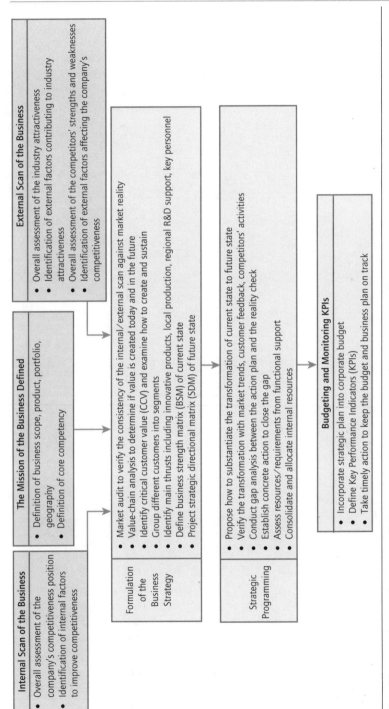

Internal Scan of the Business
- Overall assessment of the company's competitiveness position
- Identification of internal factors to improve competitiveness

The Mission of the Business Defined
- Definition of business scope, product, portfolio, geography
- Definition of core competency

External Scan of the Business
- Overall assessment of the industry attractiveness
- Identification of external factors contributing to industry attractiveness
- Overall assessment of the competitors' strengths and weaknesses
- Identification of external factors affecting the company's competitiveness

Formulation of the Business Strategy
- Market audit to verify the consistency of the internal/external scan against market reality
- Value-chain analysis to determine if value is created today and in the future
- Identify critical customer value (CCV) and examine how to create and sustain
- Group different customers into segments
- Identify main thrusts including innovative products, local production, regional R&D support, key personnel
- Define business strength matrix (BSM) of current state
- Project strategic directional matrix (SDM) of future state

Strategic Programming
- Propose how to substantiate the transformation of current state to future state
- Verify the transformation with market trends, customer feedback, competitors' activities
- Conduct gap analysis between the action plan and the reality check
- Establish concrete action to close the gap
- Assess resources/requirements from functional support
- Consolidate and allocate internal resources

Budgeting and Monitoring KPIs
- Incorporate strategic plan into corporate budget
- Define Key Performance Indicators (KPIs)
- Take timely action to keep the budget and business plan on track

Figure 7.2 Formulating a business strategy

Margin

High for Military aircraft

Medium for Large passenger aircraft (≥ 100 passengers)

Low for Regional jet (<100 passengers).

Margin

Margin

MANAGERIAL INFRASTRUCTURE

1. Very high entry barriers prevent the participation of new players and result in oligopoly
2. Low threat of substitution encourages oligo-polistic practices
3. Intensity of rivalry increases in commercial aircraft segment between Boeing and Airbus
4. Most suppliers do not have much bargaining power. But single-source suppliers do
5. Buyers of aircraft frequently are supported by local government, which tends to add complexity

HUMAN RESOURCES MANAGEMENT

1. With little competition, HR management tends to be less demanding than in other industries
2. Greater technical demands create the need for more specialist expertise
3. Up until recently, when competition intensified, there was low demand for HR management
4. Moderate training requirement to cope with buyers generally low bargaining power
5. More stringent training is needed to deal with buyers with increasing power

TECHNOLOGY DEVELOPMENT

1. Very high barriers to meet FAA (Federal Aviation Association) requirements and aircraft specs
2. Evolutionary improvement in advanced materials and engines is crucial
3. Rivalry focuses on lower fuel consumption, costs and maintenance, and "enemy-proof" protection systems
4. Suppliers with innovative ideas to deliver the desired value can improve their bargaining position
5. Buyers will influence the desired technology and target price through joint development

PROCUREMENT

1. High entry barriers for both suppliers and segment players may create more conflict as competition intensifies
2. Creation of multiple sources becomes the norm
3. Competitive procurement costs are becoming a high priority
4. Bargaining power of supplier will decrease unless remains single source of supply
5. Buyers of large companies will exert extreme pressure to compete with no-frills carriers

INBOUND LOGISTICS	MANUFACTURING	OUTBOUND LOGISTICS	MARKETING AND SALES (M&S)	CUSTOMER SERVICES
1. Few players — limited options.	1. Manufacturing process improves only slowly	1. No major change in sight	1. To build or maintain entry barriers, the giants subcontracting secondary component production	1. The major players maintain customer service models in each key country is, making it difficult for new players
2. No major change is foreseen. But, more imports from overseas	2. More automation needed to counter increasing pressure for improvement	2. Export sales become increasingly important	2. Short-range flights will face more competition from bullet-train system	2. Little short-term impact
3. Intensified rivalry raises the performance standard required	3. Increasing competition creates pressure for improved efficiency	3. Makes on-time delivery more important than ever	3. M&S team must sell value or performance; or face price war	3. Customer service need will enhance technical support level
4. Depending on whether single source or multiple sources of supply	4. Depending on whether single source or multiple sources of supply	4. Little impact	4. Little impact	4. Little impact
5. Makes just-in-time delivery capability more important	5. Pressure to outsource some components	5. Greater flexibility required to meet demand from customers with different background and in different geographic locations	5. M&S must identify the area for value creation for the firm and buyer	5. Increasing demand to cope with after-sales services

Key

1. Related to entry barriers   2. Related to threat of substitution   3. Related to intensity of rivalry   4. Related to bargaining power of suppliers   5. Related to bargaining power of buyers

Figure 7.3 Market assessment of the aircraft industry's value chain

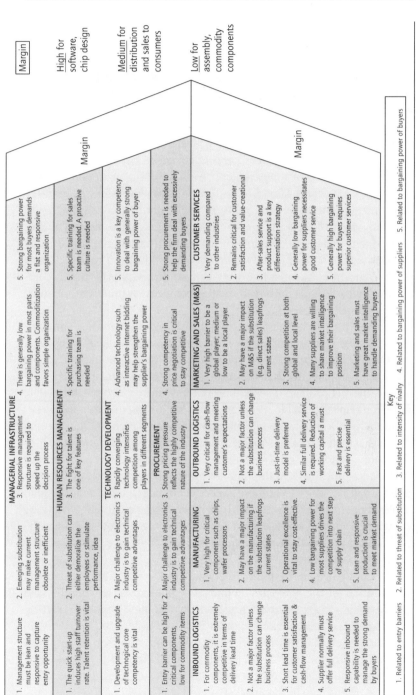

Figure 7.4 Market assessment of the electronics industry's value chain

Airbus, Now, however, facing a shrinking demand in their home markets, these two giants are becoming increasingly dependent on Asian airline companies and the localization of the manufacture and assembly of various components to Asian companies to sustain their business. This will require substantial changes to their current business models and/or production processes in order to meet increasing demands from their customers.

Ever since the electronics industry started its robust growth in the 1980s, it has had an extremely competitive market environment because of the participation of many Asian players. With the exception of a few niche players such as Microsoft and Intel, most players in this industry are constantly under pricing pressure while, simultaneously, having to stay innovative to meet the ever-increasing technical demands. The dramatic downturn in 2001, following the bust of the dot.com era, actually accelerated the pace of transformation of this industry. The value-chain analysis for the electronics industry again confirms that this highly competitive industry will continue its heated competition in nearly all industry segments.

The best way for a company to quantify the current market situation is to show the value chain for the market segment in which it is engaged, as illustrated in Figure 7.5. Starting from the horizontal level of supply point, the company needs to list the unit selling price, total quantity, total sales value, net profit as a percentage of total sales (which will ultimately determine how profitable it can expect to be) for its current market segment, as well as the same information for other horizontal market segments in which it is not a supplier. The importance of the latter is to help the company quantify the purchase cost for its products as a percentage of the total purchase by the target segment. If this percentage is relatively small, say below 5%, there is a better chance that the company can avoid frequent price haggling with its downstream customers. All these suppliers from the same market segment, as well as other horizontal players, merge into the target market segment that the company and its competitors are serving.

Of course, it is also equally important to list the same commercial information for the downstream market segment. Market conditions in the downstream segment are undoubtedly the most important driving force for the target market segment because, unless the downstream segment reaches a satisfactory state of equilibrium for its financial returns, the target market will be subject to all kinds of price reduction pressures and is likely to pass these on to its suppliers. On the other hand, if the downstream market segment is growing profitably and

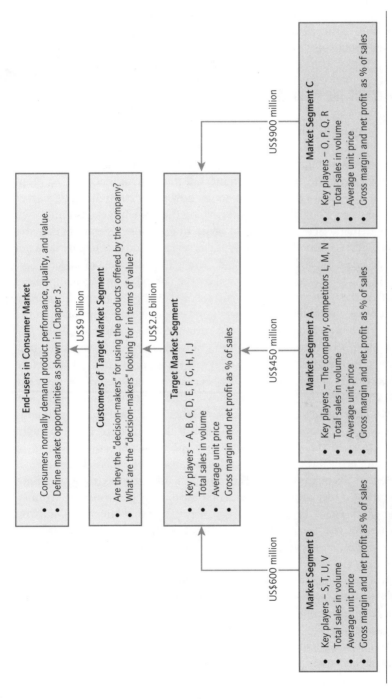

Figure 7.5 Key parameters for value-chain analysis for a typical manufacturing industry

End-users in Consumer Market
- Consumers normally demand product performance, quality, and value.
- Define market opportunities as shown in Chapter 3.

US$9 billion

Customers of Target Market Segment
- Are they the "decision-makers" for using the products offered by the company?
- What are the "decision-makers" looking for in terms of value?

US$2.6 billion

Target Market Segment
- Key players – A, B, C, D, E, F, G, H, I, J
- Total sales in volume
- Average unit price
- Gross margin and net profit as % of sales

US$450 million

US$600 million

US$900 million

Market Segment A
- Key players – The company, competitors L, M, N
- Total sales in volume
- Average unit price
- Gross margin and net profit as % of sales

Market Segment B
- Key players – S, T, U, V
- Total sales in volume
- Average unit price
- Gross margin and net profit as % of sales

Market Segment C
- Key players – O, P, Q, R
- Total sales in volume
- Average unit price
- Gross margin and net profit as % of sales

rapidly, the company will have a good chance to improve its financial position, either through price increases or through creating value-added products.

ANALYZING THE VALUE CHAIN

The purpose of conducting a value-chain analysis is to identify where the value is created at various stages of the production process. This evaluation process enables a company to see how economic value is created both for itself and its target customers. If the analysis is carried out properly, it also allows the company to see how suppliers in different market segments perform while they are serving the same target customers in a similar market environment. In order to determine overall market size and hidden economic value, both sales revenue and profitability data are needed. The information collected usually includes a list of all key players in the market segments served by the company and its competitors and in other segments not currently served by the company; the average unit price, the total volume of sales and revenue; sales margins; and net profit as a percentage of total sales revenue of all of these segments.

Figure 7.5 illustrates how this might work. Here, all three market segments, A, B and C, serve the target market segment, and it is therefore important to keep track of all three because the creation of value for the target segment very much depends on the individual contributions of each. The experiences encountered in other horizontal market segments frequently can serve as as an indicator of the conditions the firm might encounter in the segment. Obviously the most important segment to monitor is the target market segment because this is where the company's potential customers operate. Their financial and business results will have the most direct impact on the company's own performance. It must, therefore, again keep track of the key players in the target market; total sales volume and revenue within the target segment; the average unit price; sales margins; and net profit as a percentage of total sales revenue.

It is also important to keep track of who in the target segment makes the decisions regarding such things as product specification, the selection of suppliers, and the kind of value proposition they are looking for.

Whenever possible, the value-chain analysis should be extended to include end-users in the consumer market and this can be done using published economic statistics to monitor or crosscheck market trends. It is also easier to follow the trends in consumer behavior in a dynamic market environment than merely observing activities within the industry. It's worth remembering that the ultimate testament to the success or failure of a business is market acceptance.

ANALYZING INDUSTRY ATTRACTIVENESS

The attractiveness of an industry is the most important, yet least controllable, factor in determining whether a company can make a reasonable financial return on its investment. Attractiveness is strongly related to the structure of the particular industry and the way in which competition has operated within it historically. The players in an industry segment will engage in competition and, at the same time, seek a state of equilibrium. Nobel Prize laureate Dr. John Nash defined the perfect equilibrium for a market dynamic as being when everyone believes they have achieved the best possible deal. When a market reaches the state of equilibrium, it means that all suppliers and customers are receiving a good return, achieved through having a balanced input and output. However, in moving towards this state, the players may initially go through intense competition and adjust their competitive strategies in order to bring reasonable returns to their shareholders. Certain industrial segments can achieve stability in competition faster than others as a result, say, of having lower exit barriers. This means that they are less likely to have cut-throat competition and, hence, the value chain is better cushioned for any abrupt price swings that may occur.

Traditionally, the size of the industry and its growth rate are two critical factors in determining its attractiveness. In the past, when an industry was big enough and grew quickly enough, it usually represented a highly attractive opportunity because the speed of investing in fixed assets could be slow by comparison with the rapid rise in market demand. However, with increasing Asian participation in global competition, this is no longer valid. The liquid-crystal display (LCD) industry, with its large market and tremendous growth potential, is a perfect example of an industry that would have been highly attractive in the past when there were only a few dominant Western players. But, the rules of competition have changed dramatically now that the Asian players are no longer as restricted by a lack of capital and technology. The net impact of this changing market dynamic is that the size of a market is not necessarily one of the most important factors in determining the attractiveness of an industry in Asia.

Industries such as the automotive industry or the tire industry tend to have high fixed-cost structures because of their capital-intensive nature, the strong bargaining power of labor unions, and high exit barriers. Historically, these two industries are highly cyclical and are always facing ambitious new entrants. If a player in one of these industries focuses solely on maintaining a large market share, it is destined for failure unless it has an absolute advantage in costing and market acceptance. GM, for example, is the largest automotive producer in the world but has a profitability level that is way below the industry average. Likewise, Goodyear, under its previous CEO, was too preoccupied with having the greatest market share in this highly unattractive segment and made major acquisitions (of Dunlop and Sumitomo) while everyone else was trying to stay small and profitable. As a result, even with a sales turnover of roughly US$14.7 billion and total fixed assets of US$14.6 billion in 2003, Goodyear's market capitalization value was only US$1.4 billion by March 2004 — a total disappointment by any investment standard. In the same period, GM had a turnover of US$195 billion and total fixed assets of US$448 billion, but its market capitalization value was only US$27.2 billion. In both cases, the high fixed production costs were the result of expensive pension and medical benefits granted to the unions in better days. Both are now facing unprecedented challenges from both European and Asian players and how they change their fundamental cost base will determine whether these once-mighty industrial giants can survive.

Because the aerospace industry requires heavy capital investment, diversified advanced technology and substantial government support, it has only a limited number of players and, in principle, possesses reasonable attractiveness. However, 9/11 was something that no economist was able to predict and the sudden and dramatic decline in air traffic that followed changed the short-term attractiveness of the industry. Nevertheless, if passenger traffic and revenue per mile per passenger can recover to a normal level and provide reasonable financial returns to aircraft manufacturers, the industry can regain its attractiveness. Meanwhile, until full recovery is achieved, the likes of Boeing and Airbus must rely on more innovative products, such as low-fuel and low-maintenance aircraft, to stimulate demand from the airlines.

The attractiveness of an industry can be measured quantitatively using the 10 criteria shown in Figure 7.6. Each of the criteria is given a numerical

Industry Attractiveness Criteria	Weight Factor (A)%	Rating by Different Stakeholders (1 ~ 10)			Subtotal/10 (B)	Score (C) = (A)*(B)
		SBU Team Members	Customers view	Suppliers' view		
1. Size of an industry segment (↑ better)	10%					
2. Average growth rate in the next five years (↑ better)	15%					
3. Return on investment over the last five years (↑ better)	20%					
4. Rivalry among competitors in this segment (↓ better)	15%					
5. Bargaining power of buyers (↓ better)	8%					
6. Bargaining power of suppliers (↓ better)	8%					
7. Opportunities for technical advancement (↑ better)	6%					
8. Entry barriers (↑ better)	6%					
9. Exit barriers (↓ better)	6%					
10. Product substitution (↓ better)	6%					
TOTAL	100%					

Key
↑ the higher
↓ the lower

Figure 7.6 Criteria for measuring industry attractiveness

rating from 1–10 by a panel of 10 stakeholders comprising five members of the company's strategic business unit, three representatives from among the company's customers, and two from its suppliers. Obtaining a range of views like this is much more likely to produce a balanced perspective of the industry's attractiveness than relying solely on views from within the company because members of the sales team, particularly the old hands, usually have a certain mindset about an industry after working within it for a number of years. The different weight factors assigned to the criteria are determined jointly by the members of the team.

Following this scoring scheme produces a single overall rating of industry attractiveness. When this composite index is below 3.5, it indicates the industry has a low attractiveness. When it is between 3.5 and 7.0, the industry is considered to have medium attractiveness. When it exceeds 7.0, industry attractiveness is high. Whenever possible, the same analysis should be carried out across all product portfolios to get a better understanding of the attractiveness of different segments. Once the methodology has been mastered, an experienced strategy planning team can further modify the individual criteria and weight factors to take account of the changing dynamics within a specific industry.

CRITICAL CUSTOMER VALUE

A typical critical customer value (CCV) analysis consists of the key value propositions expected by customers. For example, the customers in a highly innovative industry segment would regard technical differentiation as the most important value proposition. Other important CCVs, in descending order, may include long-term commitment to an industry (because the partnership cannot be replaced without substantial damage to the customer), ability to meet future demand (because of the uniqueness of the product), technical support (again because of the special processing characteristics required to achieve special performance), and reasonable/stable price (because of the difficulty involved in finding a substitute).

For a commodity industry segment, the CCVs could well be cost position (because pricing is the most critical competitive factor), market share (because scale is important in reducing total running costs and in making it cost-prohibitive for a company to engage in unnecessary price cutting), ability to handle on-time delivery (because when everyone can make the same product, service is the remaining differentiation tool), and relationship (which brings comfort to a transaction).

For an industry segment that consists of some specialty and some commodity products, such as the electronics industry, the combined CCV actually is more critical than either of the above. In an extreme case, the CCV may consist of all of the above performance expectations.

UNDERSTANDING COMPETITIVENESS POSITION

A company's competitiveness position can usually be classified under five primary competencies and four supporting functions, as Michael Porter has pointed out. The five primary competencies are inbound logistics, operations, outbound logistics, sales and marking, and service. The four supporting functions are infrastructure, human resources management, technology development, and purchasing. The primary competencies are those directly involved in the process of creating a product and delivering it to a customer. The supporting functions, on the other hand, are only involved indirectly in that process but are closely interconnected throughout the management process. Before a company's competitiveness can be analyzed, a proper understanding of its CCV is essential because, depending on the nature of the product, customers' preferences can be very different. For certain product groups, the requirement for competitiveness may be heavily focused on price and quality, while for others it may very much depend on the areas of supply and technical support.

Therefore, the proper way for a company to assess its relative competitiveness position is shown in Figure 7.7. The first requirement is for the company to identify the leading competitor in each product group for which it acts as a supplier. Then, using a similar methodology to that employed for assessing attractiveness outlined earlier (see Figure 7.6), a set of criteria with certain weight factors derived from the critical customer value should be used to give a numerical rating for relative competitiveness. This rating will be converted into a relative scale against the leading competitor. Typical comparison criteria are shown in Figure 7.7. The weight factor ratings shown are determined by the business strategy planning team. The firm's competitiveness is calculated by dividing its score by the score of the leading competitor. Usually, when its relative competitiveness factor is more than 1.4, the company can be considered highly competitive. A relative competitiveness factor of between 0.7 and 1.4 shows medium competitiveness. Anything below 0.7 is considered to reveal low relative competitiveness. With a Y-axis range from 0.0 to 2.1, the company's competitiveness can be plotted accordingly.

Relative Competitiveness Criteria	Weight Factor (A)%	Rating by Different Stakeholders (1~10)			Subtotal/10 (B)	Score for the company $(C_1) = [(A_1)*(B_1)]$	Score for the closest competitor $(C_2) = [(A_2)*(B_2)]$	RC C_1/C_2
		SBU Team Members	Customers' view	Suppliers' view				
1. Market share	20%							
2. Product range	5%							
3. Brand name and company image	5%							
4. Competitive price	10%							
5. Competitive cost position	10%							
6. Capability to offer differentiated product	10%							
7. On-time delivery	10%							
8. Product quality	15%							
9. Technical support	10%							
10. Financial strength to support future growth	5%							
TOTAL	100%							

Figure 7.7 Criteria for measuring relative competitiveness (RC) position for a typical manufacturing company

*All criteria are measured against the leader of the selected industry segment or the closest competitor for the leading company.

BUSINESS STRENGTH MATRIX

By combining the two analyses — of industry attractiveness and relative competitiveness — we can form the basic framework for strategic analysis — the business strength matrix (BSM), originally introduced by A. T. Kearney, Inc., Chicago, Illinois.[28]

As shown in Figure 7.8, the BSM plots industry attractiveness against competitiveness position.

The generic strategies mentioned in different quadrants in Figure 7.9 offer very useful business guidelines for overall business direction. For example, if a company's business portfolio is positioned in the top left-hand corner of the matrix, it means it holds a highly competitive position in a highly attractive industry. Naturally, then, it should try to grow and seek the dominant position by maximizing its investment. On the other

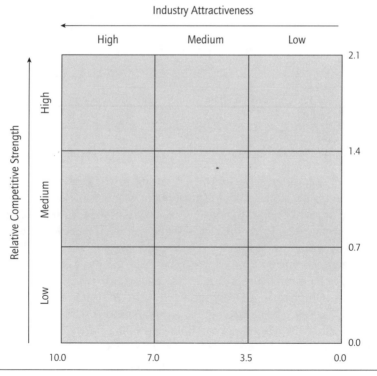

Figure 7.8 Business strength matrix based on industry attractiveness and relative competitiveness position

Industry Attractiveness

	High	Medium	Low
High	Grow Seek dominance Maximize investment	Identify growth segment Invest strongly Maintain position elsewhere	Maintain overall position Seek cash flow Invest at maintenance level
Medium	Evaluate potential for leadership via segmentation Identify weakness Build strength	Identify growth segment Specialize Invest selectively	Prune lines Minimize investment Position to divest
Low	Specialize Seek niches Consider acquisition	Specialize Seek niches Consider exit	Time exit and divest

Relative Competitive Strength

Figure 7.9 Strategic options based on industry attractiveness and competitiveness position

hand, if a business unit finds itself sitting in the center of the nine quadrants, this suggests that it must find a way to grow or face decline into unattractive areas. If a business is located at the very bottom right-hand corner, it is clearly time for it to find an exit strategy and get out of that segment.

In general, when the industry attractiveness is high, it is always highly desirable for a small player either to specialize or to expand aggressively if it has enough strength to dominate the selected segment. On the other hand, if a player has a strong relative competitiveness position, it must choose its strategic options carefully, depending on the attractiveness of the industry. For example, where an industry has low attractiveness, maintaining its overall position should be the preferred option. Where the market has medium or high attractiveness, the company should seek possible ways to expand.

DEFINING STRATEGIC DIRECTION MATRIX

Once the current and future positions have been analyzed and entered into the Business Strength Matrix, this then becomes a Strategic Direction Matrix (SDM) because it shows the road map from the current position to the future. As shown in Figure 7.10, business turnover can be represented by the size of each circle, which again highlights the growth potential for different product groups. For example, Product Group 1 (PG1) is targeted to go through an expansion phase because of its favorable competitive position in an industry with high attractiveness. However, during the expansion phase, it is anticipated that the attractiveness of the industry may be reduced as a result of increased competition. Product Group 2 (PG2) is projected to grow in selected areas because the company does not have dominant competitive advantages over its main competitor but the product group still commands attractive returns. Therefore, the best strategy for the company is not to engage in price competition with its leading competitor for the purpose of gaining short-term sales increase. Instead, it probably should try to seek long-term benefits by differentiating its

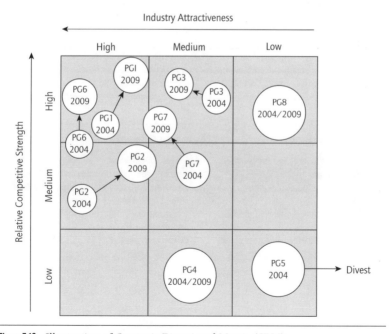

Figure 7.10   Illustration of Strategic Directional Matrix (SDM)

Current Status	Expected or Desired
Product Range	**Product Range**
1. What are the key products and our market share?	1. What are our future products? What will be phased out?
2. What is the critical customer value (CCV)?	2. What will be the future CCV? How is it different from now?
3. What are the value-creation components in our products?	3. Will the same value-creation apply to the future products? How should we change?
4. How do we maximize the value-creation?	4. Will there be a threat of substitution? How to assess risk?
5. Can we define business opportunities based on technological breakthrough and product upgrade?	5. Can we define the market size for specific innovative products year by year?
6. Can we define business opportunities based on different GDP, PPP and HDI level for individuals and countries?	6. Can we define specific products as a result of the changes of GDP, PPP and HDI in the projected period?
Market Scope	**Market Scope**
1. Who are the major customers and what are their respective market shares?	1. Besides current customers, who are the new customers? Who will be the winners?
2. Why are they buying from us?	2. What is the future CCV? Will it change from now?
3. How do we distribute our products to them?	3. How do we improve our product distribution channels?
4. Who are the customers we have not served?	4. Can we expand our customer base by a different method of distribution without hurting existing customers?
5. Can we define market opportunities based on organic growth, shifting of manufacturing base, product upgrade, etc.?	5. Can we define specific market opportunities in sales revenue year by year in the projected period?
Geographic Coverage	**Geographic Coverage**
1. What are the sales territories under our coverage?	1. Besides current geographic coverage, where are the major emerging countries for our business?
2. Where do we have adequate coverage?	2. Where are the secondary emerging countries?
3. Where should we improve our sales coverage?	3. How can we reinforce our sales coverage by allocating new resources or shifting current resources?
4. Are we better off to use a distributor to serve second-tier sales territory?	4. When do we go direct? What is the trade-off?

178

Current Status	Expected or Desired
Core Competency	**Core Competency**
1. Can our current sales organization properly serve the market and customers? 2. Do we have adequate supply chain to support the business? 3. Do we have adequate technical capability to support the business? 4. Do we have the right people and skills to serve the market and customers?	1. What kind of management organization is most suitable for future market requirement? How should we re-engineer our management infrastructure to meet the demand? 2. Where should we set up new production center? Where should we rationalize? How will manufacturing technology change? 3. How do we re-distribute our technical resources to meet future market requirements? 4. How do we develop suitable succession plan, talent pool, career development plan, etc.?

Figure 7.11 Format for market survey on a specific industry segment

current product offerings to suit a selected segment of the industry. While Product Group 3 (PG3) is positioned to improve its profitability level by strengthening its product offerings, total sales turnover will be kept at a similar level because this segment lacks big growth potential. A major change in its current market position — for example, from announcing a big expansion project — may send the wrong message to the market leader, which in turn may retaliate through a pre-emptive price reduction. Thus, any anticipated benefits to be gained from major expansion are offset by the risk of losing competitiveness in a less attractive market. Product Group 4 (PG4) is in a no-win position because the firm does not have enough competitive strength in a market with medium attractiveness. Hence PG4 can be used as a so-called market harasser, acting as an irritant to the market leader, which may dissuade the market leader from moving into another industry segment in which the company enjoys good financial returns. Product Group 5 (PG5) is self-evident. If a company does not have sufficient competitiveness to stay in a market segment that has low attractiveness, it will be always a poor performer compared to the industry leader and will only ever receive a low financial return on its investment. This product group will undoubtedly suffer the most when there is an excessive oversupply in the industry. The only sensible strategic option open to it is to get out at the right time, preferably during a boom time in the industry cycle.

Since PG6 is located in a highly attractive industry and the company has medium to high competitive strength, this business should target a further strengthening of its competitiveness position through, for example, acquiring a related industry segment in order to reinforce its core competency and to expand total business volume. For PG7, which is located in the middle of the matrix, a rational approach would be for the company to identify a segment that offers opportunities to build on its core competencies and move into a more attractive industry segment within the next five years. PG8 is more or less a good player in a bad environment. As long as the company does not have the clout to re-shape the attractiveness of the entire industry segment, the best strategy is to maintain the status quo because this avoids potential over-investment that can immediately destroy the value of the industry.

MARKET AUDIT

Once a company has calculated its overall market position, it is important to test the accuracy of that position against the reality of the marketplace. A comprehensive market audit should be conducted, incorporating key customers (by country and by region), product applications, and sales data verified against published market data. Where the introduction of a key technology is vital for the success of a business plan, the audit must also include the views of the end-users of the target customers. For example, where the introduction of an environmentally friendly electronic product, which is potentially more expensive than the products currently available, is used as the main growth engine for future business expansion, it is important to verify with the end-users, including, say, mobile-phone and notebook producers, that they are ready for this change. The market audit must confirm that the projected volume matches or is greater than the volume defined in the company's business plan. It is equally important to crosscheck with the authority responsible for approving the new product to ensure that there will be sufficient time available after approval for the necessary preparation for the launch to take place.

To ensure that the fundamental market data are properly collected, both sales and marketing teams should be involved in conducting the audit. While the former focuses on target accounts and competitors' activities, the latter normally concentrate on technical trends and collecting market data.

Figure 7.11 shows a typical market audit form. The company can start by listing its current product range, market scope, geographic coverage and core competencies. After it has identified its current position in these four areas, it can then define or project where it should be within five years.

Potential customer	Location	Market share in local market	Technical demand capability & corp. image in local market	Critical customer value (in the order of priority)
A	Taiwan	#2	#1	Technology, price, quality, long-term partnership
B	Taiwan	#1	#2	Price, delivery, customer service
C	Korea	#1	#2	Price, technical support, delivery
D	Korea	#3	#1	Technology, quality, price
E	Japan	#1	#1	Technology, quality, price, delivery
F	Japan	#3	#2	Technology, quality, price, long-term partnership
G	Singapore	#1	#1	Technical support, price
H	Thailand	#1	#2	Technical support, partnership
I	China	#1	#3	Technology, price, relationship
J	China	#3	#5	Price, partnership

	Technology-leader Group A, D, E, F	Market-share Driven Group B, C, I	Follower G, H, J
Value Proposition	(1) Define next-generation Product X with substantial performance enhancement. (2) Hold quarterly information exchange meeting to facilitate new product development. (3) Commit global technical resources to assist customer for trouble-shooting & product approval.	(1) Define low-cost Product Y targetting the largest customer base. (2) Offer exclusivity to the market-share leader in the local market for a limited period. (3) Offer technical support to shorten the product launch time.	(1) Modify Product X and Product Y to suit customers' needs. (2) Provide technical support, including process development, to help launch the product. (3) Maintain strong after-sales service.
Anticipated Results	Company image, technical supremacy, sales margin	Market exposure and dominance, top-line growth	Higher sales margin, incremental sales

Figure 7.12 Customer grouping based on market survey and analysis

CUSTOMER SEGMENTATION

From a marketing viewpoint, there are obvious benefits to grouping customers according to the key value propositions revealed by the earlier evaluation of CCV. Since every organization always has limited resources for dealing with multiple tasks, any effective marketing plan must identify business priorities based on appropriate customer segmentation. A typical customer segmentation for a specialty product group could be divided into technical leaders, market-share leaders and followers. For a commodity product group, customers could be categorized as market-share leaders, market followers, new entrants and survivors.

Once the customer segmentation process has been completed, a common value proposition for each segment should be clearly stated. For example, as shown in Figure 7.12, for a technology-leader group, the common value proposition would probably include new-product development capabilities, processing and equipment expertise, and customer support. For a customer group driven by market share, there is a need to design and produce a low-cost product in order to capture the largest customer base. The company may have to offer limited exclusivity in certain markets in order to secure the total market share of the selected account. For the follower group, the value proposition would normally involve modifying a product designed for the technical-leader or market-share groups. This might also entail giving special attention to technical support and after-sales service as part of a package for market followers.

Once these customer segmentations have been organized properly, functional support teams must examine if the necessary support requirements can be met.

CUSTOMERS' PURCHASING TERMS AND CONDITIONS

At this point in the process, the data collected by the sales team comes into play. For example, a specialty product group may find that a customer demands quarterly technical meetings. Another may ask for a written commitment to meet future demand for the next 10 years. A commodity customer may ask for a price reduction in exchange for an increased volume commitment over the contract period. Another may demand a guaranteed turnaround time or an extended payment period. All of these purchasing contacts and their minimum requirements must be recorded for review before a total commitment is made because the implications of these commitments involve much more than sales revenue alone.

			2004		2009	
			Sales	Margin	Sales	Margin
Target Customer Segment – Technology-leader Group	Main targets for this business within 5 years	(A) Use the patented technology to capture an emerging industry	US$5m	55%	US$240m	40%
		(B) Upgrade current product performance to improve margin	US$160m	30%	US$190m	35%
		(C) Set up new R&D center in China to support new business development	US$25m	35%	US$120m	30%
		Total	US$190m	31%	US$550m	36%

Detailed action plan to fulfill the main targets (action/completion date/responsible person)

(A)
1. Broaden patent coverage to related area/2005.03/AC
2. Obtain approval in Japan, Korea, Taiwan/2005.09/PH
3. Launch product in Japan, Korea, Taiwan/2006.05/PH
4. Product promotion in global trade shows/2006.10/PH

(B)
1. Benchmark against major competitors/2005.09/AC & CC
2. Formulate the improved version in lab/2005.03/AC
3. Field test to confirm the results/2006.09/CC
4. Launch the improved product/2006.10/PH
5. Replace the existing product/2007.05/PH

(C)
1. Conduct market survey in China/2005.06/PH
2. Define the product range & target price/2005.11/PH
3. Confirm suitable cost position internally/2005.12/PH
4. Launch the products in target customers & city/2006.03/PH
5. Modify successful products and pass on to next tier of customers & location/200609/PH

Pricing strategy to support the business plan & detailed action plan (action/completion date/responsible person)

(A)
1. Ensure our current selling price accepted by the industry/2005.03/PH
2. Promote the product based on volume discount/2006.06/PH
3. Pass on the benefit of economies of scale to stimulate further growth/2007.06/PH

(B)
1. Establish price/performance relationship/2005.09/PH
2. Identify the premium for extra performance 2005.09/PH
3. Confirm the premium by key customers/2006.09/PH
4. Mark up for second-tier accounts/2006.11/PH

(C)
1. Determine our target price based on relative competitiveness position
2. Confirm that our internal cost delivers target margin/2005.11/PH
3. Define price list and discount level/2006.01/PH

Internal and external resource requirements* & detailed action plan (action/completion date/responsible person)

(A)
1. Global coordination for patent registration/2005.02/JM
2. Patent department completes registration/2005.02/JM
3. Public relations department prepares the announcement with marketing manager/2006.04/PR & MC

(B)
1. Global coordination on product offer/2005.09/JM.
2. Push for public awareness by public relations department and marketing manager/2006.08/PR & MC

(C)
1. Obtain capex approval for R&D center/2005.06/JM & PH
2. Transfer R&D manager from Japan/2005.10/PH
3. Assemble R&D team/2005.10/PH
4. Incorporate new business development into KPI/2005.10/PH

Figure 7.13 Business implementation plan for a target customer segment

Note: *For consumer-oriented industry, need to include brand-name promotion campaign and eye-catching advertising.

TARGETING SELECTED SEGMENTS

The next step is to decide on key business strategies. If the eight product groups shown in Figure 7.10 are presented for decision, naturally the company's priority will be to grow the high-value PG1 and to prune the low-value PG5. However, depending on its current financial position, it may not be feasible for the company to grow PG1 without making an acquisition or investing in a new factory. It may then have to choose the less capital-intensive strategy to build the business while waiting for an upturn in the industry to improve its strategic position. But while it is awaiting better times, it may be weakening its competitive position as healthy players in the industry make timely investments for expansion. Therefore, solid financial strength and sound planning are vitally important in formulating an effective growth strategy. Likewise, for PG2 to grow into a specialized area, the company may need to have certain technological know-how ready to cope with the market demand. At this point, it will need to assess if its R&D capabilities are adequate to cope with future technical upgrades and business expansion. If the targeted expansion is in a highly specialized area, internal resources may not be sufficient to make the transformation, which may mean that the company will have to seek an alliance with another firm or acquire another company that has the required technical competency.

In the case of PG3, the company is probably best advised to keep a low profile while seeking opportunities to reinforce its competitive position in the segment. This may require that discretionary funds for a specific new technology in its infancy are made available or it may involve the purchase of an appropriate patent or technology that has yet to reach the commercial stage. Any investment in this category will probably be relatively small because the company has no intention of engaging in heated competition that will only reduce the attractiveness of the industry. However, the seeds for future growth must be planted in advance if the anticipated harvest defined in the business plan is to be realized.

The strategic options for PG4 are relatively limited because the company has nothing to lose and probably nothing significant to gain, either. Because of its unfavorable position in the SDM, it will not want to invest substantial capital in trying to improve its strategic position. It can, however, use this position to assist other SBUs that may be engaged in competition with the same industry leader. This obviously would only occur when the total benefit to the company outweighs the sacrifice of the position in PG4.

While these guidelines and principles are applicable across all industry segments, when such studies are being carried out in the Asia Pacific region the evaluation criteria may have to be extended to include the leading players in the region, many of whom appear in the various case studies in this book. A different set of CCVs and a different market analysis are required for the Asia Pacific region before the BSM and SDM can be prepared. The CCVs for this region may be linked to Asian cultural characteristics (such as the importance of brand name and relationships, for example) and business practices (such as speed and pricing). The selection criteria should be determined primarily by the Asia Pacific team and then balanced by views from other regions. Likewise, the attractiveness of an industry will be heavily linked to affordability or parity purchasing power.

A systematic way to present a business implementation plan for a specific target segment is shown in Figure 7.13. Here, continuing the example shown in Figure 7.1, the company undertakes detailed preparations for achieving its three main targets: to use its patented technology to capture an emerging industry; to upgrade its current product performance to improve margins; and to set up a new R&D center in China to support new business development. These preparations include drawing up a detailed action plan, a pricing strategy and an itemized list of resources, internal and external, that will be required. If these plans are meticulously implemented, the anticipated financial results will be as shown exactly in the top right-hand corner. The key financial targets, agreed on and committed to by the entire team, must be kept at the forefront at all times so that no one loses sight of the goal.

MARKETING OBJECTIVES AND GAP ANALYSIS

Once a company has made up its mind on where it is and where it would like to be in five years' time, its various business units across different market segments must decide on a clear set of marketing objectives. Essentially, the company may categorize its own portfolio into three groups: grow, keep and divest. For market segments that are classified under the growth mode, the company needs to consider whether there are any synergies to be had from combining these segments into the same SBU to unleash the growth potential. If there is not sufficient justification for this, the firm must initiate some sort of new-business review procedure to keep those target growth areas under close control. For those market segments belonging to the "keep" mode, the company must ensure that the cost position is kept in line with the competitive market position in order to maintain stable financial returns on investment. These segments may still have robust growth opportunities in the Asia Pacific region and hence are entitled to special resource allocations to take advantage of such opportunities. However, it is unlikely that these market segments will receive major new capital investments on a global scale. The high sales growth in Asia may or may not be sufficient to close the gap between the company's actual and targeted global sales revenue. A gap analysis will reveal whether sales growth in Asia will be sufficient to bring benefit to the company overall. Where strong competitive advantages no longer exist, the company may wish to keep its sales in Asia stagnant during growth periods to protect the margin for the Asia Pacific and other regions.

For market segments classified for divestment, the marketing objectives can be extremely simple: either milk the business while it is still possible or exit at the right time. If a business is at the milking stage, it may be a perfect fit for another company that takes a different view of value creation.

Let's say, for example, that when our WMN established a business 30 years ago, it was highly profitable because there were only a few players in this high-growth segment. However, as the market continued to grow, it attracted new players, the technology barriers gradually disappeared and a glut in supply led to a dramatic reduction in the attractiveness of the market. While the WMN may no longer find that segment attractive, to a regional player who enjoys cost benefits from vertical integration, it may still present an attractive proposition.

If a business is marked for divestment, the timing of its exit from the market is crucial. A company normally will not want to divest while that business still has value, but, equally, it will not want to wait until the business hits rock bottom and have no suitable buyers. It must therefore have a clear SDM for each product group at all times and build its annual budget under the framework of the five-year business plan.

FUNCTIONAL SUPPORT REQUIREMENTS

Research and development

If a WMN builds its differentiation strategy around technical competency, the role of R&D will be crucial. When the five-year business plan is ready for final review, the R&D team must gauge whether the company has the technical competencies to sustain the plan. It must ask whether the company has enough in-house technical capabilities to support any proposed expansion. If not, will it acquire the necessary expertise by hiring specific technical experts or should it consider buying a technology firm? Alternatively, should it consider obtaining a license from the technical leader in the same industry segment?

Once this review has been completed, the R&D team will add its recommendations to the implementation plan. Where there are substantial gaps between the R&D recommendations and, say, the view taken by the SBU team assigned to spearhead the development of a revolutionary new product, there may be a need for a second iteration of the review process, which may in turn lead to a pragmatic adjustment to the timetable or achievable sales outlined under the business plan.

Manufacturing

The successful delivery of any business plan is dependent on the ready supply of products and thus on the manufacturing function, which is also required to ensure that the cost structure can support the targeted selling price. The cost structure may, in turn, be dependent on a commitment by the sales team to deliver a higher sales volume. When the planning process has been properly concluded, the manufacturing function should come back with its fixed-cost position, the necessary fixed-asset investments, and its timetable to meet the proposed business plan.

Customer services

Given the current trend towards downsizing and outsourcing, the company must decide how many customer service centers and how much customer service support can be justified within the scope of the business plan. To deal with the increasing pressures to reduce costs, a WMN may be forced to reduce the number of customer service centers it currently operates across the region. The company must start identifying precisely which of these best fits into the needs of the current ordering and delivery process and build these into the five-year business master plan.

Finance and control

There are at least four finance and control (F&C) issues to be considered for business planning purposes. The first is the need to develop proper financial reporting in line with the newly proposed market segments and SBUs. The second is the need to calculate the profit and loss (P&L) statement defined for different stages of the five-year plan and any other key financial performance indicators, such as cash flow, capital expenditure, EBITDA, and A/R, related to the proposed business plan. The third critical task is to ensure compliance with any local statutory regulations that may affect its accumulated tax benefits which, in turn, will affect the cash flow. The final consideration concerns ensuring compliance with the Sarbanes-Oxley Act of 2002 (enacted after the disastrous downfall of Enron and WorldCom) covering statutory filing to the US Securities and Exchange Commission (SEC) for routine and special reporting on various strategic moves, including acquisitions and divestments. The SEC rules are very strict and cannot be taken lightly. Any failure to comply, albeit inadvertent, can have severe consequences and can undercut any perceived benefits the company may see in investing in the Asia Pacific region.

From a historical viewpoint, it is during the active acquisition and divestment period that the role of the F&C team is most crucial in ensuring total compliance with statutory obligations.

Figure 7.14 illustrates the functional support required for achieving the defined business objectives.

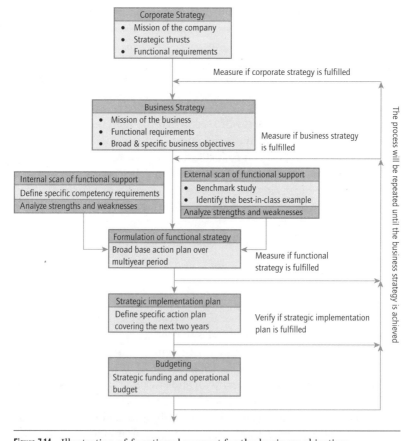

Figure 7.14 Illustration of functional support for the business objectives

Case Study:

TSMC vs. TEXAS INSTRUMENTS

Taiwan Semiconductor Manufacturing Company, Ltd. (TSMC) has been one of the brightest stars in the hi-tech industry segment ever since it was incorporated in 1987 under a partnership between the Taiwan government, Philips Electronics and other private investors. Under the strong leadership of its chairman, Dr. Morris Chang, and his team, TSMC has become a role model for how to transform vision into business success in a rapidly evolving industry. The TSMC business strategy has from the very beginning been geared towards being a dedicated integrated circuit (IC) foundry for fabless design houses (FDHs) such as Altera, Broadcom, Nvidia, Qualcomm, VIA and integrated device manufacturers (IDM) such as Analog Devices, Motorola and Philips. In order to prevent any potential conflicts of interest with its customers, TSMC strictly excludes itself, as clearly defined in its articles of association, from the design, manufacture or marketing of IC products under its own brand name. With his uncompromising integrity, Morris Chang had no problem gaining the target customers' acceptance, which is often considered to be one of the strongest barriers to entry into the contract manufacturing industry. Dr. Chang has further defined TSMC as a service company that creates value for its customers through its unique competency in technology and manufacturing at a competitive price. In order to work more closely with its customers, TSMC has established e-foundry programs on the Internet that cover joint design, joint engineering and joint logistics.

TSMC's business strategy has proven to be both visionary and prudent as it continues to hold a global market share of more than 50% in the dedicated IC foundry industry regardless of the heavy investments by several other Asian competitors, including UMC of Taiwan, Hynix of Korea, SMIC of China, Chartered of Singapore, and Toshiba of Japan. At the time of writing, TSMC enjoys the best net profit as a percentage of sales in this industry, at a mind-boggling 23% and, at 18%, had the best return on equity in 2003, based on a total turnover of US$6.0 billion. Most customers prefer to work with TSMC rather than make a multi-billion-dollar investment in their own state-of-the-art foundry because TSMC provides a full range of services at a competitive cost. The outlook for TSMC and its main competitors continues to look bright because the IC industry is projected to grow at between 8% and 10% per annum, with the contract IC industry growing faster than the IC industry overall. The current challenges to TSMC come from its smaller rival in Taiwan, UMC, and some newcomers in China that are using a very similar business model. Some seasoned executives from Taiwan's foundry industry have invested in China via their overseas investment arms to form companies such as SMIC, while TSMC has only recently received approval from the Taiwanese government to move forward with its plans to expand into China. Given the challenges being posed by Chinese start-ups,

	TI			TSMC		
Financial Results	2003	2002	2001	2003	2002	2001
1. Revenue (US$ million)	9,834	8,383	8,201	5,968	4,674	2,518
2. Net income (US$ million)	1,198	−344	−201	1,389	622	289
3. Total assets (US$ million)	15,510	14,679	15,779	11,977	11,247	7,330
4. Return on equity, or ROE (%)	10.1	−3.2	−1.7	14	7.0	5.0
5. Return on assets, or ROA (%)	7.7	−2.3	−1.3	11.6	5.5	4.0
6. EBITDA (US$ million)	2,493	1,977	1,246	3,541	2,782	1,362
7. EBITDA/Sales (%)	25.4	23.6	15.2	59.3	59.5	54.1
8. Net income/sales (%)	12.2	−4.1	−2.5	23.3	13.3	11.5
9. Sales growth (%)	17.3	2.2	−30.9	27.7	85.6	−49.5

Figure 7.15   Texas Instruments and TSMC: A comparison of financial performance
Source: Mergent Online database[29]

TSMC will most likely have to diversify its product range on each technology platform in order to counter the assault across a range of industry applications. SMIC will exert increasing pricing pressure in China as it moves into mass production mode. However, with the strong partnership between TSMC and its key customers in FDH and IDM, other competitors may find it difficult to replicate TSMC's successes. Building an IC foundry is not as difficult as establishing a relationship built on trust – an area in which Dr. Chang and his team have clearly set the industry benchmark. In a design industry that is critically dependent on the protection of intellectual property rights, all would do well to learn from the business conduct and ethical standards set by TSMC.

Since high profitability such as that achieved by TSMC always invites competition, a number of global giants, including IBM, have decided to plunge into contract wafer production. IBM's entry through its Services Division in late 2003 was the first time that a major WMN had entered an electronics industry segment as a latecomer following the commercial success of an Asia-based company. IBM will have to catch up with its Asian competitors in technology, productivity, quality, speed and services. Surprisingly enough, apart from in a few niche applications, IBM no longer has obvious competitive advantages over the leading Asian players in this industry and is unlikely to pose a major threat to TSMC. The most genuine threat to TSMC will mostly come from its fellow Asian players, including the formidable Samsung Electronics, which entered the semiconductor contract production service in 2004.

Texas Instruments (TI) is another US hi-tech icon lauded for inventing the microchip in 1958. This revolutionary invention was patented in 1973 and won its inventor, Jack Kilby, a Nobel Prize in 2000. The invention of microchip technology is acknowledged to mark the beginning of the massive transformation that has taken place in information technology, ranging from the hand-held calculator, the personal computer, radio and television, to electronic control and wireless telecommunication. Texas Instruments was also the first company to introduce the 4-megabit Digital Random-Access Memory (DRAM) chip in 1985, a field from which it exited in 1998.

The company generates 85% of its revenue from semiconductor products such as programmable digital signal processors (DSP) and high-performance analog chips (HPAC). These two products are vital for broadband communication and mobile Internet because both products convert real-world signals into digital form on a real-time and power-efficient basis. Thanks to its technical supremacy in these two highly specialized areas, Texas Instruments has enjoyed a strong competitive advantage in these industry segments. However, just like other WMNs, it also outsources its wafer production because by doing so it eliminates a major financial risk by avoiding excessive capital investment and hence is capable of maintaining a stable profit margin. Therefore, Texas Instruments is a customer of dedicated wafer producers, including TSMC. TI performs better than most other Western hi-tech companies largely because it maintains a dominant technical leadership position in its key market segments, including in Asia. Its sales revenue in 2003 was US$9.8 billion, with a net profit of US$1.2 billion, or 12% of sales.

Between TSMC and Texas Instruments there is no direct competition. On the contrary, these two companies enjoy considerable synergies arising from TSMC's contract foundry work, without which TI may have been forced into making a costly investment in a foundry of its own. Each company has excelled because it chose to focus on its strengths and each is the beneficiary of ingenious product development and intelligent strategic planning.

CHAPTER 8

STRATEGIC OPTIONS FOR INVESTMENT

Many people refer to joint ventures as marriages that may end up dysfunctional. Some see them as extra-marital affairs that are sometimes inevitable. But the provocative question should be why people cannot plan better from the beginning.

JOINT VENTURE

In the period after World War II, most Asian countries lagged behind their Western counterparts in industrial technology, market knowledge and manufacturing expertise. Thus the formation of any kind of co-operative agreement with a mighty multinational was often considered to be a short-cut to prosperity or, at least, a learning experience. Asian governments often stepped into the negotiation process to assist local companies by imposing certain protective conditions. As most Asian countries were fight-ing for foreign investment, it was generally not difficult for the stakeholders to reach an agreement. WMNs came to Asia to re-export manufactured goods (Texas Instruments and RCA in the electronics industry, for example), to secure the supply of natural resources (BP and Shell in the oil industry), or to explore local market opportunities (Ciba-Geigy and ICI in the chemi-cals and pharmaceuticals industries). Most Asian countries, including Japan, were not in a position to bargain for favorable terms in any joint venture.

But, as we have seen, this has changed dramatically over the past 30 years as Asian countries have become increasingly competitive in many industry segments. Now, most developed Asian economies are competing with WMNs for any high-potential projects in emerging markets such as China and India, where there is a history of strong government intervention whenever there is substantial foreign investment. For Western multinationals, the search for a good joint venture (JV) deal is becoming increasingly complex.

Justifications for a joint venture

Legal requirement

Fear of losing control over their markets often led governments to limit the formation of wholly owned or majority-owned foreign enterprises in certain industry segments. This was particularly true in countries with a large domestic market which, they believed, should be served by local companies on a preferential basis. In Japan, China and India, the governments actually forbade wholly owned foreign enterprises.

In 1992, the Chinese government finally announced its acceptance of wholly owned foreign enterprises but, in doing so, defined a group of pillar industries, including telecommunications, automotive, banking, energy and transportation, that were excluded from this open-door policy. These remaining restrictions have since been loosened as a result of China's accession to the WTO and under political pressure from the US government. It should not be taken for granted, however, that access to a local market segment is automatic. In most cases, the Chinese government reserves the right of final approval, depending on how the proposed investment will benefit the local people and government.

Hoping to attract foreign investment, some Asian countries offer incentive programs for investors. The Singapore government, for example, has reduced corporate income tax and adopted a policy of "positive discrimination" for those companies that already have a local joint venture to participate in other infrastructure projects.

Risk-sharing requirement

Investing in Asia can be a risky business for a WMN that has had little or no experience in the region. For such companies, a joint venture may be a way of reducing the financial risk. In considering whether to undertake a project on its own, the company must weigh the potential payoffs against the risks involved. Whenever these risks outweigh its financial capabilities, the company probably needs to opt for a JV. A risk-sharing

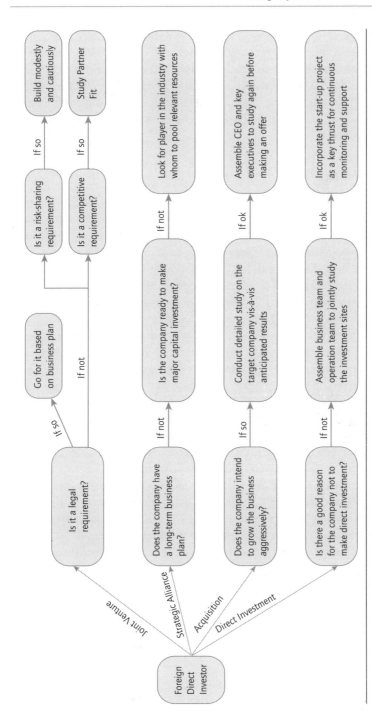

Figure 8.1 Selecting and implementing a strategic investment option

model can be effective only if the partners share the same commitment and sense of urgency in tackling imminent risks. Some WMNs that engage in heated competition outside Asia may become JV partners in China simply because the risk-sharing requirement outweighs other considerations. It is worth bearing in mind that sharing risk can sometimes lead to the loss of ownership of a project as a result of ambiguities arising from the JV partnership.

Competitive requirement

In the pursuit of market opportunities in Asia, a WMN will have to consider whether it has the required local competencies to take on the business challenge by itself. A lack of local market knowledge, of local manufacturing capabilities, of an experienced management team or of a complete distribution network may lead the company to have second thoughts about operating a wholly owned business venture.

A WMN may decide to go for a joint venture because it needs timely access to a market or because it wants to follow one of its existing downstream customers which has established a presence in a particular marketplace. This scenario is particularly applicable in the automotive and electronics industries where often a complete network of suppliers have to decide if they want to continue serving a particular customer when it moves into a new market. If they decline to participate in the new geographic location, it may backfire and affect their supply relationship with a powerful global account. As time is of the essence in such circumstances, the company may be forced to enter an emerging market with little preparation and it is here that a JV with a local partner may turn out to be a feasible option.

However, as Asian players become more competitive in their manufacturing and financial capabilities, the WMN may have to contribute more in the way of selected technology to demonstrate its value to a proposed partnership. There is always the risk that this valuable technology will eventually proliferate and become standard, setting the stage for more intense competition. Thus, when a WMN uses technology as a major part of its JV package, it must be able to update its own technology through innovation to stay ahead of the competition.

Selecting a JV partner

There are five important criteria for selecting a suitable JV partner. These cover how well the proposed partner fits in with or complements the company's strategy, competencies, culture, infrastructure and long-term objectives. Strategic fit refers to whether the partners can pool their individual resources into a JV that will perform better than they can individually. For example, in China Nike found a strong local partner in Pao-Chan, a Taiwan-based company that had an established distribution network across China's vast marketplace but lacked a strong brand identity. Because the cost of setting up a country-wide distribution network in China can be extremely high, it made strategic sense for Nike to form a JV with Pao-Chan to gain immediate access to a big market. The local partner then benefited from Nike's strategic decision not to build its own production base.

Competency fit in a specific marketplace refers to how both parties of the JV can utilize their respective competitive strengths within the local environment to achieve their agreed business targets. To continue our earlier example, Pao-Chan contributes its low-cost production base and comprehensive distribution network, while Nike contributes innovative marketing and a strong brand name. The combination of the two companies, each with unique competitive strengths, makes a strong competency fit, as demonstrated by the strong market share of the JV in China.

Culture fit usually means more than it appears at first sight. It is not simply a matter of speaking the same language but also includes such considerations as the structural differences between the Western company and the local player and what impact these may have on the way they conduct their joint business. It also refers to how compatible they are in their responses to, say, an unforeseen conflict. How the partners respond to a crisis may determine if they have a culture fit. While most WMNs do not know the history of their JV partners well enough to determine how they might handle a potential business conflict, there are ways to verify the culture fit. However, the WMN must first understand how it will respond before it can determine how its JV partner will behave in a similar situation. A close historical review is required before a decision can be made on their compatibility in this area.

While compatibility between the respective infrastructures might not be critically important, it does have a strong influence on how a JV will perform. Often, one of the JV partners insists on using its management organization as the platform for running the joint business. In doing so, it may well create a one-sided decision-making process that can undermine the whole purpose of the JV. Where loyalty is directed to one partner rather than to the JV, there is clear potential for conflicts of interest across every business activity. Therefore, to avoid the possibility of being mired in endless and often trivial debates, wherever possible the WMN may find it better to choose qualified employees from outside and pick only a few key managers from the majority equity partner.

The last and yet probably the most critical of the compatibility criteria relates to long-term objectives. Many JVs fail only because the partners have totally different perceptions about how long the partnership should last. At the outset, in a well-defined market, this question may not arise. But as the market dynamic changes over a period of time, the partners may have their own ambitions in pursuing the market opportunities defined by their respective parent companies. Often, under the terms of the JV agreement a local partner is not allowed to engage in export business. But as it becomes competent in mastering the technology and meeting market demands, there is very little chance of stopping it from tapping into the global market. This is why most of the JVs formed in the 1970s between Japanese companies and WMNs later ended up in an equity takeover by the Japanese partner. Since most JV agreements leave the duration of the contract open, such conflicts between the partners' respective long-term objectives are almost inevitable at some stage. In short, the company must decide whether the partner could eventually become a competitor and, if so, whether the company could still benefit from the JV in terms of its overall market position on a global basis.

Once the selection criteria are set, the next step is to match the respective expectations of the potential JV partners.

The WMN's expectations

Normally the foreign partner invests in a JV with a view to gaining access to a new business opportunity, or to learning about the market potential, or to getting a speculative deal. In the first case, the WMN has a venturing motive and this is best managed by giving the JV full responsibility for the business. In the second case, the WMN is in a cultivating mode, which implies that short-term business results are not necessarily its main priority. Nevertheless, the financial burden on the JV and the parent company must be kept to a minimum so as not to hamper the WMN's long-term prospects. In the last case, the WMN is in an opportunistic mode and is looking for a quick completion of its objectives for the JV.

The expectations of local players

Local players usually choose to participate in joint ventures because they expect their Western partners to have certain technological and financial competencies which they currently lack and which will enable them to participate in other market segments. Local players, too, may be looking for a new business opportunity or a speculative deal and many see the possibility of opening up export opportunities.

Matching capabilities

As long as the joint venture can meet the expectations of both partners, there is a good chance that a harmonious business relationship will result. However, this depends on two factors: market realities and the matching of capabilities. The best way to ensure the matching of capabilities is to undertake the business planning process over the span of the JV contract period as mentioned in Chapter 7 to see if the company will be better off through the setting up of the JV. The business plan for the JV must also define the respective contributions required of the partners. The capabilities of each of the partners and how they can contribute to the venture must be assessed, preferably by the management team assigned to run the JV because such an assessment is usually feasible only after a period of direct hands-on interaction.

Anticipating potential conflict

Many foreign investors make market assessments based largely on intelligence provided by their local JV partner. While the local partner may not set out to mislead, inconsistent or conflicting information can lead to tensions between the partners at different times. The remedy for this type of conflict is to properly document any communication and make the person responsible for providing the key market information accountable for the ongoing operation and sales activities.

Another major area of conflict relates to the transfer price of finished goods and raw materials that WMNs often use to conduct transactions with their affiliates. Without understanding the exact tax benefits brought to a JV and its shareholders by such transfer-pricing arrangements, the local partner often feels the victim of foul play. This area of course is best defined in the JV agreement so that there are no gray areas that can give rise to complaint from either party.

Another potential source of major conflict is the treatment of expatriate costs, which often exceed the expectations of the local partner. The difficulty for expatriates who, frequently, are among the key decision-makers for the JV company, is in justifying a level of costs of which local parties will have had little or no experience. If this perception of excessive management charges is left unresolved, it is a sore that will continue to fester into the future. It is for this reason that experienced multinationals usually deal with the majority of expatriate costs through their regional headquarters rather than run the risk of upsetting the local partner over something that he cannot understand anyway.

Negotiation techniques and processes

Before initiating any formal negotiations with a potential local JV partner, the company must undertake a detailed internal review of the business plan proposed for the JV by the SBU team. Normally a commercial representative from the SBU will eventually be either responsible for running the JV or serving as the company representative at the JV board. The review should include as many experts on the target market as possible, its primary purpose being to define the financial targets to be achieved by the company. These in turn will be used to determine sales turnover and cost structure.

Once there is consensus on what should be achieved, a draft JV agreement, based on similar legal and commercial arrangements for that specific market, can be drawn up. This will be subject to further internal discussion and verification before formal negotiations begin.

Effective negotiation is an art for which there are no simple rules. The best deals are usually achieved when the negotiation team is not in a hurry to make a decision, when it has a clear understanding of local practice and when it knows how to play the game according to local rules. Asian players sometimes save the most important topics to the final moment of negotiation. Both sides may intentionally create conflicts on certain relatively inconsequential issues to give themselves room for compromise on other, more essential, issues. Keeping detailed notes and issuing minutes of these discussions is always a good idea. After several rounds of negotiation, both sides may walk away from a meeting without agreement on many of their financial and business targets. At this point, the negotiation team must review progress with the senior management team and decide whether it makes sense to continue with the negotiations. The temptation to rush on with the JV simply for the sake of meeting certain quotas assigned by the corporate board should be resisted Sometimes with a little patience, a cooling-off period can be very effective for both parties to resolve their internal problems and to stay focused on what will prove to be beneficial for both.

Good faith and reality check

During the process of forming a JV, partners must remain cautious about market conditions and their anticipated financial returns must be built on a realistic cost base. Whenever possible, the partners should benchmark their JV to a similar operation to assess its cost position. Likewise, they should conduct a joint market audit and allow full disclosure of any information that the potential partner needs to help determine compatibility. Transparency in the early stages is the key to eliminating the possibility of conflict later on. Provided each side respects the confidentiality of the other, a reciprocal audit of this kind should serve to draw the partners closer together in a mutual understanding of their strengths and weaknesses. Most of all, it can help create a culture of openness that is conducive to constructive suggestions for their common interests.

Unless some kind of realistic crosscheck can be carried out in advance, there is a good chance that a poorly structured JV will fall apart once it goes into operation.

Staying on track

Once the JV is up and running, its management team must be committed to resolving any differences of opinion that arise. For example, during an industry downturn, the WMN may want to rationalize its global production sites in line with reduced market demand. But under the specific terms of the JV agreement, it may not be always feasible for the WMN to change the scope of its investment or even its routine operation. Under these circumstances, the best way to achieve cost savings is to obtain a commitment from the JV partner to adopt a market-oriented approach on its own operation. To do this, the WMN needs to develop a target-specific plan to reduce the cost elements that are under the control of the respective JV partners. In order to develop an effective rescue solution, partners must understand that subsidizing a JV production site by artificial means will only weaken the JV's competitive position in the long run. Any true solution must be checked against the reality of the market.

In addition to possible financial ups and downs, JV companies are often beset with problems arising from personality clashes between key members of the management team. As soon as such cases arise, senior management from the parent companies should become involved. The majority shareholder, of course, usually reserves the right to appoint the key posts. After proper fact finding and diplomatic maneuvers, the partners must quickly find a way to reconcile differences and move forward. Ultimately, the general manager or chairman of the JV must remain fully accountable for running the business. Any attempt to control the JV from a distance will jeopardize the efficiency of the JV organization and eventually defeat the object of setting it up.

Benefits beyond a joint venture

While many WMNs and local players doubt the value of forming joint ventures, the fact remains that there is an increasing number of successful JVs, even in traditionally difficult markets such as China or India.

Some parent companies even point to the major contributions made by their JVs in a difficult business environment. For example, while Xerox USA was experiencing unprecedented difficulties in its home market, the Fuji-Xerox joint venture, after many years of success in Japan, was able to contribute innovative products and brand-new manufacturing technology to the parent company. Xerox USA traditionally relied on large copy machines as its main source of revenue and profit, and it wasn't ready when the home-office boom drove the office-equipment market towards more compact and cost-effective models. But the strong technical and marketing expertise that Fuji-Xerox had gained in the Japanese market in the miniaturization of copy machines came to the rescue of the parent company.

In certain instances, a successful JV can also provide the parent company with a testing ground for a market in which the WMN does not have sufficient experience. For example, Western finance corporations wishing to enter China can only do so under a JV arrangement. But this arrangement gives the WMN time to learn how consumers respond to the issuance of credit cards or how an asset-disposal company settles a non-performing loan, and to prepare itself for when it will have complete access to the market.

STRATEGIC ALLIANCE

Many Western companies have proved that strategic alliances can be established without them having to make a substantial equity investment. It may be the case, for example, that several industry players decide to pool their money for an emerging technology that may require a long time to pay back. Ford and Nissan decided to form such an alliance to produce a hybrid fuel cell for the next-generation engine by devoting common resources to the project. Since neither company regards the other as an imminent threat, either in geographic position or market share, they are willing to set aside minor differences in a cost-effective approach to preparing for a key technology. Acer sponsors the Ferrari Formula One Racing Team and jointly the two companies have developed a strong market presence, particularly in Europe. Thanks to a series of good marketing and sales campaigns, Acer gained the top spot in the notebook computer industry in Europe for the second quarter of 2004. The alliance developed in Europe is now helping it regain its market position in the US. Likewise, Lexus has been working with Bridgestone in Formula One to develop the best synergy between racing car performance and tire compound formulation. The money they have pooled for the strategic alliance is also used to promote the image of both companies.

Strategic alliances are also common in the electronics industry. When Intel came out with its Wi-Fi chip for the digital mobile industry, it looked for strategic partners who could contribute the most to its commercial success. In Asia, Intel normally works with the leaders in various sectors to develop a concerted marketing program for a successful product launch. Likewise, in the software industry, Linux looks for strategic alliances with numerous Asian governments which, out of concern for security of information, are seeking an alternative to the dominant Microsoft software.

The advantages that come from forming a strategic alliance include the fact that no long-term commitments are required and there is minimal capital investment. If things work well, the alliance partners may choose to continue to work together. If they don't, they can go back to working on their own. The use of strategic alliances is becoming increasingly common in Asia.

DIRECT INVESTMENT

Direct investment in a selected marketplace has been the method most favored by Western companies, especially after most key Asian economies joined the WTO, which requires a level playing field in various industry segments.

Whenever possible, the Western company should look for ways to make its own investments, particularly in fields where it possesses limited but critical technological know-how in manufacturing. By making its own decisions concerning future business directions, a company can be sure that it will not be helping to create a future competitor. It is also much easier to build a team for a wholly owned enterprise than for a JV because the company's goal automatically becomes that of the subsidiary.

According to the sixth American Business in China White Paper,[30] the trend towards more wholly owned manufacturing operations was reflected in the responses of the 236 companies that participated in a questionnaire survey. It is encouraging to note that 73% of these companies considered themselves profitable or highly profitable; 23% considered themselves to be at break-even point or experienced a small loss; while just 4% suffered large losses. While the 2004 survey's overall financial results were more or less in line with those of 2003, there were twice as many companies that were looking to increase their investment in China as there were the previous year. According to the survey, the top challenges for doing business in China are, in descending order, unclear government regulations, bureaucracy, lack of transparency, inconsistent interpretation of regulations, poor protection of intellectual property rights, difficulty in enforcing contract terms, and corruption.

ACQUISITION

Acquisition can provide a fast track for a company looking to boost its size, as long as it has adequate internal funding. Where there is insufficient funding, the company is forced to resort to heavy external borrowing, which in turn can reduce its chances of success in the future. For companies that use leverage funding as a way of expanding their business, the odds on experiencing a dramatic decline are much higher than for a company with more conservative financial planning. Leverage borrowing usually neglects fundamental principles, assuming that the industry can defy the business cycle and maintain continuous growth. There are many more failures than successes when it comes to managing acquisitions, particularly for those companies that engage in leveraged borrowing based on high-yield bonds to fund growth. However, surprisingly enough, financial buyers tend to do better than corporate buyers in delivering the anticipated financial results in the first few years, a trend that probably reflects the fact that a failure to match corporate cultures or competencies is often the biggest stumbling block to a successful acquisition. Companies that truly believe in the correctness of their own culture and management systems are often confronted by different realities as they try to impose this predetermined framework onto the company they have just acquired.

China is one of the world's fastest-growing markets for mergers and acquisitions (M&A). According to a recent report by Dealogic Thomson Financial,[31] the leaders of M&A in China over the past 20 years are China International Capital (US$72 billion), Goldman Sachs (US$62 billion), Rothschild (US$49 billion), Morgan Stanley (US$25 billion), JP Morgan (US$19 billion), Citigroup (US$10 billion), and HSBC Holdings and Credit Suisse First Boston (US$6 billion each). Since M&A are still in their infancy in China, there is great potential for future development.

A related Dealogic report[32] showed that the value of M&A for the Asia Pacific region excluding Japan had exceeded 2,940 deals, or US$161 billion, in the year to date, a rise of 65% over the same period the previous year. The two leading countries in the region, Australia and China, made up more than 55% of the total transaction value. While M&A activities targeting emerging markets will undoubtedly increase, it is important to note that outbound M&A activity is also likely to become increasingly important as Chinese companies look to secure energy and raw material and to gain greater access to overseas markets. The high-profile acquisition of IBM's personal computer and notebook business by Lenovo of China in 2004 is another clear indication that Chinese companies are becoming active players in global M&A deals.

Corporate and financial buyers

The *Harvard Business Review* made an interesting comparative study of corporate and financial buyers in the period 1994 to 1998, when corporate M&A activity was at its peak.[33] The study's authors, Patricia Anslinger and Thomas Copeland, gave financial buyers high marks for generating substantial financial returns without the benefits of corporate synergy. What made these leveraged buyouts (LBOs) successful, they said, was financial discipline in reducing the debt load quickly and the adoption of effective turnaround operating principles. Statistics showed that LBOs had an 80% success rate in covering their cost of capital and also had a return to shareholders roughly twice that of corporate buyers. LBOs normally reduced their debt ratio substantially within the first two years while implementing a series of major restructuring programs.

These figures may well have benefited from the favorable investment climate that prevailed during that period, when Western stock markets were on a good run. Nevertheless, the high success rate of LBOs vis-à-vis corporate buyers could well be due to the simplicity in communicating business objectives and the effectiveness in delivering the expected results by a well-delegated management team.

Identify a target

As with identifying a potential joint-venture partner, the company must conduct a systematic study of the players within target segments that may create additional value. If the company has operational excellence, it would normally target those with a strong sales history but poor cost position. If the company has a strong brand name, it would naturally search for candidates with strong manufacturing competencies but a poor sales history.

Unfortunately, not all the necessary financial information is readily available in the format required by WMNs. Many Asian firms still lump various unrelated business units together in consolidated financial results, giving the seller plenty of room to argue about its asset value. Furthermore, many Asian companies still consider fixed assets to be the main consideration in any assessment of business value, while WMNs generally assess a business on its capacity to generate cash flow or net profit. Financial investors, too, make their assessments on a net cash-flow basis. Given such differences in approach, skillful negotiation is required if the WMN and a targeted Asian company are to reach an agreement on a reasonable market value.

Making it work

The general guidelines on how to make an acquisition work include insisting on innovative operating strategies; picking the best leader for the integration period; rewarding the executive team generously; emphasizing cash flow; pushing the pace of change; and fostering a dynamic relationship between owner, managers and board.

Judging whether an acquisition works or not can often depend on the timeframe over which an evaluation is made. In general, LBOs score better than corporate buyers in the first few years. But, without a clear, long-term business strategy, LBOs are often unable to grow the business after years of ruthless cost-cutting and, lacking the necessary resources to handle new business opportunities, slide into an irreversible decline.

To sustain the long-term success of a buyout firm, a business growth strategy must be in place to guide the company from the initial cost-cutting phase into a dynamic growth phase. The growth plan should be based on the recommendations of the existing business unit and supported by the entire executive team. Whenever necessary, the buyout firm should be preparing adequate funding, preferably from its own profits, to spur additional business expansion through further investment or additional acquisitions. Taking such a systematic approach will ensure that the buyout firm is able to address both current and future performance issues. The methodology outlined in Chapter 7 can be used as a guide for preparing a business plan for the acquisition target.

TOLLING

As outlined in Chapter 6, tolling is another type of strategic alliance that can provide some momentum for business growth or simply for improving the cost position of a product. Tolling arrangements between WMNs and Asian players are common and provide an opportunity for both sides to learn how to deal with a partner from a different cultural background and with a different management philosophy. Tolling can therefore be used as a stepping-stone into a target market or as a testing ground for two partners to see if they can work together in a future joint venture.

Since there is usually minimal, if any, capital investment required to start a tolling project, the WMN's financial burden can be easily covered. The biggest challenge for the company is to have its product manufactured in accordance with its precise specifications without disclosing all vital know-how and proprietary technology. In an uncertain business environment, many tolling arrangements can break down when, for example, the WMN decides to divest itself of certain business units. When this happens, the local tolling partner usually receives financial compensation as well as free technology transfer. Thus, the tolling partner may gain free access to a market that is fully paid for by the WMN. This suggests that even a seemingly low-cost, low-risk investment for the WMN must be analyzed systematically and captured within the company's strategic business plan. While many companies gain short-term financial benefits by avoiding making certain fixed-asset investments, it is prudent to review the trade-off between tolling and internal production. In general, tolling may make sense when a firm is no longer able to maintain its manufacturing supremacy over its competitors or does not consider a certain product portfolio crucial to its long-term competitiveness.

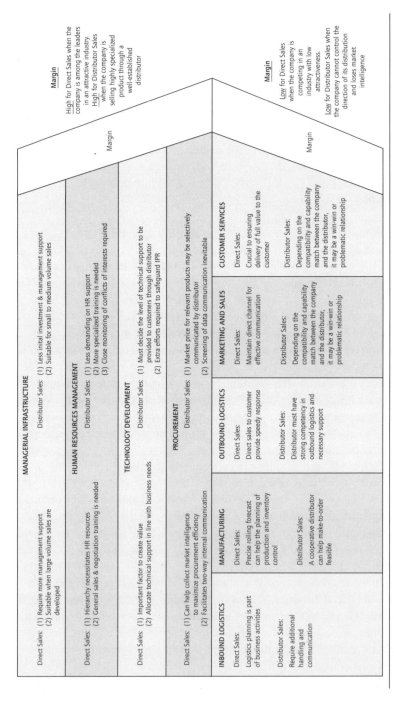

Margin

High for Direct Sales when the company is among the leaders in an attractive industry. High for Distributor Sales when the company is selling highly specialized product through a well-established distributor

Margin

Low for Direct Sales when the company is competing in an industry with low attractiveness. Low for Distributor Sales when the company cannot control the direction of its distribution and loses market intelligence

MANAGERIAL INFRASTRUCTURE

Direct Sales: (1) Require more management support
(2) Suitable when large volume sales are developed

Distributor Sales: (1) Less initial investment & management support
(2) Suitable for small to medium volume sales

HUMAN RESOURCES MANAGEMENT

Direct Sales: (1) Hierarchy necessitates HR resources
(2) General sales & negotiation training is needed

Distributor Sales: (1) Less demanding on HR support
(2) More specialized training is needed
(3) Close monitoring of conflicts of interests required

TECHNOLOGY DEVELOPMENT

Direct Sales: (1) Important factor to create value
(2) Allocate technical support in line with business needs

Distributor Sales: (1) Must decide the level of technical support to be provided to customers through distributor
(2) Extra efforts required to safeguard IPR

PROCUREMENT

Direct Sales: (1) Can help collect market intelligence to maximize procurement efficiency
(2) Facilitates two-way internal communication

Distributor Sales: (1) Market price for relevant products may be selectively communicated by distributor
(2) Screening of data communication inevitable

INBOUND LOGISTICS	MANUFACTURING	OUTBOUND LOGISTICS	MARKETING AND SALES	CUSTOMER SERVICES
Direct Sales: Logistics planning is part of business activities	Direct Sales: Precise rolling forecast can help the planning of production and inventory control	Direct Sales: Direct sales to customer provide speedy response	Direct Sales: Maintain direct channel for effective communication	Direct Sales: Crucial to ensuring delivery of full value to the customer
Distributor Sales: Require additional handling and communication	Distributor Sales: A cooperative distributor can help make-to-order feasible	Distributor Sales: Distributor must have strong competency in outbound logistics and necessary support	Distributor Sales: Depending on the compatibility and capability match between the company and the distributor, it may be a win-win or problematic relationship	Distributor Sales: Depending on the compatibility and capability match between the company and the distributor, it may be a win-win or problematic relationship

Figure 8.2 Value-chain analysis on Direct Sales versus Distributor Sales

DISTRIBUTOR AND COMMISSIONING AGENT

Another cost-effective way for a Western company to build a sales network in the Asia Pacific region is to find an experienced distributor or commissioning agent to serve a certain market segment on its behalf.

As usual, the company should begin the selection process by collecting market intelligence that will give it a complete picture of the market, its players and the channel of supply to customers. Unless the company has a special competency in distribution, the best way to proceed is to follow existing industry practice — appointing a suitable distributor for indirect sales while making direct sales to big customers, for example.

The next step in the strategic planning process is to conduct a value-chain analysis, as illustrated in Figure 8.2, to generate a general profitability profile. Once a short-list of potential candidates who have an established distribution framework within the chosen industry segment has been drawn up, the selection process follows that for choosing a JV partner.

Over the years, good Asian distributors have proven to be very helpful in developing the business of many WMNs. Under tremendous competition in the market, they are usually willing to settle for a lower commission rate than their counterparts in Western countries. Some Asian distributors can even offer customers extended financial terms which, in turn, provides additional cash-flow support for the WMN. The selection of a suitable distributor can also pave the way for future joint ventures involving major capital investments in a selected market segment. However, a knowledgeable distributor can also become a fierce competitor if the business relationship cannot be sustained. Some WMNs suffer because certain distributors have set their own agendas and priorities.

Case Study:

NESTLÉ vs. WAHAHA

With annual sales of US$70 billion and net profits of US$5.0 billion in 2003, Nestlé is the largest food company in the world. Famous for its branded milk, chocolate, coffee, tea and ice cream products, Nestlé also owns numerous other famous brands, including Carnation, Friskies, Purina, Libby's and Perrier, across a range of product areas.

Nestlé is the undisputed leader in the food production industry because of its unrivaled ability to manage such a diversified portfolio of food products on a

	Nestlé			Wahaha		
Financial Results	2003	2002	2001	2003	2002	2001
1. Revenue (US$ million)	70,146	64,133	49,972	1,230	NA	NA
2. Net income (US$ million)	4,954	5,441	3,942	196	NA	NA
3. Total assets (US$ million)	71,407	62,832	55,334	NA	NA	NA
4. Return on equity, or ROE (%)	16.9	21.7	19.9	NA	NA	NA
5. Return on assets, or ROA (%)	6.9	8.7	7.1	NA	NA	NA
6. EBITDA (US$ million)	12,151	10,867	7,786	NA	NA	NA
7. EBITDA/Sales (%)	17.3	16.9	15.6	NA	NA	NA
8. Net income/sales (%)	7.1	8.5	7.9	15.9	NA	NA
9. Sales growth (%)	9.4	28.3	−1.0	NA	NA	NA

Figure 8.3 Nestlé and Wahaha: A comparison of financial performance

Sources: Mergent Online database[34] and authors' research

global basis. Built around a Swiss work ethic, the company has established a reputation as a producer of high-quality goods.

Nestlé entered North America more than 100 years ago and has since established a strong foothold in the largest consumer market in the world. Likewise, it has also been among the pioneers entering any major emerging market, be it China, India or Brazil. Today, its sales revenue is almost equal to the GDP of some of the countries in which it operates. The company's CEO, Peter Brabeck, is fully aware of the importance of emerging markets and has provided strong support for business development. For example, he insists on adopting a medium- to long-term approach in emerging markets, recognizing that it takes time to build core competencies and allowing cyclical change. Because of the strong credibility of its leadership team, Nestlé has been successful in persuading investors to support its future investment strategy. Today Nestlé draws around US$13 billion, or 20% of its global sales revenue, from the Asia Pacific region and is one of the most successful multinationals in the region.

Wahaha is the largest beverage company in China and provides a clear illustration of the business potential that exists in the world's most populous country. With annual sales of US$1.2 billion and a net profit of US$196 million in 2003, Wahaha (the name means "Baby Giggles and Giggles" in Chinese) is hardly a match for a global food giant such as Nestlé. But, given the huge market potential in China, there is no doubt that this burgeoning company could one day become one of the largest food companies in the world. Wahaha's success is undoubtedly related to its cost-effective marketing and distribution capabilities. It is also worth mentioning that it learned about automating its production lines from its Western JV partner, Danon of France. This, in turn, has given it an improved cost position, which is essential in the beverage business if the company is to gain market share and stay profitable when the competition intensifies.

Wahaha has also taken on global giants such as Coca-Cola and Pepsi in China with a cola drink of its own – Future Cola. Few would have bet on Wahaha surviving the contest, given the superior brand name and advantageous cost position of the respective giants. However, because Wahaha in general has a good quality image with Chinese consumers, it has been able to attract its target customers at a price that is reasonably rewarding to Wahaha but not necessarily so for the two global giants. In the first round of this contest the company has captured a greater market share for soft drinks in China than either of its major rivals, despite their vast sales and marketing experience. Where Chung Chin Ho, CEO of Wahaha, has excelled is in his ability to mobilize his gigantic sales team, distributors and retailers in every village and city, while the two multinationals have concentrated mainly on metropolitan areas. The company's broad market exposure in fruit and milk drinks has enabled immediate penetration into every corner of the consumer market. In a matter of two years, the competition in carbonated drinks within China has clearly swung in favor of Wahaha.

These results have given Wahaha the confidence to pursue new business opportunities in other segments, including the instant-noodle industry, which is currently worth around US$3 billion per annum in China, Hong Kong and Taiwan. The industry is dominated by suppliers such as Chef Kang and Uni-President of Taiwan, who have been in the China market for more than 10 years. It is unclear how Wahaha is going to break into their market but its strategy seems to be to make full use of its home-court advantage, particularly in the countryside where distribution can be much more difficult for the overseas players. It will undoubtedly seek to leverage its strong brand name to lure its current customer base into this new business.

Not all of its business ventures have been so successful, however. Its latest endeavor to enter the children's clothing business was a flop. Quite obviously, Wahaha still lacks a comprehensive strategic plan that will allow it to enter a totally different industry segment. Essentially, the food and clothing industries have few direct links in core competency requirements and market segmentation. No global conglomerate has achieved success in these unrelated industry segments simultaneously. Another weakness for Wahaha is its complicated ownership of, or connection to, some 50 local legal entities that it was asked to acquire or to support as part of its social responsibilities. For the most part, these acquisitions were made at the request of local party leaders. As a result, it is difficult to obtain a complete picture of the company's financial performance.

There is little direct competition between Nestlé and Wahaha as Nestlé continues reinforcing its position in the high-end segment and gradually moving its customer base into the sector of the newly affluent. Given its excellent record of global portfolio management, Nestlé should have little need to engage in price wars with local players.

Wahaha's customer base extends from middle-range to low-end. As long as it can continue to build on its good corporate image and reputation for quality, it should outpace the average market growth rate and gradually rise in the global rankings in the food production industry.

CHAPTER 9

DEFINING AN EFFECTIVE ORGANIZATION

As great a basketball player as Michael Jordan was, he could not possibly have won a single NBA Championship — never mind six — without the support of the versatile Scottie Pippen, the hard-working Bill Cartright, the three-pointer shooter, Steve Kerr, and even the controversial Dennis Rodman.

THE MAIN OBJECTIVES

In the past there was an unfortunate tendency amongst Western multinationals to lump the Asia Pacific region in the "rest of the world" category, along with anywhere else that was not North America, South America or Europe. As the Asia Pacific region is becoming an important part of global business, this approach to financial reporting results in a lack of transparency and, thus, of accountability for the region. This often leads to a situation where a company's headquarters fails to understand the economic contribution made by this region and thus finds it difficult to justify allocating the resources necessary for future growth. Likewise, because of its poor profile, the region is seldom seen as providing a rewarding executive career path, resulting in a critical shortage of executives with Asian experience in company headquarters. Such a deficiency in Asia management expertise is frequently the bottleneck that prevents WMNs from expanding their business. Worse still, the micromanaging of Asia from a long distance by people without substantial regional expertise is unlikely to be effective.

Western companies must give the Asia Pacific region due recognition within their global business strategy by according it equal weight as a global SBU and allocating adequate resources to support its growth.

The main objectives for the Asia Pacific organization, therefore, are to develop a growth strategy for the region, to engage in appropriate business activities within the region, to channel critical market intelligence back into the global organization, and to reinforce the competency of the global organization. The regional organization must be given responsibility for enacting a local business plan that reinforces the corporate identity and is in line with the company's worldwide strategy. The regional team must be authorized to work as a division with its own P&L responsibilities.

ORGANIZATIONAL FACILITATORS FOR THE REGION

In 1993, based on a study of three major European companies that had achieved success in the region, Lasserre and Butler proposed five major facilitators for the implementation of business development in Asia Pacific markets.[35] These are as follows:

Legitimization   Top management must constantly show commitment and support for the successful development of the Asia Pacific region because of the tremendous market potential for the company. A board director or a member of the executive committee should be given responsibility for the region so that the board is kept fully aware of progress. The company chairman and/or CEO should make regular visits to the region to support the regional team and to keep up to date with customer requirements.

Regional drive   The Asia Pacific region should be treated as a special business unit, with the same authority as any other global SBU and subject to the same assessments against the targets set out in the five-year business plan and annual budget. The regional team should also be responsible for updating the global management team on market intelligence, especially in providing an analysis of the strategic activities and direction of key competitors in the region. It goes without saying that developing and implementing a growth strategy geared specifically to the unique competitive environment is another of the regional team's major responsibilities. It has to ensure that strategic expectations and specific sales plan are met in full. In order to make the management team truly accountable for its performance, the operation must be given greater autonomy than is the case in other regions in which the WMN traditionally has strong competencies and considerable experience.

Networking   This can include quarterly or monthly regional meetings, the setting up of regional task forces to address specific market opportunities, and regular training activities to cover all the local organization's responsibilities, including country-specific legal issues. Regular networking meetings between business and function teams across different geographic areas can lead to constructive discussion about the benchmarking standards for the region.

Transformation/Adaptation   A WMN must ensure that the core competencies of its global organization can be replicated or tailored to suit the Asia market. With a highly competitive environment in Asia, the ability to transform the core competency from the home market to the local environment can play a crucial role in determining success or failure.

Commitment through people   The senior executives at corporate headquarters must be willing to learn from local human resources and management experts and adopt the best practices of other successful companies in the region — Western or Asian. Once the company has decided on how it intends to structure its regional management team, it should recruit prudently, both from within its own ranks and externally, and have appropriate incentive and training schemes in place to ensure that it can then keep hold of the right people. Managing human resources correctly is vital in Asia. While building an effective team can take a considerable amount of time, it only takes a short time to destroy it. If a manager is capable of winning the trust of co-workers, there is a tremendous potential to be unleashed from every single member of the team. On the other hand, if the manager has to rely on threats and force to push co-workers to cooperate, there is obviously something wrong with the leadership. Where there is trust, there is mutual respect and support. Once a manager has the wholehearted support of the team members, there is almost a guarantee of gaining extra mileage from everyone in the team. Wherever there is a high turnover of managers and staff, there are likely to be underlying problems. If the company has constantly to resort to the services of headhunters, this generally signals a deficiency in developing a sustainable succession plan within the organization. This subject will be explored in greater detail in Chapter 10.

A LEAN AND EFFECTIVE ORGANIZATION

The shape chosen by a Western company for the structure of its local organization in the Asia Pacific region is best determined by the competency requirements to fulfill its business objectives and the specific needs of the market or markets in which it is to operate. For many major WMNs, this consists of a country head or legal representative, a financial controller, and an HR and administration manager in each major country or territory. In addition, there is usually a sales manager or sales team in each major sales territory. A typical country management organization might comprise a country head, and heads of finance, HR, the various SBUs, sales & operational planning, and, where there is a production facility, of production. However, a full-time country-head is becoming increasingly difficult to justify and it is quite common nowadays for a senior SBU head to take on that role.

The same concept can be applied to the regional management structure, depending on the complexity of the business activities and the number of legal entities the company has within the region. Where there are four or more entities, this is usually enough to justify having a full regional management team. Otherwise, where the company has had sufficient operational experience in the region, it is possible that all SBUs or divisions can share the same corporate platform with minimum duplication. Normally, the best scenario is for the regional head to have regional or global business responsibilities so that it is much easier for the management team to stay business-focused. Whenever possible, the role of regional head should be combined with that of the regional business head. The dual-head leadership system, which is also called the "matrix management structure", has proven to be difficult to follow in many Asian countries, particularly in China. Unfortunately for global companies, the matrix management system is an eternal dilemma about balancing empowerment and control. The only thing that a company can do is to minimize the complexity of its organization. Two possible models for regional organization are shown in Figure 9.1.

Whenever a multinational sets up a corporate platform in a country it must ask itself how much it can afford to spend to support the business activities. Most, however, rarely ask this question because corporate general and administrative (G&A) expense tends to be perceived as a sacred cow that cannot be challenged. But, in reality, as the business environment gets tough, G&A as a percentage of sales revenue or a percentage of sales margin should constantly be measured against that

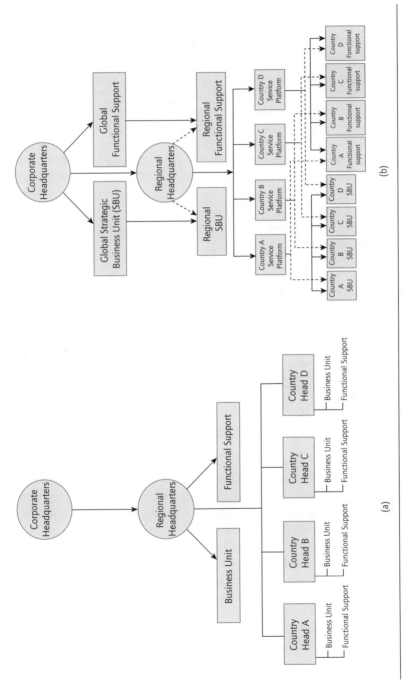

Figure 9.1 Two models for Asia Pacific regional organization: (a) Fully autonomous regional structure; (b) Service-platform regional structure

of its main competitors. As a matter of fact, the best way to justify the G&A charge is to track the ratio of G&A as a percentage of sales margin because it reflects whether a company can afford its management infrastructure.

If the company cannot create enough economic value to justify its supporting infrastructure — either through product differentiation or increased productivity — it must learn to live with lighter corporate support. In fact, having a lean Asian organization is the norm for multinationals because of the highly competitive nature of the market and the generally lower wages offered by regional or local players. Any WMN must therefore focus on the quality of its people and the business process that is needed to stay efficient and productive. Keeping abreast of competitors' cost structures should be treated as one of the major benchmarking criteria, especially for those companies engaged in commodity industry segments.

BUSINESS-ORIENTED REGIONAL MANAGEMENT

Each SBU must be given autonomy in defining its marketing plans and business strategies. Likewise, an effective and responsive regional organization must be similarly market-driven and stay focused on business planning and implementation. Therefore, in principle, the regional management team should consist of regional business heads as well as the heads of key functional support areas such as HR, finance, IT, product safety, supply-chain planning, manufacturing and purchasing. Ideally the regional head should have a strong commercial background and track record within the region.

All too often, Western companies appoint people who have demonstrated loyalty at home to key executive positions in Asia simply to enforce corporate governance and ethical standards, rather than for their ability to contribute to the organization's commercial or functional competencies. Any compromise on professional competency in these key appointments will automatically jeopardize the effectiveness of the team. Executives working in Asia must learn to appreciate the diversity of talent available to them and realize that language skills or culture compatibility do not in themselves guarantee business excellence. The success or failure of an Asian organization should be measured primarily by its business results and its ability to sustain success.

REGIONAL HEAD AND GLOBAL LEADERSHIP TEAM

In recruiting a regional head, the company's selection criteria should include the following key qualifications and qualities:

- a proven track record in managing a diversified regional team
- the ability to formulate effective implementation plans to achieve business goals
- commitment and skills to implement the strategic plan
- decisiveness in implementing plans, even under adverse conditions
- effective communication and consensus-building skills
- the ability to focus on creating opportunities as well as on learning from past failures
- uncompromising ethical standards in protecting the company's best interests
- a willingness to be flexible in finding pragmatic business solutions
- responsiveness in meeting customers' demands and competitors' challenges
- an ability to convert the suggestions of the global leadership team into concrete action.

The role of the regional head can be extremely difficult without the full support of the CEO because it involves reconciling the often conflicting approaches of local and global organizations. There are several drawbacks to having direct involvement from the global leadership team in managing local affairs. The most common relate to inaccessibility arising from time differences and/or distance, cultural gaps, and a general lack of experience in Asian business, which can often lead to fixed and inappropriate attitudes that can be counterproductive to the business in Asia. For example, commodity-oriented multinationals often divest themselves of redundant assets or under-performing business units via e-auctions. However, to do so in Asia could be disastrous and result in a complete loss of credibility in the eyes of customers for all the company's business units, or possible manipulation by competitors to extract the company's sales and technology.

Another potentially hazardous intervention in local matters can occur when the global leadership team makes a critical strategic decision to acquire a new business based on the erroneous assumption that the same levels of profitability that could be expected in the US or Europe are applicable to Asia.

Western companies that place the Asia Pacific region under the remote control of a member of the global leadership team also run the risks associated with having an overly complex reporting structure and too many decision-makers. Experience has shown that this remote-control organizational model hardly ever works for Asia unless the region is adequately represented on the global leadership team. Such representation can be in the form of an official appointment or quarterly participation in global leadership team meetings. But to ensure sound communication, the best solution is to have the regional head as part of the global leadership team. In both General Electric and Philips, for example, the Asia Pacific head sits on the board so that ambitions to expand the Asia market are strategically aligned with each company's overall direction. On the other hand, companies that have yet to embrace cultural diversity as a corporate strength prefer to have all directors or members of their global leadership team from the same — Western — background. While such decisions may, on the surface, appear to be simply a matter of professional judgment, in reality they are more reflective of the fact that the management of diversified human resources is not yet a core competency for those companies.

RESPONSIBILITIES OF THE REGIONAL MANAGEMENT TEAM

The head of finance occupies the second-most important position in the regional management team because this area serves as both a control mechanism and a support function. Apart from the standard professional accounting qualifications and expertise, the head of finance must be familiar with the US Generally Accepted Accounting Principles (GAAP), International Accounting Standards (IAS), and a range of other accounting standards. He or she must enforce strict adherence to the company's own ethical policies and business practices and total compliance with its statutory obligations. For example, the Sarbanes-Oxley Act, introduced in mid 2002 by the US Securities and Exchange Commission (SEC) for improved corporate governance, has substantially raised internal control standards. The regional finance head must be proficient in implementing the control mechanisms in all the company's operations in Asia because non-compliance with the Act can lead to heavy punishment.

Another key position on the regional management team is that of financial analyst. The incumbent is required not only to master the key financial figures related to the business operations but also to calculate the financial benefits of any major business decisions to be made by the team. The financial analyst is also responsible for tracking how the business is performing against the agreed key performance indicators (KPIs) on a regular basis. The setup of KPIs should be considered as one of the key tasks for the regional team. Once the KPIs are agreed upon, the team should have the discipline to measure, review, and react on a routine basis to ensure that the team is able to deliver what it aims for. Another important function for the financial analyst is to work with the team members to explore the financial benefits to be derived from any potential improvement opportunities.

The role of the regional head of human resources (HR) is to serve as the gatekeeper to recruit and retain talent within the region and to monitor the personnel management system in line with corporate guidelines. Because most WMNs have reduced their workforce in recent years during the economic slowdown, few regional heads will have an opportunity to develop future leaders in any systematic way. To cope with the massive growth potential in emerging Asian markets, Western companies will have to come up with a realistic business plan that incorporates the development of sufficient local talent capable of meeting the challenges for future growth.

The primary responsibility of the regional manufacturing head is to coordinate the production sites in the region to create synergies in manufacturing efficiency, quality benchmarking and engineering expertise. The position also entails responsibility for ensuring that all corporate and statutory environmental, health and safety standards are complied with. When a company places the safety of employees at the top of its operational priorities, this can give a tremendous boost to morale within the workforce. This is particularly important in Asia because it provides a sharp contrast to many local competitors that are operating with different priorities in mind.

The person in charge of regional sales and operational planning (S&OP) works closely with the different business units and manufacturing sites seeking synergies in the management of working capital. The S&OP head must understand where the economic value is released and set manufacturing priorities accordingly. In some structures, the S&OP team also has substantial customer service functions, processing orders and following up on deliveries. The most obvious advantage of using a centralized S&OP is the cost benefit that comes from having shared services across different business units and reduced working capital as a result of consolidated inventory management.

Every member of the regional team should be skilled in managing people as they fulfill their various planning and review functions. The team must understand the objectives set by the global team and transform them into action plans with regional characteristics. Ideally, the team should be drawn from different geographic locations so that it is capable of assessing the overall strengths and weaknesses across all territories in the region. The leader of the regional team in particular must be able to harness the diverse talents available within the team into assets for the company.

A STRATEGY-FOCUSED ORGANIZATION

Robert S. Kaplan and David P. Norton have written extensively on the subject of the strategy-focused organization.[36] They emphasize that company vision and business strategy must be translated into manageable targets and tested against measurable performance indicators. The cause-and-effect relationships that lie at the heart of the strategy involve four perspectives — learning and growth; internal; customer; and financial — as shown in Figure 9.2.

For each of the four perspectives, there must be clearly defined objectives, measures, targets and initiatives so that the entire organization can be mobilized to implement a common vision and strategy. If properly aligned and implemented, this will open up new business opportunities, enhance operational excellence through the prudent management of manufacturing, and increase customer value through the value-added services offered by a well-organized supply chain — all of which will enable the company to deliver on its promises.

When the strategy-focused organization is properly empowered, it can be linked into a continuous process for reviewing the budget and business operations.

THE STRATEGIC PLANNING CAPABILITY

Any company's regional management team must be given the power to make strategic plans that take into account the complexities peculiar to the Asian market. As we have seen, for a multinational to impose a one-size-fits-all approach from above is fraught with difficulty and would represent a huge, and probably costly, miscalculation. If business in Asia is important to the company's global business portfolio, this is sufficient justification for having a separate regional business strategy which, though requiring different action plans, must still complement the overall global strategy.

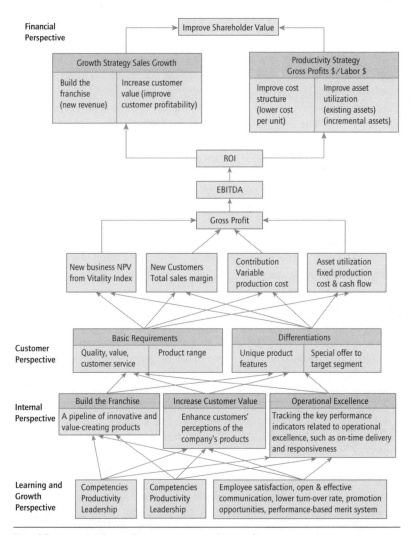

Figure 9.2 Strategy-focused organization and its application

The task of preparing region-specific strategic plans could be undertaken either by a dedicated regional strategic business development department or by senior executives within the region. Once the mechanism and responsibilities are agreed upon, there must be clear accountability for delivering results. During the implementation phase, the regional team will be able to monitor market dynamics and provide the timely feedback that is required to keep the business plan updated.

REALIZING SYNERGIES

Whenever a company can clearly define its vision, strategic objectives and business targets, it is likely to create synergies between different business units. The business of creating synergies is not something that is naturally at the forefront of people's minds; it has to be nurtured from the top down. The process begins with the CEO and the members of the executive committee, who should foster productive interaction between the various business units by encouraging them to share their respective strategic business plans at the global, regional and local level by sharing their experience in new business areas or with an innovative technology that may have different applications in other business units. When a proper example is given by the top executives, the chances are that it will take root throughout the regional organization in Asia, where employees tend to follow rather than to challenge. Executives must clear the problems related to business processes and management systems so that the employees can embrace the concept of synergy with enthusiasm.

Case Study:

DELL vs. FOXCONN

Founded only 20 years ago by Michael Dell, Dell Computer had annual sales of US$41.4 billion in 2003. Through a unique business model that focuses on product design and distribution, Dell Computer reached the Fortune 500 roster of the world's largest companies in 1992 and became the largest computer hardware company in 2001.

Acutely aware that there was an abundant supply of computer hardware and associated peripherals on the market, particularly in Asia, Michael Dell adopted a totally different business model to differentiate his company in a crowded and highly competitive environment. Through concentrating on an information-management system that covers market segmentation, customer differentiation and an online information exchange with key suppliers and customers, and an innovative supply-chain planning model, Dell Computer is able to enjoy high sales growth and good financial returns while most of its high-profile competitors are suffering from excessive asset investment, fluctuating values in inventory and uncertain market conditions.

Michael Dell considers his direct involvement with customers and an innovative supply chain as the two most important factors behind the company's success. By dealing directly with customers, his company gets to know and understand

	Dell			Foxconn		
Financial Results	2003	2002	2001	2003	2002	2001
1. Revenue (US$ million)	41,444	35,404	31,168	10,793	7,455	4,553
2. Net Income (US$ million)	2,645	2,122	1,246	663	488	387
3. Total assets (US$ million)	19,311	15,470	13,535	5,965	3,820	2,954
4. Return on equity, or ROE (%)	42.1	43.6	26.5	25.7	24.3	23.5
5. Return on assets, or ROA (%)	13.7	13.7	9.2	11.1	12.8	13.1
6. EBITDA (US$ million)	3,809	3,055	2,029	875	734	537
7. EBITDA/Sales (%)	9.2	8.6	6.5	8.1	9.9	11.8
8. Net Income/Sales (%)	6.4	6.0	4.0	6.1	6.6	8.5
9. Sales Growth (%)	17.1	13.6	−2.3	44.8	63.7	45.3

Figure 9.3 Dell and Foxconn: A comparison of financial performance
Source: Mergent Online database[37]

their needs and is thus able to provide customized products and services to match their individual requirements. Because this system eliminates the need for retailers, Dell is able to offer customers powerful and richly configured systems at competitive prices. It is also able to introduce the latest technology much more quickly than companies with slow-moving, indirect distribution channels, turning over inventory every three days on average. The simplicity of this business model does not allow for excessively high profit targets. For the past five years, Dell has been making an average net profit of 6%, which is quite remarkable considering that it does not own too many assets and in a period in which the entire electronics industry has undergone a major shake-up. Dell's ambitious business target is to grow its sales to US$60 billion by 2006, which translates to an annual growth rate of 15% from 2003. This will necessitate an increase in its market share in Japan and China, its third- and fourth-largest markets, and an expansion into other electronics segments such as consumer electronics, printers, servers and storage. It will most likely continue to focus on a low-cost, high-efficiency approach to leverage growth on its abundant market knowledge and superior distribution capabilities. Given its track record over the past 20 years, few doubt that Dell will achieve its ambitious goals. However, some Asian markets, particularly China, are projected to get tougher as competition continues to cut prices even though raw-material costs are edging up. In China, the lowest-priced PCs offered by local producers such as Lenovo, Founder and Tongfang have dropped to around US$360 per unit. Because of the depressed profitability, Dell has had no choice but to trim its growth projections in China from three times to twice the market rate. In this increasingly competitive market, Dell will have to weigh its profit and market share targets carefully. Dell traditionally excels in corporate accounts and the extent to which it can maintain this competitive advantage over local competitors on their home turf will determine if it can continue to outgrow its local competitors in a closely contested market.

Foxconn, or Hon Hai Precision Industry Co., Ltd., is an ambitious and capable electronics manufacturing service (EMS) company based in Taiwan and China but with additional production facilities in Europe and the United States. After initial success in international trading in the tooling business, Foxconn's founder, Terry Kuo, stepped into the consumer-electronics industry in the 1980s and, rather than operating as a typical OEM contractor, set his sights on Foxconn becoming one of the two leading companies in any market segment in which it chose to participate. The company has continued to grow, regardless of the boom-and-bust cycle in the electronics industry. The Foxconn Group generates global sales approaching US$11 billion per annum and had a net profit of US$663 million in 2003. As one of the world's major EMS companies, Foxconn has defined a global business strategy based on strong partnerships with industry leaders, unparalleled competency in its global production capability, efficient global logistics, market-oriented legal support, and superior technological capabilities for providing technical support and developing new products.

In order to fulfill its founder's vision to work with global leaders in different industry segments — such as Dell, IBM, Apple, Cisco, Nokia and Sony — Foxconn has adopted a business model that supports the complete value chain, from product design to manufacturing to distribution, based on a strong competency in delivering the results in line with an aggressive timetable. The emphasis is on efficiency and customer service. Terry Kuo takes an active, hands-on approach to managing the company. When a customer such as Intel requires a new CPU connector, this approach ensures that the design engineers, whether based in Taiwan, in mainland China or on the US West Coast, work around the clock until the required product is delivered to the customer. Once a product design has been approved, Foxconn can usually move quickly into mass production while most competitors are still trying to figure out how to satisfy the volume or quality demanded by a customer. As with Michael Dell's business model, Terry Kuo also emphasizes the importance to the company of its enterprise resource planning (ERP) computer system, which gives it the online global inventory control and build-to-order production planning that are crucial in this highly competitive industry. This online supply-chain computer system is directly connected with those of key global accounts and is also integrated with some 1,800 subcontractors in order to improve response times and reduce the inventory. Foxconn firmly believes that only companies that are capable of saving money for their customers will remain as long-term leaders. The company will undoubtedly face persistent pricing pressures from many new competitors, particularly those from China, which will become the leading electronics manufacturing country within the next five years. The cluster effect again will induce a new wave of local competitors that will challenge the Taiwanese transplants in China. On the other hand, the competition against other EMS players such as Flextronics will no doubt be intensified by growing anxieties over shrinking margins and increasing demand from their OEM customers. Because the successful Foxconn model provides full services to OEM customers, there is no doubt that other EMS companies will start replicating this strategy. However, Foxconn has a reputation as a strong leader in responding to the changing market environment and will continue its expansion into other electronics segments or technologies in order to maintain its remarkable growth momentum.

Even though Foxconn has repeatedly confirmed that it is not in a position to compete with its global alliance partners, it is difficult to predict how a rapidly converging electronics industry will shape up in the future. In the past, Acer managed to become a global computer brand while, at the same time, remaining a major supplier to OEMs. Later, after encountering strong resistance from its OEM customers, it was forced to split into three divisions to be able to continue to serve its OEM customers and to develop its own brand-name products without a conflict of interest. This strategy is clearly paying off, as Acer has climbed to third position in the global notebook industry and its sister company, BenQ, is a rising star in the consumer-electronics market.

With the strong EMS competency possessed by most Asian players in communication, computer and consumer (3-C) electronics industries, the only thing preventing them from selling their own products directly onto the global market is the lack of an influential brand name. The emergence into global markets of the new electronics giants from Asia will drive down already-thin margins and possibly lead to a showdown between the big EMS companies and the global brand-name giants who no longer have the manufacturing competency to cope with the fast-evolving technology. If the 3-C electronics industry segments cannot quickly return to a healthy financial state, further pressure on the EMS companies from the big global brands will no doubt create an irreparable chasm.

Eventually, the combined market and financial conditions will decide the future landscape for competition in the electronics industry. The convergent technologies, such as the merging of video, audio, wireless and computing technology, will bring rapid change to the structure of the industry. Only 10 years ago, few could foresee that Acer or Samsung or TCL would become such powerful competitors in the global market. Market-focused companies that have sustainable competitive advantages will eventually be the long-term winners. In the computer industry, while some of the battles may have been won and lost, the war is just beginning.

CHAPTER 10

MANAGING HUMAN RESOURCES

Managers or staff within a company fall into four basic categories: those who are competent and passionate about their work; those whom we respect for their performance but not necessarily their personality; those who are friendly but contribute little to the success of the business; and — the most dangerous — incompetent and unethical executives.

VITAL FACTORS FOR DELIVERING RESULTS

A business plan can be turned into a sequence of vibrant business actions only when there are adequate resources available to drive the business process. Having a competent and committed business team is the most crucial factor in implementing an effective Asia Pacific business plan. Normally the assembling of the business team starts from the appointment of the regional head who, preferably, will be experienced in marketing as well as an execution expert. The selection and matching of staff to the various leadership roles should be the company's top priority. Management talent can come and go depending on whether the environment within the company is conducive to retaining and cultivating talent. When a company cannot recruit and retain competent managers and staff, it is unlikely to be able to achieve its strategic goals because only people can deliver the anticipated results.

THE ROLE OF EXPATRIATES

From taipan to business executive

A hundred years ago, at the height of the colonial period, almost the entire Asia Pacific region was under the control of the Western empires. Humiliating and unfair treaties, imposed and enforced through military might, placed trade into the hands of powerful Western businessmen, known as "taipans", who exploited the region's natural resources and abundant cheap labor and traded everything from tea, whisky and typewriters to arms and ammunition; from pianos to fashion and dresses. Just like their modern-day counterparts, the taipans made use of economies of scale to produce glycerin, carbolic soap and shampoo for the local market. Communication with the home office in Europe or the US was mostly reliant on surface mail, which took roughly five weeks to arrive.

The taipans were both adventurers and entrepreneurs, who had to be healthy and lucky to survive the variety of contagious diseases, including yellow fever, malaria and cholera, that were rampant. They had to be hardy and determined to endure the hardships of life in the outposts of the empire. Regardless of the lingering resentments they left in their wake, there can be no denying that the taipans bridged the gap in trade and cultural exchange between the East and the West. They were a special group of entrepreneurs who sowed the seeds of the free economy in Asia.

Nowadays, the business executives of Western multinationals, properly equipped with ultra-modern communication tools, can no longer depend on the free ride of imperialism and dominant technology. The challenges facing today's taipans are different but no less daunting than those faced by their predecessors. The playing field these days is much more level, thanks to the wide spread of free economy and the advance in living standards in the East. The fundamental rules of the free market have been well accepted and practiced by most Asians, who are now redefining their competitive advantages by raising the standards of quality, productivity, teamwork and, sometimes, technology. Seasoned Western business executives must be aware of the strengths of Asian countries, particularly those derived from their respective cultures and from their overall diversity. They must have the humility to recognize that Asia is catching up fast and they must become part of this ongoing learning process. They must rediscover the passion for entrepreneurship and the sense of adventure that are becoming hard to find in most WMNs. Only those Western companies that are willing to free their imaginations will spot opportunities for growth that will be denied them if they remain blinkered by the outmoded demands of hierarchy and mindset. Equally important for executives stationed in Asia is to quickly develop the skills required to suit local market conditions and to assess any business risks pragmatically.

Modern business executives must also be prepared to listen to any feedback and to react in a constructive way in Asia. They must question if they are operating dual standards, demanding one set of ethical standards from their subordinates and a different set from themselves. They must be seen to practice what they preach. They need to be mindful that people will judge them by their deeds rather than by their intentions. These universal rules of good management practice apply equally in Asia as well as in the West.

Cultivating diversity

Given the highly diversified cultures within the region, companies must recognize the need for a management team that reflects that diversity without discrimination of any kind in the workplace. Any deviation from these principles should never be tolerated. Perhaps the most obvious advantage to having a diversified management team is that the members can bring a broader range of understanding of local markets and what is required to achieve the objectives within those markets.

The management team should work to cultivate a team spirit based on common objectives and shared results, and avoid politically or religiously sensitive issues that have the potential to give offense to other members of the team or to customers and hinder open and constructive communication. Equally, there should be no room for emotion or personal prejudice in the decision-making process and, wherever possible, all contributory factors should be subjected to a joint review by the team before a final decision is made. From time to time, matters will arise which cannot be resolved simply with facts and figures but which require wisdom and people-management skills. In Asia, where there is so much emphasis on interpersonal relationships, a manager who is able to build a reputation of being fair-minded and trustworthy will usually succeed in winning people over. Draconian or Machiavellian styles of management, on the other hand, will only jeopardize the mutual trust that is essential for teamwork.

Localization or globalization?

One of the main responsibilities for expatriate executives in any WMN is to identify the available talent in the local team and provide the necessary career-development programs to maximize their potential. Cultivating local talent may help to minimize the long-term financial burden associated with maintaining certain expatriate positions in the region. However, experienced expatriates will always be needed to spearhead the expansion into new business or geographical areas. Therefore, building an effective team of expatriates and local managers is one of the key tasks in the business strategy. There should also be a transition plan for the gradual transfer of responsibility to local management staff. Provided that the transition is conducted smoothly and supported by an effective professional-development program, any localization of an expatriate position usually serves to motivate other local managers, though the hand-over is likely to take longer for technical positions than for operational roles.

As the borders between countries and markets disappear in an increasingly globalized world, the company that is capable of quickly mobilizing or sharing its global brainpower will have an edge over its competitors. While many Western multinationals are searching for economic benefit through outsourcing customer services to low-cost countries, industry leaders such as GE, which has a proven track record in managing its global human resources, have long been sharing global service platforms, including finance, customer service and even R&D, with their affiliates around the world.

A similar process can be applied to senior-level appointments. For example, Dow Chemicals has recently appointed its Asia head to lead one of its global SBUs. Du Pont appointed the president of its Taiwan operations to head its global micro-electronics materials division. IBM has appointed the president of its Japanese operations to the company's global executive committee. While all of these companies are able to make use of this extensive cross-functional experience and draw the best candidate for any position, some American companies are still struggling with a US federal law that requires them to fill a certain percentage of senior posts with people from specific racial backgrounds. The basic difference between these two concepts — one driven by statutory requirements, the other by an appreciation for talent — reflects the fundamental management philosophy of these firms and sets apart a great company from an ordinary one. A truly seasoned global executive understands the difference between a cult and a team; where the former seeks collective strength from homogeneity, the latter builds competitive advantages from diversity.

Qualifications and career paths

Traditionally, an outpost position in Asia was hardly the best career path to the top executive positions within a Western multinational. It is only recently that WMNs really began to wake up to the tremendous business opportunities available in Asia, particularly in the manufacturing segments. Because the average WMN currently derives only 5% to 15% of its global sales from Asia, an expatriate with experience in Asia does not necessarily stand out when it comes to considering candidates for a key executive position in the global operation.

An expatriate working in Asia should, like the taipan of old, have entrepreneurship (to spot a growth opportunities) and stamina (to overcome the challenges associated with an emerging market). In addition to the professional expertise necessary to meet business expectations, the candidate must be open-minded, to appreciate the diversified culture; be adept at communication, with or without a language barrier; be resilient, to endure certain frustrations; be flexible in dealing with customers' requests; and be ready to travel into a harsh environment. A relocation with the family is always helpful for the expatriate to cope with the new environment, provided that the family members also share the same appreciation of cultural diversity.

The biggest challenge in the career path of an expatriate is whether there is a suitable position lying ahead at the end of the overseas assignment. Relentless restructuring and downsizing at home make it less likely that a good position will be waiting when the expatriate returns home. In fact, most expatriates change their employer upon their repatriation. Many multinationals see the high costs associated with maintaining expatriates as an investment; it is a pity, then, that most of these investments are wasted. The skills and experience acquired by expatriates in Asia could be put to good use in strategic-planning departments and human-resource teams, broadening global horizons and reinforcing competencies on new business frontiers.

SUCCESSION PLANNING

Performance-based selection

A recent article in the *Harvard Business Review*[38] has some interesting insights into how companies can identify talent or potential problems within their ranks. The article examined a matrix used by the Bank of America to gauge the performance of its managers. The matrix, as shown in Figure 10.1 maps performance results ("what" was delivered against written goals and financial results) against individual performance ("how" the leader behaved in achieving those goals). Those revealed to be poor

Performance Results
(the "what")

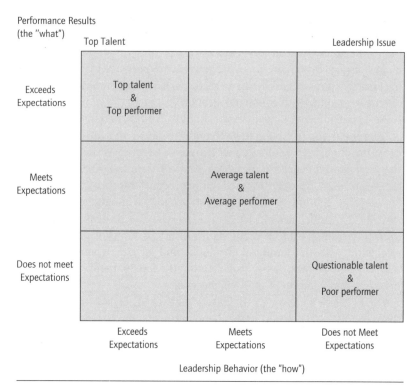

Figure 10.1 Performance appraisal based on leadership behavior and performance results

performers (as shown in the bottom right-hand corner of the grid) are placed on probation for immediate corrective action. If they fail to make the required progress, they may then face further disciplinary action. Those who perform slightly better but whose management behavior is still unacceptable, are given individual coaching to improve their performance. Should they fail to respond to this training, they too are placed on probation. Managers classified in the center of the matrix need to develop further skills, though this is not as urgent. For the top performers, as well as those who achieve a satisfactory level of performance, the company's goal should be to retain them and to develop them professionally.

Normally, the line manager and the HR manager will independently assess the leadership behavior of the employees. The HR manager will then compile the data and present the consolidated performance results on each employee to a joint committee consisting of regional or country management team members for approval. In order to make such an appraisal system work, proper definition of the business targets and leadership behavior must be included in the job description and annual target-setting. In general, leadership behavior can cover compliance with business conduct guidelines defined by the company and the ability to develop a high-performance team.

Development programs for local talent

It is important that the required management skills and competency expectations are well defined for different job levels. For example, manufacturing, logistics and sales positions require strong communication skills and teamwork. Supervisors in these areas will also need to be able to read financial and operational analytical reports, to give individual coaching when required and to have team-building skills. At the next level, managers need to be well versed in all issues relating to corporate governance, business planning, resource allocation, value creation, handling ambiguity, and building a winning team.

Such requirements will obviously vary by industry segment and in accordance with the needs of specific business units. At all times, the company should be looking to identify leaders who can operate across different functional areas. These so-called linchpin positions require that a leader is capable of operating across several areas at once and, in the process, producing results that add up to more than the sum of the individual contributions of those areas. In most companies, this is usually the best testing ground for leadership and a true leader will have a track record of leading diversified business and functional support teams for a minimum of three years.

As part of their standard recruitment processes, companies try to ensure that they have the right people in the right positions. They look first of all for a candidate who has the correct educational background. The second criterion is to look for relevant working experience. That is, they map the candidate's intelligence quotient (IQ) against the emotional quotient (EQ) or skills to manage the environment. This mapping process can be represented more formally, as shown in Figure 10.2.

However, following this simple selection process can often overlook the enormous potential hidden behind the EQ. Increasingly, recruiters are placing more emphasis on exploring and understanding a candidate's emotional and leadership capabilities, either by qualitative ranking or by

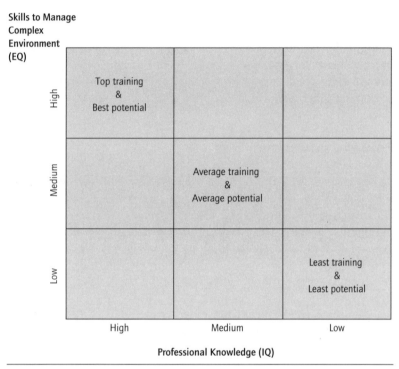

Figure 10.2   Talent selection based on professional knowledge and skills to manage environment

quantitative measurement using scientific methods. The information revealed on a matrix similar to that shown in Figure 10.1 can be invaluable to any company's human-resources data bank for matching available skills and experience to current and future managerial requirements. Once again, the specific definition of these criteria will vary in accordance with the specific needs of a particular area of the organization. In general terms, the higher the position, the more critical the need for someone with both the ability to deal with adversity or to spot talent (the EQ component) and the ability to manage a cross-functional team or to use KPIs to track performance against agreed targets (the IQ component).

A close matching of individual capabilities (as shown in Figure 10.2) with performance appraisal (as shown in Figure 10.1) will help ensure that the right people are going to the right jobs, to the benefit of both the company and the individual. However, if the matching process reveals that people with a high rating for individual skills and job potential do not show up in the high-performer category, this suggests the company must improve its delegation of power to these high-caliber employees. If, on the other hand, those who rate as top performers in the company's performance ratings are shown to lack necessary skills or levels of competency, this suggests that the career-development program is probably not sufficiently linked to business performance, in which case the company is probably ageing and in need of restructuring to rejuvenate its human resources.

Balancing expatriate and local talent

Despite a widely accepted view among many Western multinationals that it is better in the long term to localize all expatriate positions, there are certain synergies to be gained from maintaining a team consisting of both expatriates and local managers.

Regardless of technological advances, there is still no substitute for an effective face-to-face meeting. In an environment conducive to open discussion and debate, direct interaction between expatriate and local managers often generates a wider diversity of views and delivers a more balanced perspective on current business realities. A diversified team approach can also capture the broad market dynamics in an efficient way, filtering and processing information about customers' perceptions and requirements from frontline employees through to the decision-makers.

The beauty of having a mix of expatriate and local managers is that it allows a cross-breeding of cultures while maintaining a free flow of information. Companies that have developed a cultural diversity tend to perform better in the Asia Pacific region.

MARKET-ORIENTED COMPENSATION

In order to develop a market-oriented management culture, a WMN's compensation scheme should be set up to reflect the performance of the SBU, the division and the firm. While companies stress the importance of keeping their compensation schemes competitive, they often fall short in two important areas: stock options and the weight factor of performance bonuses. If a company is genuinely interested in enhancing value for its shareholders, the best way to ensure that a consistent message is sent across the company is to offer stock options to all employees, managers and executives. Many successful companies — Acer, GE, Samsung, TSMC and Foxxcon, to name but a few — take advantage of such plans, enabling them to maximize growth potential and earning power through creating a can-do corporate culture.

The other factor that is frequently forgotten by many companies is the weight factor applied to performance-based bonuses as a percentage of salaries. Some companies boast performance-oriented bonus schemes and yet these often come in at less than 10% of annualized base salaries. If it truly believes in the value of building entrepreneurship from within, the company must be consistent in structuring the bonus scheme in such a way that it is market-oriented and performance-driven. An effective bonus scheme should allow a higher weight factor to the senior executives, while offering a 15% to 20% weighting to frontline employees. The bonus scheme must be defined in accordance with the big picture, giving consideration to such things as the cash flow for the company, division, SBU or region as well as the operational considerations such as working-capital reductions, days of outstanding receivables, asset turnover rate, vitality index and delivery fill rate.

MANAGING HUMAN RESOURCES IN ASIA

As we saw in earlier chapters, Asians are culturally and socially inclined towards subordinating their individual views and aspirations, to being responsive to authority, however it may be defined. This willingness to listen and respond to their superiors often comes as a surprise to Western expatriates raised in a very different climate.

In Asia, managers are often expected to act as mentors as well as bosses in guiding subordinates on the job and, sometimes, off the job. This can lead to fulfilling professional and personal relationships that continue long after the expatriate returns home.

For many Western expatriates, being assigned to work in Asia gives them an opportunity to escape the usual hierarchical constrictions and gain exposure to different activities and responsibilities that they would not get at home. In general, when an employee, local or expatriate, is properly challenged and rewarded, there is always a higher level of job satisfaction. When expatriate managers are willing to cross the rigid rules of job level or working hours, they tend to be recognized as true contributors and leaders and can inspire the team to a higher level of performance.

TAPPING INTO LOCAL TALENT

In addition to developing the talent available within its own ranks, a company will sometimes need to fill certain strategic positions from outside. If properly balanced with internal promotions, external hiring serves to stimulate intellectual debate that can lead to creative management thinking. In fact, the success of moves by Samsung Electronics of South Korea and Wipro of India to bring in experienced Western business executives from different industries underscores the value of learning from companies with different cultures and management backgrounds.

Other valuable sources of potential recruits are Asian schools offering Executive MBA (EMBA) programs. These English-based programs can be found across Asia. For example, in Singapore, the National University of Singapore and Nanyang Technological University both offer high-quality MBA programs. The Hong Kong University of Science and Technology (HKUST), in conjunction with Northwestern University–Kellogg School of Management, offers a similar program. In South Korea, Sungkyunkwan University is collaborating with Massachusetts Institute of Technology to deliver an English-based MBA program with funding from Samsung. In Taiwan, there are at least four top MBA schools striving for recognition by the international business community but, for the most part, falling short because of their limited success in developing world-class curriculum and global business vision. Aspire Academy, an advanced management training institute, offers probably Taiwan's most internationalized curriculum including courses in leadership, brand name and change management.

As with all other industry segments, the global education industry has high hopes of the potentially abundant opportunities in China, where numerous cooperative programs between Chinese colleges and internationally reputable MBA schools are gaining rapid acceptance. The top MBA schools in China include Qin-Hwa University and Jiao Tung University. In India, the top MBA schools, such as the Indian Institute of Management in Ahmedabad and the Indian Institute of Management in Bangalore enjoy the privilege of being able to choose from a vast pool of the brightest applicants, with an acceptance rate of less than 1%.

The biggest problem for Asian MBA programs is the lack of a global brand name, which explains why so many are hooking up with renowned Western institutes. Another major obstacle to Asian countries developing top-quality MBA or EMBA programs of their own is government intervention in educational matters that some Asian countries are still subjected to from time to time. Providing an academic environment free from political influence is an area in which Asian countries clearly still have a lot to learn from their Western counterparts.

Case Study:

MICROSOFT vs. WIPRO

As the most profitable hi-tech company in the world, Microsoft generates net profits of around US$1 billion per month, which gives it the second-highest market capitalization behind General Electric. In the 1990s Microsoft became the supreme stock-market performer, when its innovative software transformed the PC into a powerful and user-friendly tool for average people and gave the company an astonishing 38% average annual growth rate. Microsoft reached its first US$1 billion sales faster than any hi-tech start-up and maintained its impressive profit levels even when the whole industry was in a serious downturn in 2001.

However, after the daunting performances of the last 29 years, Bill Gates, co-founder and chairman of Microsoft, is now facing his first major crisis in charting the future direction of the company. Until such time as competitors such as Linux are ready to replace Microsoft's operating and software products on a

	Microsoft			Wipro		
Financial Results	2003	2002	2001	2003	2002	2001
1. Revenue (US$ million)	32,187	28,365	25,296	1,350	929	732
2. Net Income (US$ million)	9,993	7,829	7,346	233	173	178
3. Total assets (US$ million)	79,571	67,646	59,257	1,262	885	642
4. Return on equity, or ROE (%)	16.4	15.0	16.3	27.5	23.6	34.2
5. Return on assets, or ROA (%)	12.6	11.6	13.0	18.5	19.5	27.6
6. EBITDA (US$ million)	14,656	12,994	13,256	317	247	223
7. EBITDA/Sales (%)	45.5	45.8	52.4	23.5	26.6	30.5
8. Net Income/Sales (%)	31.0	27.6	29.0	17.3	18.6	24.3
9. Sales Growth (%)	13.5	12.1	10.2	45.3	26.9	17.1

Figure 10.3 Microsoft and Wipro: A comparison of financial performance
Source: Mergent Online database[39]

massive scale, the company will continue to enjoy success in these areas. However, in most other areas, including games, the Internet, business software, and cellular phones, Microsoft has yet to deliver the anticipated financial returns. The long-awaited launch of Longhorn — an upgraded version of the Windows operating system — scheduled for the first half of 2006, is still in the balance pending completion of complex litigation proceedings. The EU Antitrust Commission is challenging the company over whether the bundling of advanced software programs is in violation of free-market competition. Having had this matter settled in its favor in the US in 2004, it is vital to Microsoft's future prospects that it replicates this success in Europe.

Meanwhile, Linux has been actively pursuing new business opportunities at the expense of Microsoft in Asia, particularly in China. As a later-comer, Linux is able to offer more flexible and cooperative conditions to its customers, including the sharing of software codes — something that Microsoft had not been willing to consider until recently. Since many Asian governments are genuinely concerned about securing their computer software from attack by hackers, the business model proposed by Linux is quickly gaining acceptance. Because Linux software can be run on less-powerful PCs than many Microsoft products, it is banking on being able to pick up even more business, because to install Longhorn will require that consumers invest in expensive hardware upgrades.

As the second-largest PC market in the world, China offers Linux an opportunity to challenge Microsoft's domination in the global software market. It has been very difficult for Microsoft to make money in China because of the rampant piracy of its products. Pirate copies are frequently sold at local computer software shops at less than 1% of Microsoft's global price. After 12 years of fruitless market testing, Microsoft has finally changed its strategy for China by developing cheaper and less-sophisticated software to meet local requirements.

Wipro and Infosys Technology Ltd. are the two most well-known Indian software companies that have caught the attention of the IT software industry as a result of the seemingly unstoppable trend of outsourcing by Western companies. Today, it is not only the multinationals who outsource their back-office support functions to India; many US government agencies are doing the same thing in an effort to offset their shrinking budgets. From a purely commercial viewpoint, outsourcing can benefit both customers and suppliers, enabling the former to reduce their total operating costs by as much as 40% and the latter to tap into a highly profitable industry segment. However, from a political standpoint, this is probably the most controversial issue, with politicians in the US and Europe coming under increasing pressure at home to restrict the levels of overseas outsourcing.

Nevertheless, the robust growth in outsourcing by clients from Western countries enabled Wipro to exceed US$1 billion in annual sales for the 2003 calendar year and is set to continue.

Wipro was originally founded in 1945 as Western India Vegetable Products and was mainly engaged in processing of vegetable oils for products such as soap. When the socialist government asked IBM to leave the country in 1977 for political reasons, Wipro decided to take advantage of this opportunity and to enter the computer hardware industry. However, as India lacked the clusters of computer component producers that were available to Northeast Asian countries, it was unable to compete in the hardware industry on the global stage. Hence, Wipro chose to tap into the great depth of homegrown scientific and technological skills and entered the software industry. Such a strategic decision has proven to be visionary because Wipro was able to concentrate on an industry that does not need large sum of fixed assets and efficient infrastructure. Wipro's chairman, Azim Premji, was able to achieve this remarkable transformation through a series of key strategic plans, of which the recruitment and training of talent was the most crucial. Through close cooperation with many successful WMNs, including General Electric, Premji had not only learned how to run a successful global business but also had direct access to top-notch business managers within the ranks of his Western partners. Wipro's ability to attract highly skilled business and engineering talent proved to be critical in an industry segment that is heavily dependent on intangible assets. In order to keep itself abreast of market trends in technology and human resources, Wipro set up a technical headquarters in Silicon Valley, California. Having recruited the talent he needed, the managers were given responsibility for executing business plans under a master strategy defined by Premji and his CEO, Vivek Paul, who was recruited from GE Medical System.

Another of Wipro's business strategies is to acquire the leading company in any business area that it wishes to enter. For example, it paid US$90 million for Spectramind, the leading call-center in India, to secure a position in a market segment that has attracted global giants such as IBM and Accenture. It also acquired several specialized American software companies that focus on corporate financial-information management. These strategies are now paying off, with Wipro beating Oracle, the longtime industry leader, in some new contract bidding. As a result of these strategies, Wipro's first-quarter revenues for 2004 were 45% up on the same period in 2003, while its net profits jumped by 43%. If business continues to grow at this robust pace, it won't be long before Wipro's annual sales exceed US$1.5 billion and propel it into the top 10 global IT companies, a longtime goal of Azim Premji.

The question now is whether Wipro can ever pose a threat to the mighty Microsoft, which has an annual R&D budget four or five times bigger than Wipro's total annual sales. The short-term prospects for any direct head-to-head competition are slim because Wipro has yet to develop a global brand name. But, as it continues its impressive growth pattern, few can rule out the chance that Wipro and other Indian IT software companies will be in a position to compete with any of the global software giants.

CHAPTER 11

IMPLEMENTING BUSINESS STRATEGY

A company should never claim victory until it has implemented its business strategy and got the anticipated result. Very often, companies introduce ambitious business plans or great management tools but continue to perform poorly. This only confirms one fundamental principle for sound management; which is, nothing is worse than failing to deliver the agreed result.

DEFINING TARGETS AND RESOURCES

After the comprehensive process of preparing a business plan, the RMT and SBU team must be able to identify the strategic goals and to translate these into business and operational targets. For example, after a thorough study of market expectations, the company may believe that through fine-tuning its current product platform it can overtake the current market leader in another industry segment. Having set this as a strategic goal, it must then prepare a solid business plan built around clearly defined sales and marketing targets that can be both understood and measured. All targets must be measurable; those that are not are usually not manageable either.

But there is not much point in having targets if it is not clear how these will be achieved. The RMT and SBU team must also identify the critical factors that will ensure success in outperforming its rivals. These critical factors may possibly include the development of patented technology or proprietary know-how to manufacture a product that will offer the company a unique cost position and superior product performance. This, of course, will entail mapping out and acquiring whatever resources are necessary for this to happen. These might include capital investment, technical expertise, specific sales knowledge, or a certain type of salesmanship for dealing with the specific industry. It may necessitate hiring industry specialists from a different field.

Once the resource allocation plan has been agreed, the RMT and SBU is ready to submit the business plan for assessment by decision-makers further up the company chain of command.

ASSESSING THE PROBABILITY OF SUCCESS

Positioning

An effective business plan must clearly define where the company is today and where it would like to be at the end of the next three or five years. While ascertaining the current status is generally a straightforward sales and marketing exercise to collect the relevant data, it can still be something of a hurdle. When the sales team has worked in the same industry for a long time, the market data it records is often based on perceptions rather than actual market surveys, which increases the chances of obtaining a skewed picture. An assessment of the overall position of a business unit should therefore be based on a team approach, one in which the entire global SBU leadership team sits down to work through the strategy planning process outlined in Chapter 7. The industry attractiveness and competitive strength scores can then be mapped on the strategic directional matrix. Any decision is then justified on the basis of a track record of measurable data rather than on individual intuition or imagination.

Sustainability

A strategic business plan can be effective only when the key assumptions on which it is based, such as technical competency and market coverage, are sustainable. If a company is being forced to cut corners in order to meet its short-term financial objectives, the business team must seriously ask itself if the company can retain its core competencies and build upon them. One of the most common mistakes in preparing a business plan is to commit to a fuzzy target based on ambiguous assumptions under pressure from the top. Whenever there is a lack of ownership or accountability, it is likely that the implementation will be unsustainable. Another big problem for sustainability arises when implementation is heavily dependent on a few key players. Should these key players leave the organization, sustainability is thrown into doubt. It is important, therefore, that a workable succession plan is also in place throughout the span of the business plan.

Valuation

The valuation is a measurement of economic value over the anticipated period based on a discount rate reflecting the cost of the capital. Any good business plan must constantly deliver value above the cost associated with the capital employed. Even under the worst-case business scenario, a good business plan must demonstrate its viability. The key assumptions about market conditions, such as the segment growth rate, the cost of raw materials or the strategic directions taken by the industry leader, will have a significant impact on the company's viability in the particular segment. There must be a systematic way to verify these assumptions, particularly in a low-margin business where a company cannot afford any sudden shortfall in its business targets.

Flexibility

The business plan's flexibility can be tested by investigating its ability to survive the worst-case scenario, in which most of the key assumptions on which it is based completely fail to match market realities five years down the track. This is not an exercise in paranoia, because such scenarios can and do occur, particularly in dynamic markets which experience rapid technological developments. There have been a number of notable examples of telecommunications companies that made billions of dollars-worth of fixed-line investments in anticipation of, say, the arrival of upgraded Internet technology in five years, only to find that their assumptions were erroneous or were not matched by market realities. Such was the case for Global Crossing, which went bust in 2002. Knowing the unpredictable nature of telecommunications technology and knowing that there are always penalties attached to bad business decisions, the company must ask itself how much risk it is willing to take and how it will cope with the risk. That flexibility should be assessed systematically to eliminate the possibility of deluding itself or its shareholders.

IMPLEMENTING A SALES AND MARKETING PLAN

Walk the talk by a committed team

The greater the involvement of the entire business team, the greater the chances of success. Where decisions are made and passed down from the top, the less likely it is that these will have the wholehearted agreement of those charged with implementing them. Where a plan has been championed by a particular individual and that person leaves the company, considerable disruption is bound to follow. It is important, therefore, that plans are drawn up by a team and reviewed by that same team on a regular basis. The routine review process by a committed team is an important one because it enables modifications to be made where fundamental changes in key assumptions have taken place. Obvious examples of this would be the dramatic changes to the structure of the aerospace industry after 9-11. Even after substantial modification, the team remains accountable for delivering the agreed results.

Creating value through customization

Customization is one of the many options for releasing value from the value chain but it can only add value when the customer is willing to pay for the additional complexity it imposes on the supplier. Therefore, it is important that the company implements three best practices for smart customization, as defined by Oliver, Moeller and Lakenan:[40] to understand the sources of value that customization provides to customers; to evaluate the "virtuous variety" — the ever-changing point at which customization adds value to both the company and its targeted customer; and to tailor the business streams to provide value at the lowest cost. A good example of this can be seen in the banking sector, where 60% to 80% of customer transactions take place through online banking, which is easier and faster for clients and cheaper for the bank after the business process is tailored and streamlined for specific customer requirements. As the authors make clear, though, two-thirds of companies fail to turn their customization into business success on the top line as well as the bottom line. A company needs to differentiate its product for the sake of creating value rather than simply fulfilling the ever-increasing demands made by its customers. When a custom-made product is created, it must command a premium over the original product. This can be tracked against changes in net present value (NPV), as described in Chapter 5.

A concerted approach with business partners

In many industry segments, it is becoming increasingly important that any new product launch or new sales campaign must be conducted in conjunction with business partners. For example, before Intel introduced its Wi-Fi chip for short-distance wireless applications, it incorporated the views, needs and capabilities of its major wireless partners — wafer producers, semiconductor packaging companies, computer software companies, phone companies, and communication equipment companies. Using its huge bargaining power, Intel was able to orchestrate a major sales and marketing campaign that eventually brought together each piece of the core technology for the final launch. As a result, it is projected that Intel will capture the majority of a Wi-Fi chip business that will be worth US$ 3.5 billion per annum by 2008.

SONY employed a similar approach in developing and launching its halogen-free notebook. Since SONY did not own the appropriate technology itself, it had to identify a company that did and obtain its commitment to the project. SONY orchestrated a concerted sales and marketing approach because it recognizes the commercial value in being perceived as the market leader in environmentally friendly products such as this. Without SONY's clout, it is extremely unlikely that the other partners in this venture — raw-material suppliers, copper-clad laminators and printed circuit-board producers — would have been able to effect the deal.

Therefore, while a company is planning a differentiation strategy to increase its competitive position, it is increasingly important for it to consider a concerted sales and marketing approach. Any company that wishes to introduce an effective sales and marketing plan must consider the feasibility of creating new industry demand through harnessing its own competencies to those of other powerhouses in different industry segments in working towards a common business objective.

FUNCTIONAL SUPPORT, FINANCIAL ANALYSIS AND SENSITIVITY STUDY

At this stage, the company should take its business plan one step further by involving the corporate manufacturing, technology and finance teams to assess whether the company has the necessary resources in each of these areas to implement the blueprint. This review process should provide the necessary checks and balances in providing specialist views that are not always available to top-level management.

Another key function that must be involved in certifying a business plan is the manufacturing department. Once the plan reaches its final approval stage, it is vital that the key production parameters such as volume, specifications and quality-control systems are thoroughly reviewed and validated by the manufacturing department. Through this review process, it is likely that certain capital expenditures will be needed in order to cope with the three- or five-year business plan. The necessary fixed-asset investment will naturally have an impact on the project's financial payback.

Following the manufacturing analysis, the functional team should then revisit the financial analysis to verify the financial targets. Any financial analysis must include a sensitivity study to gauge how changes in the key assumptions underlying the business plan over the course of the following five years will affect the company. For example, the company may have a projected growth of 8.0% per annum for that five-year period. The sensitivity study will assess the effects on the company of any variation on that figure, say, from 5.0% to 10.0%, and of any other figures such as selling price or raw-material costs, on which its assumptions have been based. The results of a properly defined sensitivity study will serve as a strategic guideline for the company's executive committee. For example, the company should know in advance the implications of a rise in oil prices or in the cost of raw materials for its entire cost structure and how it would cope with the new cost structure under a leaner organization. Proactive business management relies on a thorough understanding of the company's financial statement based on a comprehensive sensitivity study.

BENCHMARKING FOR REALITY CHECK

With few exceptions, a business plans can find a point of comparison within the given industry segment. Benchmarking is particularly important for any new business seeking to enter a new emerging market or territory in Asia. As discussed earlier, the company's business planning department should collect as much market intelligence as possible from the current leader within the chosen segment. The information sought will include details of its business model, organization chart, manufacturing capability, unit production cost and selling price, as well as notes on key personnel and their competency levels. If the company cannot match the segment leader in any of these areas, it should take immediate steps to close the gaps within a reasonable timeframe so that the validity of the business plan is not affected.

Without this information, the company will be forced to rely on its usual preconceptions, which can be a very dangerous ploy — particularly in Asian markets.

DRAWING NECESSARY RESOURCES AND EMPOWERING STAKEHOLDERS

In Chapter 10, we mentioned the crucial importance of appointing the right regional head and business team to work in Asia. Great attention must also be given to the allocation of other resources that are crucial for the successful implementation of the business plan. Often, companies are not prepared to spend any money unless the business demonstrates sustainable financial returns. Such an approach, however, can be short-sighted because it is often necessary to invest in building technical competencies through the acquisition of know-how or through market testing based on products made in a pilot plant. Such proactive investment costs should be captured in the overall NPV for the new business development. As outlined in Chapter 5, the vitality index should be treated as a key performance indicator for the measurement of a company's overall achievement in managing its future product portfolio. The justification for investing in the future is best decided by the track record of the particular RMT and SBU. A current market downturn should not necessarily rule out the funding of future high-potential projects. But the SBU team has to be able to demonstrate its ability to deliver on its promises.

In this regard, the members of the RMT and SBU team should be given the opportunity to review the key business decisions on a regular basis. Modern communication technology is such that it is fairly straightforward for team members to be kept up to date on any developments or suggestions that may have an impact on the project, without the interruptions that come from having to seek approval from above.

DELIVERING RESULTS BY DEFINING MAIN THRUSTS

A good way to ensure that the business plan is executed smoothly is to break it down into key components to be achieved within a specific timeframe. This process determines the main thrusts that will propel the business forward towards its targets. Individually, these mini-targets provide impetus at crucial stages. Together, they help ensure that the company is able to deliver the promised results in a timely fashion. The fulfillment of these transitional targets should be incorporated into the quarterly performance review and annual target-setting processes. Only through the constant tracking of these milestone targets will the company be sure that it is on track.

DEVELOP A BACK-UP PLAN

Knowing the complexity and variability of market conditions, an experienced business executive will always have a back-up plan. Normally, a company's overall budget figure must be based on an aggregate of the budgets allocated to individual business teams. There is also a need to develop a back-up plan to address possible downturns in business but still meet the budget figure. The most common back-up plan will have a broader scope for developing new business than that defined in the business plan. Depending on how volatile an industry segment is, the business team must constantly prepare a list of target business accounts as the back-up for the master business plan. A good company can constantly hit the agreed targets because it has the discipline to carry out the agreed action plan. But, the really superior company can hit the agreed targets even during a sudden downturn because it always has a back-up plan in its pocket.

DEFINE, MEASURE, ANALYZE, IMPROVE AND CONTROL

This book has proposed a systematic approach to defining and implementing a business growth strategy for the Asia Pacific region. Because the methodology used can be quantified either in a strategic directional matrix (SDM) or in numerical targets, it lends itself to a statistical analysis such as employed in Six-Sigma methodology. That is, it defines, measures, analyzes, improves and controls (DMAIC) the entire business growth plan. Once a company has identified certain planning processes as the most crucial areas for its industry segment, the DMAIC can be readily applied. For example, if the company knows from past experience that its competitive position against its closest market rival is the most crucial area in which it needs to define a precise growth strategy, it should adopt the relative-competitiveness scoring system given in Figure 7.7. This process gives the company a means of learning how to improve both its performance vis-à-vis its main rival and its market standing in the eyes of its customers. An increased understanding of the market will increase the company's chances of attaining and retaining a position of dominance in its chosen market segment.

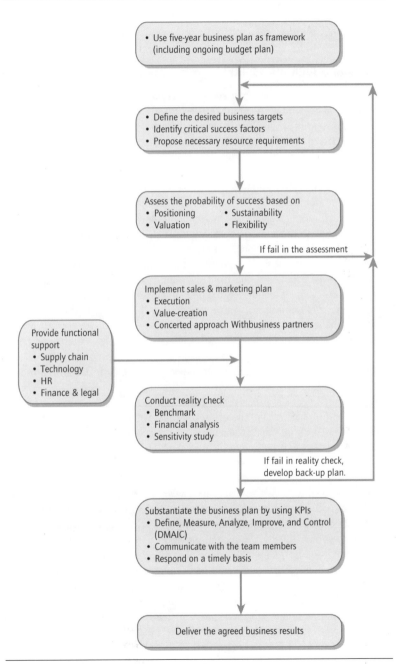

Figure 11.1 Flow chart for implementing business plan

Case Study:

JOHNSON & JOHNSON vs. CIPLA

Johnson & Johnson has established itself as one of the most admired companies in the world because of its robust top-line growth, strong brand name, unparalleled marketing capability and impressive financial performance. With a market value of US$161 billion, an annual sales turnover of US$41.8 billion and a net profit of US$7.1 billion in 2003, Johnson & Johnson was ranked seventh on *BusinessWeek*'s Global 1000 list published in July each year.

While the Johnson & Johnson parent company focuses on formulating overall business strategy, each of its 240 subsidiaries operates like an independent company. Through well-known household brands such as Band-Aids and Johnson's Baby Shampoo, the company is widely recognized as a leading supplier for pharmaceuticals, consumer products and devices and diagnostic equipment. The company generates almost half of its revenue and 60% of its profits from its pharmaceuticals. The devices & diagnostics division, best known for introducing Cypher, a potentially multibillion-dollar drug-coated stent for keeping arteries clear, provides it with a unique growth option based on synergies with its pharmaceutical products.

Johnson & Johnson's business growth strategy over the past six years has been built around the acquisition of 35 companies at a total cost of US$49.4 billion dollars. Johnson & Johnson utilizes its strong competency in global marketing to turn high potential drugs, made available to it through its acquisitions, into blockbusters for treating such conditions as arthritis. The company's acquisition strategy is likely to remain one of its key strategies for the foreseeable future. However, given the increasing competition for attractive acquisition targets, and the fact that its sales turnover is already at such a high level, it is unlikely that acquisition by itself can contribute enough revenue growth to the company. As a result, its stock price has not been keeping up with the rest of the big pharmaceuticals companies such as Novartis, Aventis and GlaxoSmithKline.

The second growth option for Johnson & Johnson is to tap into the synergies available among its 240 subsidiaries to jointly develop cross-divisional products similar to Cypher. Ideally, this type of teamwork can spur a wave of innovation that can put Johnson & Johnson on top of its major competitors. Another option for improving its bottom line would be to rationalize its massive infrastructure costs, which, until now, have stayed untouched because of its long history of exceptional financial performance. For an industry that traditionally relies on product innovation and marketing clout to create economic value, it is unclear how this type of cost-control measure will affect the company's morale and productivity. Johnson & Johnson's new CEO, William Weldon, will have to spend a lot of time analyzing the potential impact of various options before he makes a prudent strategic decision.

	Johnson & Johnson			Cipla		
Financial Results	2003	2002	2001	2003	2002	2001
1. Revenue (US$ million)	41,862	36,298	33,004	314	293	217
2. Net Income (US$ million)	7,197	6,597	5,668	52	48	35
3. Total assets (US$ million)	48,263	40,556	38,488	374	282	209
4. Return on equity, or ROE (%)	26.8	29.1	23.4	23.2	26.4	24.7
5. Return on assets, or ROA (%)	14.9	16.3	14.7	14.1	17.1	17.2
6. EBITDA (US$ million)	12,207	10,857	9,200	72	67.0	51.0
7. EBITDA/Sales (%)	29.2	29.9	27.9	22.9	29.9	23.5
8. Net Income/Sales (%)	17.2	18.2	17.2	16.6	16.4	16.6
9. Sales Growth (%)	15.3	10.0	13.3	7.2	35.0	36.5

Figure 11.2   Johnson & Johnson and Cipla: A comparison of financial performance

Source: Mergent Online database[41] and author's research

Cipla, with an annual turnover of US$314 million dollars and a net profit of US$52 million dollars in 2003, is, by Asian standards, a highly successful pharmaceuticals company, though dwarfed by global giants such as Johnson & Johnson. The question here is whether, and how, an Asian company like Cipla will affect the competitive nature of the global pharmaceuticals industry.

In the 1970s, the socialist Indian government took a number of measures designed to boost the standard of healthcare within its vast population. These included revoking its recognition of international medical patent laws and introducing price-control regulations on basic medicines such as aspirin. Under the protection of these measures, Indian companies simply copied the leading pharmaceutical products in the world. Cipla is capable alone of producing 400 of the top 500 pharmaceutical products sold in the world, and at a small fraction of the global market price. Bayer's patented anthrax medicine, Cipro, sells for around US$6 per pill in the US but is sold for only 12 cents in India. It is estimated that the average Indian pharmaceuticals company has a production cost advantage of about 70% over its big Western rivals. Now that India has joined the WTO, however, with effect from 2005 it will have to abide by the international trade laws governing intellectual-property rights. Therefore, the first possible consequence of having Indian competitors back in the international arena in 2005 is the massive pricing pressure on those drugs without patent protection. As Cipla's financial performance shows, it is capable of making 16% net profit on sales even though its typical selling price is, at most, only 15% of its Western counterparts. This means that for generic drugs, steep price pressure is almost inevitable. Indian companies will undoubtedly be the biggest beneficiaries of this. India already has a 2% share of the global pharmaceuticals market. But in the generic drug segment its market share is 20%, which is very bad news for the mighty Western pharmaceuticals companies that have so far enjoyed tremendous advantages conferred by the current business model consisting of product development, medical testing, FDA approval, and launch onto the global market. Some estimate that a generic-drug business worth at least US$3 billion will be available to companies such as Cipla, Wockhardt, Ranbaxy and Reddy's Laboratory when the barriers come down in 2005. Meanwhile, the big Western pharmaceuticals companies will try to extend the lifecycle of their drugs before their patents expire through licensing arrangements opened up by a loophole in the current FDA and patent regulations.

In order to expedite growth opportunities, some Indian pharmaceuticals companies have begun to make acquisitions overseas. For example, in July 2003 Wockhardt acquired CP Pharmaceuticals of the UK for US$19.5 million, thereby gaining access to the UK National Health Service. Though acquisitions by Indian companies to date remain relatively insignificant compared to the overall market size, it is clear that these companies are becoming increasingly confident of their ability to compete with the global giants.

Another challenge confronting Western pharmaceuticals companies is whether it would now be better for them to tap into the enormous resources of know-how available within India's scientific community at a fraction of the cost of their counterparts in the US or Europe. Since Indian companies are already well prepared to produce nearly all drugs currently manufactured by major pharmaceuticals companies, there would be little investment or time needed to transfer a major pharmaceuticals R&D center into India. On the other hand, the Western pharmaceuticals companies still remember how their market share collapsed from 75% in 1970 to 30% in recent years as a result of government intervention in the market. While there is a lot to be gained from formulating strategic partnerships with certain Indian companies or from making their own investments in India, they have to weigh this against the risk of having their fingers burned a second time. Those who are capable of tapping into the enormous competency of Indian scientists will have a much better chance of dealing with their competitors, current and future, in the global arena.

REFERENCES AND BIBLIOGRAPHY

1) *1421 The Year China Discovered the World*, Gavin Menzies, Bantam Books, 2003.
2) *Japan as Number One: Lessons for America*, Ezra F. Vogel, Harvard University Press, 1979.
3) "Dreaming with BRICs: The Path to 2050", Goldman Sachs, Global Economics Paper No. 99, October 2003.
4) Economist Intelligence Unit (EIU), 2004. See http://www.eiu.com.
5) Ibid.
6) United Nations Human Development Reports 2004. See http://www.un.hdi.org.
7) "The Myth of Asia's Miracle", Paul Krugman, *Foreign Affairs*, November/December 1994.
8) Transparency International Corruption Perceptions Index 2004. See http://www.transparency.org.
9) EIU, op. cit.
10) *IMD World Competitiveness Yearbook 2004* available from http://www02.imd.ch.
11) *Jack Welch*, Jack Welch and John A. Byrne, Headline Book Publishing Company, 2001.
12) At http://www.mergentonline.com
13) "The Chinese Negotiation", John L. Graham and N. Mark Lam, *Harvard Business Review*, October 2003.
14) EIU, op. cit.
15) United Nations, op. cit.
16) *Re-engineering Acer*, Stan Shih, Commonwealth Publishing Co. Ltd., 1996.
17) "Cool Companies", *Fortune*, May 24, 2004, pp.44–65; "Next Frontier", *Newsweek*, June 14, 2004, pp.42–82; "A Hybrid Future"; *Newsweek*, September 6, 2004, pp.36–72; "The Innovation Economy", *BusinessWeek*, October 11, 2004, pp.76–111.

18) Mergent, op. cit.
19) *Competitive Strategy*, Michael E. Porter, The Free Press, 1985, p.94.
20) *Strategies for Asia Pacific: Beyond the Crisis*, Philippe Lasserre and Helmut Schutte, Palgrave, 1999.
21) *The Six Sigma Way*, Peter S. Pande, Robert P. Neuman, and Roland R. Cavanagh, The McGraw-Hill Company, 2000.
22) Mergent, op. cit.
23) "Copycars", Graeme Maxton in "The World in 2004", *The Economist*, December 2003, p.115.
24) "Beijing Toughens Stand Against Piracy", Charles Hutzler, *The Asian Wall Street Journal*, December 22, 2004.
25) Mergent, op. cit.
26) Mergent, op. cit.
27) Porter, op. cit.
28) Reproduced in *The Strategy Concept and Process*, Arnoldo C. Hax and Nicolas S. Majluf, Prentice Hall, 1996.
29) Mergent, op. cit.
30) "American Business in China", White Paper, American Chamber of Commerce in China, September 2004.
31) See http://www.dealogic.com
32) Ibid.
33) *Strategies for Growth — Growth Through Acquisition*, Patricia L. Anslinger and Thomas E. Copeland, Harvard Business School Press, 1998, pp.55–77.
34) Mergent, op. cit.
35) "Strategic Development in Asia", Philippe Lasserre and Charlotte Butler, paper presented at the 8th LVMH Conference, INSEAD Euro-Asia Center, February 5–6, 1993.
36) "The Balanced Scorecard", Robert S. Kaplan and David P. Norton, Harvard Business School Press, 1996.
37) Mergent, op. cit.
38) "Developing Your Leadership Pipeline", Jay A. Conger, *Harvard Business Review*, December 2003, pp.76–84.
39) Mergent, op. cit.
40) "Smart Customization: Profitable Growth Through Tailored Business Streams", Keith Oliver, Leslie H. Moeller and Bill Lakenan, *Strategy + Business*, Spring, 2004.
41) Mergent, op. cit.

In addition to the specific sources referred to above, we found the following books to be valuable sources of information on business strategies:

Attaining Manufacturing Excellence, Robert W. Hall, Dow Jones-Irwin, 1987.

Benchmarking, Robert C. Camp, ASQC Quality Press, 1989.

Business Strategy, Irene Chow, Neil Holbert, Lane Kelley and Julie Yu, Prentice Hall, 1997.

Doing Business Internationally, Danielle Walker, Thomas Walker and Joerg Schmitz, The McGraw-Hill Company, 2003.

The Best of Branding, James R. Gregory, The McGraw-Hill Company, 2003.

The Essential Drucker, Peter F. Drucker, HarperCollins Publishers Inc., 2001.

The Strategy-focused Organization, Robert S. Kaplan and David P. Norton, Harvard Business School Press, 2001.

A range of regular general and finance publications such as *The Far Eastern Economic Review*, *Finance Asia*, *The Financial Times*, *Forbes Investment Guide*, *International Herald Tribune*, *South China Morning Post* and *Time* also have useful information pertinent to this topic.

INDEX